RoadhouseBLUES

STEVIE RAY VAUGHAN AND TEXAS R&B

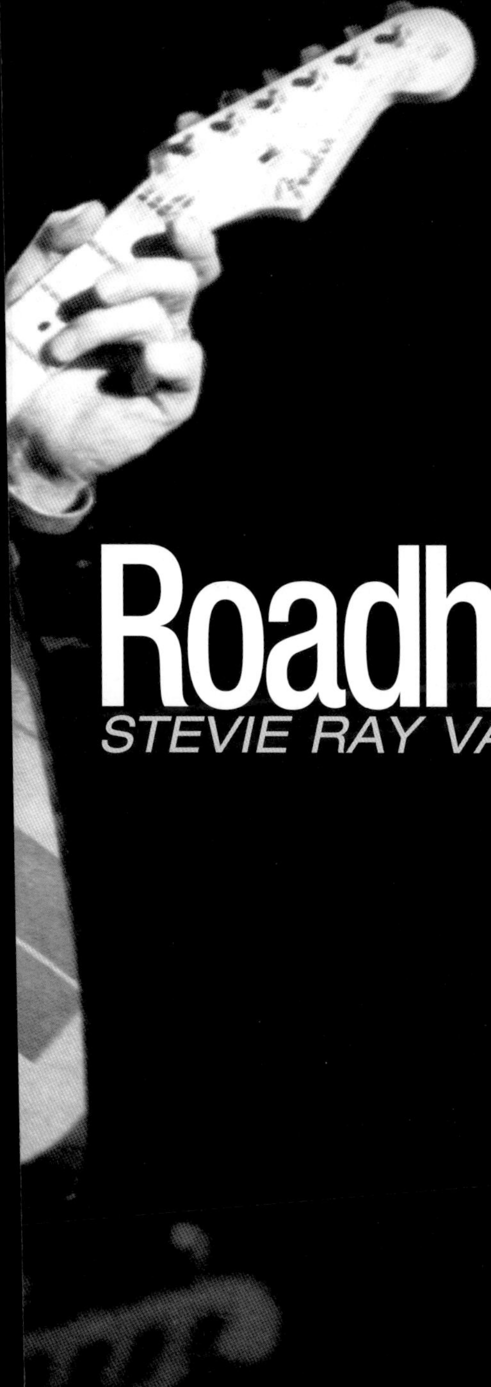

RoadhouseBLUES

STEVIE RAY VAUGHAN AND TEXAS R&B

by **Hugh Gregory**

Roadhouse Blues

STEVIE RAY VAUGHAN AND TEXAS R&B

A BACKBEAT BOOK

First edition 2003

Published by Backbeat Books

600 Harrison Street,

San Francisco, CA94107

www.backbeatbooks.com

An imprint of The Music Player Network United

Entertainment Media Inc.

Published for Backbeat Books by Outline Press Ltd,

Unit 2A Union Court, 20-22 Union Road,

London SW4 6JP, England.

ISBN 0-87930-747-1

Art Director: Nigel Osborne

Design: Paul Cooper

Editorial Director: Tony Bacon

Editor: Paul Quinn

Origination by HK Scanner Arts International Ltd

Printed by Colorprint Offset (Hong Kong)

03 04 04 06 07 5 4 3 2 1

Contents

6 Introduction

CHAPTER 1 8 **Working The Triangle** – Texas pioneers: Durham, Christian, T-Bone, Gatemouth...

CHAPTER 2 24 **Blues Masters** – local heroes, from Freddie King and Albert Collins to Billy Gibbons...

CHAPTER 3 40 **Groover's Paradise** – early years of the Vaughan brothers in Dallas and Austin...

CHAPTER 4 54 **Double Trouble** – shifting line-ups, via The Cobras and Triple Threat Revue...

CHAPTER 5 70 **Texas Flood** – Bowie's 'Let's Dance' and Double Trouble's debut album...

CHAPTER 6 84 **Entertainer Of The Year** – new bandmember, new manager, old habits...

CHAPTER 7 96 **Live Alive (Just)** – hitting rock bottom, and starting afresh...

CHAPTER 8 106 **Musician Of The Decade** – new era: *In Step*, *Family Style*, and a sudden stop...

CHAPTER 9 120 **Stevie Ray & The Guitar** – his influences, his technique, and his sound...

CHAPTER 10 132 **Legacy** – the blues after Stevie Ray: brother Jimmie and other keepers of the flame...

CHAPTER 11 148 **Walk That Walk** – update on Double Trouble, The T-Birds, and the next generation...

CHAPTER 12 162 **Here To Stay** – Texas roadhouse blues today, and the lasting impact of Stevie Ray...

172 Discography & Bibliography

189 Index

192 Acknowledgements

Introduction

"You can't hear American music without hearing Texas."

CASEY MONAGHAN

Long-time director of the Texas Music Office, Casey Monaghan, hit the nail on the head when he claimed, "You can't hear American music without hearing Texas". And if you apply his maxim to American *guitarists*, it takes on an even greater resonance – especially as so many great guitar players have originated from the Lone Star State: from electric guitar pioneers like Eddie Durham and Charlie Christian, to legendary R&B performers like T-Bone Walker and Johnny Guitar Watson, and modern blues-driven icons such as Freddie King, Albert Collins, Billy Gibbons, and the man on the cover of this book, Stevie Ray Vaughan himself.

So, you might wonder, why Texas? Why has this cattle-ranching haven recently become a recognised centre of musical excellence, rivalling internationally famed cities such as Detroit, Chicago, New York, LA, even Nashville? Apart from its sheer size, perhaps the most significant reason is its location. With the Gulf Of Mexico laying along the eastern seaboard, and the bayous of Louisiana to the east, Mexico to the south, New Mexico to the west, and Oklahoma and Arkansas to the north, Texas is culturally rich – as well as being oil rich since the 1920s. The state was and is a melting pot, where different shades and influences have coalesced to create an indefinable hybrid – a unique feel and sound that can't be replicated.

Yet for all its growing popularity over the years, the sound of Texas still seems almost 'rural', resisting assimilation into a broader cultural identity – they don't go for the easy, streamlined pop or rock found in abundance elsewhere. It's true that local boys like Charlie Christian and T-Bone Walker ultimately moved to New York or Los Angeles, and were followed in their turn by many other talented Texans, but this didn't mean the music scene at home was insufficient to support them. They could have made a good living if they'd stayed in Texas, as many before and since have done, graduating from the regular low-paid suburban 'roadhouse' gigs to the more illustrious halls and venues, be it in Houston, Austin, Dallas, Forth Worth or wherever. It's more that these individuals' ground-breaking talents could grow and flourish to an even greater extent in a larger environment – and at the same time the wider world got a chance to hear what Texas had to offer. To hi-jack an old phrase, you can take the musician out of Texas, but you can't take Texas... you know the rest.

Stevie Ray Vaughan was another who required the larger stage for his talents to become fully realised, but he was nonetheless the quintessential Texan guitarist. His style and technique was always passionate and committed – even in the midst of the most frenzied bout of soloing, the discipline still remained, and he always knew where he was going. Stevie Ray understood the blues, and recognised the value of dressing up the standard pentatonic scale with fades and passing tones – but articulation was always the key: irrespective of how fast he was playing, each note stood out, hard and fast. (There's lots about Stevie Ray's technique and tone in Chapter Nine.) The bottom line was the feeling – Stevie Ray always played from the gut. There might have been a formula in his approach, but it was rarely discernible: he claimed he never knowingly played the same thing twice. To some extent that's why Stevie Ray's live albums – especially those issued posthumously – are far more accurate records of his artistic development than any amount of biographical data will ever be.

Though he required the larger stage for his talents to be fully realised, Stevie Ray was the quintessential Texan guitarist

So why this book? Simply because Stevie Ray Vaughan's influence was such that he needs to be placed within the context of a broader picture – which means not only other electric guitarists, but the music of Texas itself, and its neighbouring states. Tracing his history, his inspiration and his legacy, helps explain the secret of why the blues has survived and thrived through changing fashions, seemingly against all odds. Taking a basically simple, traditional musical form, which he loved and cherished, Stevie Ray Vaughan inspired others to explore and interpret, and to have faith in their own intuition – promoting the idea that when it comes to the blues, anything goes.

CHAPTER 1

Working The Triangle

"When I first heard T-Bone Walker's solo on 'Stormy Monday', it drove me crazy. I could never believe a sound could be that pretty on an instrument."

B.B. KING

Tracing the roots of Stevie Ray Vaughan's music inevitably involves an overview of the history of electric guitar playing in general, and its impact on the R&B and blues bands of Texas in particular. For that we need to go back, way back. Back in fact to the mid 1930s, before the guitar was amplified as a matter of course. And there are three major names that are indissolubly linked to this development – all three of them Texan-born guitarists: Eddie Durham, Charlie Christian and T-Bone Walker.

Others played a part in the history, of course: Floyd Smith, a member of Andy Kirk's Clouds Of Joy in the 1930s, played an amplified steel guitar, Hawaiian style – like the lap steel, it was held horizontally, using a metal bar to slide along the strings. Such was the value of Smith's contribution that he had a feature spot at the Clouds Of Joys' gigs, where he could let rip on 'Floyd's Guitar Blues' – a number which was made into a successful recording in 1939, and later covered by Muddy Waters. (Some say that by the time of the 1939 recording Floyd was using Gibson's revolutionary 'electric Spanish' guitar, the ES150, having been introduced to it by Eddie Durham.)

Bob Dunn, from Braggs in Oklahoma, joined Milton Brown's Musical Brownies in 1934; interestingly Dunn had first seen the Hawaiian steel guitar back in 1917 in Kusa, Oklahoma, when it was used by some visiting Hawaiians. Dunn was completely absorbed by electronics and guitars, and he adapted a "standard Martin acoustic by magnetizing the strings and raising them above the box," according to Bill C. Malone's *Country Music USA*. "He then attached an electric pickup to the guitar, which was connected to a Vol-U Tone amplifier that Brown had bought in Mineral Wells, Texas." In 1935, when the Musical Brownies took part in recording sessions in Chicago, Dunn became arguably the first country musician to use a set-up like this.

In September that same year Eddie Durham played an electric guitar on 'Hittin' The Bottle' with the Jimmie Lunceford band; jazz chronicler Leonard Feather, ever controversial, noted that this was, "probably the first recorded example of any form of guitar amplification." Durham was born in San Marcos, Texas, on August 19th 1906, and started his career as a trombonist in Lunceford's band until he spotted the potential for an amplified guitar – so he added a resonator, a metal cone inside an acoustic guitar's body, which acted like an in-built megaphone, enabling him to play at a much greater volume. Durham, though, was primarily a composer, who happened to play the guitar, and it was in this capacity that he joined Count Basie's band in 1937, assembling trademark compositions such as 'Topsy', 'Out The Window' and 'Time Out'. The story goes that Durham first encountered Charlie Christian in Oklahoma City around this time.

Christian was born in Dallas, Texas, on July 29th 1916, then in 1921 the Christian family moved to Oklahoma City. Christian's father, Edward, was a blind musician and singer, while Charlie's brothers, Clarence and Edward, both played a variety of stringed instruments. Although the family earned its living in bands of strolling players, Charlie and his brothers stayed in one place long enough to attend the Douglas School in Oklahoma (one of their contemporaries there was writer Ralph Ellison, whose classic *Invisible Man* novel gives a black perspective on 1950s America). The Douglas School encouraged and developed the musical talents of its students, teaching harmony from the ninth through the 12th grades, maintaining a concert band and an orchestra. The Christian family may not have been affluent but they were certainly very cultured.

By 1931 Charlie had left school, and was playing in a variety of local bands. From an early age he was exposed to the full gamut of musical styles: jazz was developing rapidly, but the blues and gospel were a fundamental part of the musical landscape, as was the influence of Irish ballads, German polkas, the cajun of the bayous, and the canciones of the Mexican border. Also, in the mid 1920s and early 1930s, Oklahoma City was seen as the crossroads of the South West – bands from Chicago or Kansas City, or the east coast, passed through as a matter of course en route to Texas or Los Angeles.

Over the next few years Charlie continued travelling and playing, including a spell in his brother Clarence's band, the Jolly Jugglers, as well as Alphonso Trent's Orchestra in 1938. It's difficult to pin down with any certainty when it was that he started experimenting with the electric guitar: certainly Eddie Durham later claimed, "I don't think Christian had ever seen a guitar with an amplifier until he met me." But by 1938, Mary Osborne (who herself went on to become one of the the top guitarists of her era) recalled hearing Christian in Bismark, North Dakota, and seeing a display in a music store which boasted: 'The latest electric guitar model as featured by Charlie Christian'.

This guitar was the Gibson ES150, which made its debut in the company's catalogue in 1937, and again was probably introduced to Christian by Durham. It was the instrument with which Christian would change the perception of the guitar. It perhaps seems paradoxical that a stylist of Charlie Christian's evident calibre should have been enthused at the prospect of merely playing more loudly. But what Christian heard in the electric guitar was something very different – it could assume a distinct voice, particularly when delivering single-note solos. So when the ES150 came along, Charlie already had a vocabulary for its use; and the conviction and authority with which he applied this new language did not escape anyone's attention. By 1939, Columbia Records' A&R supremo John Hammond was on the case, travelling down to Oklahoma City to audition Charlie. In October of that year Charlie was cutting his first sessions with bandleader and clarinet player Benny Goodman.

Curiously, for all the suspicions that usually greet any new invention, most people seemed to recognise that the electric guitar transcended novelty and, in Leonard Feather's words, would help "re-orient the whole concept of jazz guitar". Charlie's all-round ability, learned on the road throughout the south-west, had imbued him with considerable technical skills, and he could augment the rhythm with filigree figures of great intricacy or little riffs that would became catalysts in their own right, taking tunes off in a new direction and inspiring fellow bandmembers. Although he never recorded as a leader, and had a brief recording career – he died of TB and the rigours of life on the road in 1942 – Charlie was the charismatic figure that guaranteed the electric guitar's longevity. As Dave Gelly observes in *Masters Of Jazz Guitar*, "Without Charlie Christian the electric guitar might have remained a mere curio in the attic of musical history".

Christian was already acquainted with Aaron 'T-Bone' Walker. In 1935, Walker and his new wife had decided to move to Los Angeles, and he arranged for Christian to take over his current position in Lawson Brook's band in Fort Worth. Later on, the guitarists would room together in New York when Christian was working with Goodman at the Hotel Pennsylvania.

Christian revolutionised the role of the jazz guitar, but Walker is the main man for blues guitarists. Quite apart from his inventive, lyrical, melodic lines, Walker was a showman par excellence, the template for every guitar-wielding superhero ever since. Armed with a bejewelled guitar, Walker would play on bended knees, or with the guitar clasped behind his head, or manipulated in some other unconventional way. He had every trick in the book. But, as B.B. King said, "When I first heard T-Bone's single-string solo on 'Stormy Monday', it drove me crazy. I could never believe a sound could be that pretty on an instrument … T-Bone has a way of using ninth chords … I like his singing too, but he always killed me with the guitar. Just killed me." Through Walker's influence the electric guitar became one of the most emotive and evocative vehicles for musical expression. His soloing techniques and sophisticated chording illustrated his debt to jazz, while he remained firmly grounded in the blues.

Aaron Thibeaux Walker was born on May 28th 1910 in Linden, Cass County, Texas. His parents split up when his father, Rance Walker, decided to become a farmer. His mother, Movelia, decided that the rural life was no place for the young T-Bone, and promptly moved to Dallas in 1912, where she soon re-married. Her new husband, Marco Washington, was a musician – bass fiddle player in the Dallas String Band, who combined minstrelsy with an early form of the blues. The young T-Bone's household could hardly have been more musical. He later recalled: "I think the first thing I can remember was my mother singing the blues in the evenings in our place in Texas." Soon he had learnt to play the guitar as well, encouraged by relations and friends such as Big Bill Broonzy and the Texan guitarist Blind Lemon Jefferson – "a great friend of my family," Walker later recalled; "I was really crazy about him. My whole family was crazy about him. He'd come over every Sunday and sit with us and play his guitar, and they'd sing and they'd have a few drinks."

By late 1929 Walker had toured across the south west as a tap dancer with Dr Breedings' Medicine show. This had led to a period playing the banjo in Ida Cox's outfit, a three-day stint with the 'Mother Of The Blues' Ma Rainey, and a week-long engagement with Cab Calloway (as a consequence of winning a talent contest). By the time Columbia Records talent scouts hit Dallas, renting a building on Young Street where they set up a portable recording unit, Walker was, if not a seasoned professional, certainly able to give a good account of himself. Recording under the pseudonym of Oak Cliff T-Bone (derived from the area of Dallas where he lived) Walker was accompanied by pianist Douglas Finnell – inspired by the success of duos like Scrapper Blackwell & Leroy Carr and Tampa Red & Georgia Tom.

The resulting single, 'Wichita Fall Blues' and 'Trinity River Blues', was a reasonable enough holler, but it failed to sustain his career in the short-term – because the great depression that was just around the corner, put paid to any further efforts from Oak Cliff T-Bone. Walker still gigged around Dallas and its environs with Lawson Brook, basically a former high-school band, sometimes venturing as far as Abilene or San Antone or even Oklahoma City. By around 1935 Walker was ready to make the move up Route 66 to the City Of The Angels. In Los Angeles, Walker first made his name in Big Jim Wynn's band: Wynn, who played baritone sax, later recalled that Walker, "was a song and dance act back then – the guitar came later." This confirms that Walker's ability as an entertainer was already finely tuned, and the acrobatics and contortions with the guitar were merely an expression of his desire to perform. Wynn also noted that Walker was experimenting with amplification: "He had a funny little box … a contraption he had made himself."

In 1937 Walker joined Les Hite's Orchestra, and for the next two years he toured solidly, playing from coast to coast. This culminated in some recordings, which included 'T-Bone Blues' for the New York-based Varsity label. Dramatically at odds with Hite's prevailing big-band style, it had the jump-style beat that would become synonymous with the embryonic sound of R&B. With that in the bag, Walker left Hite in Chicago and headed back to the west coast, where he took up the electric guitar and put together his own outfit. More touring followed until, in 1942, Walker settled down to cut 'Mean Old World' and 'I Got A Break Baby' for the fledgling Capitol label. With Freddie Slack (piano), Jud De Naut (bass) and Dave Coleman (drums), these sides give an indication of what was to follow. Although black artists had been recording in Los Angeles for many years, their records were aimed at a white crossover audiences. Walker broke that particularly divisive mould.

Throughout the war years, with recording restrictions in place, Walker (who was exempt from war service because of flat-feet) enjoyed a prestigious stint with Milt Larkins' Orchestra at the Rhumboogie Club on Chicago's south side. Larkins later commented: "Anytime there's a Texas band, blues and jazz fit together ... T-Bone was a picker … He played blues and other things." Walker's vocal style was easy and conversational, and made no attempt to utilise the cadences and patterns of the standard blues delivery; and what's more, his incisive and ringing guitar lines offered inspiration to the other youngsters now flocking to the coast.

Although Walker remained a big draw on the club circuit, his recording career was curtailed by the war. When it resumed in 1945, it was with the Chicago-based Rhumboogie label, where he cut six sides including 'I'm Still In Love With You' and 'Sail On Little Girl', alongside a re-working of the earlier 'Mean Old World'. But these failed to sustain his earlier momentum – if anything, they showed him in slightly regressive mood.

When Rhumboogie shut up shop in 1945, Mercury acquired the catalogue, and issued a few

Walker titles, but in 1946 that all changed when he started to record for the Black & White label. Owned by Paul Reiner, the label had started to operate at the end of the war and had hit paydirt with 'Open The Door, Richard', a novelty item confected by tenor sax man Jack McVea and comedians Dusty Fletcher and John Mason, under the auspices of a youthful A&R man named Ralph Bass. With Bass on his side, Walker set about changing the face of contemporary music. Often accompanied by Jack McVea on tenor, Walker issued a steady flow of gems for Black & White, such as 'Don't Leave Me Baby', 'T-Bone Shuffle' and 'Hard Pan Blues'. Even 'Bobby Sox Baby', which could be construed as a notional attempt to cross over into the mainstream of popular music, was entrenched in the R&B tradition.

Fronting a band that comprised tenor and trumpet and a rhythm section that swung as effectively as any big-band, Walker's flamboyant showmanship – for instance playing his jewel-encrusted guitar behind his head, while doing the splits – provided a role model for others such as Guitar Slim and Johnny 'Guitar' Watson.

In the late summer of 1947, McVea – who had basically led the Black & White house-band – left to capitalise on the success of 'Open The Door, Richard', and was replaced by pianist Lloyd Glenn as the in-house arranger. Walker's sessions with him produced 'Call It Stormy Monday, But Tuesday's Just As Bad'. Although it was to be many years before Walker would make a cent on the publishing, 'Stormy Monday' is as emblematic of his style as it is the distillation of R&B. In the tradition of all great songs, it has been covered by everyone, from Count Basie to Chris Farlowe, from Woody Herman to Isaac Hayes, and from Lou Rawls to the Allman Brothers Band.

This was the busiest period of Walker's studio career. Another recording ban was due at the end of 1947 (called by The American Federation of Musicians to force a better deal for musicians in the new mass-media world), which meant record labels and producers were trying to stockpile as much as possible before the impending drought. In such a climate it might be reasonable to assume that quality would be the first thing to get thrown out the window. In Walker's case this was far from true.

His band at this juncture featured Teddy Buckner (trumpet), Hubert 'Bumps' Meyer (tenor), Willard McDaniel (piano), Billy Hadnott (bass) – who incidentally was one of Charles Mingus's early teachers – and Oscar Lee Bradley (drums). This line-up, perhaps because of the volume of material they cut in two short months, has all the hallmarks of a classic R&B band: a pumping unit that drove all before it but never lacked finesse or variety. At its heart were the ringing, stinging lines from Walker's guitar – flash but always heartfelt. He created a template for everyone from B.B. King to Stevie Ray Vaughan. The lyrics of Shifty Henry, later Walker's bassist on the road, also deserve recognition for their acuity and cogency.

But even the excellence of these sessions, and the fact that all of Walker's records sold consistently well, could not stop Black & White going to the wall – largely due to the recording ban, and also Reiner's business policy: he thought all records would sell over 500,000 copies, just as 'Open The Door, Richard' had done, and he simply kept on issuing them until he went bankrupt. So in 1950, Walker signed with Lew Chudd's Imperial label. Irrespective of the recording ban, Walker's profile remained high, maintained by a touring schedule that was as intensive as it was debilitating.

With an 11-piece band that variously included Eddie 'Lockjaw' Davis on tenor and Big Jim Wynn on baritone, Walker was on the crest of the R&B wave. He would keep this band in place until 1955, during which time he recorded over 50 sides for Imperial. Again these are characterised by their consistency and urgency, but with Mari Young in place as pianist and arranger (they had worked together in Chicago on the Rhumboogie sessions) there is a harmonic sophistication that ultimately belies R&B's reputation for simplicity.

Although Walker was a welcome addition to the Imperial roster, the label was already prospering thanks to the consistent hit-making of pianist Antoine 'Fats' Domino, who (in partnership with arranger and bandleader Dave Bartholomew) had managed to fuse the rolling, loose-limbed feel of New Orleans with R&B in a string of hits such as 'Blue Monday', 'Blueberry Hill', "I'm Walkin'", and 'Walkin' To New Orleans'; records which defined the spirit and laissez-faire feel of The Big Easy, in contrast to the hectic urgency and bustle of Chicago where Howlin' Wolf, Jimmy Reed and Muddy Waters ruled the roost. The result of Imperial's prosperity meant that Chudd could pack Walker off to New Orleans to work with Bartholomew. The sides cut in New Orleans represent another facet of the Walker canon.

With his 11-piece band, which he kept in place till 1955, T-Bone Walker was on the crest of the R&B wave

In 1955 Walker was hospitalised, and when he got out, rock'n'roll had danced in. Now signed to Atlantic, in 1959 he cut the immaculate *T-Bone Blues* with tenor man Plas Johnson and jazz guitarist Barney Kessel. Throughout the 1960s, Walker continued to champion his brand of blues and R&B in Europe, with visits to the first *American Folk Blues Festival* in 1962, then again in 1965, and in 1966 with jazz impresario Norman Granz's Jazz At The Philharmonic. In 1968 he made another visit to the festival and tied in recording dates with the French Black & Blue label, cutting *Feeling The Blues*, which was followed by the Grammy-award-winning *Good Feelin'* (1970), with African multi-instrumentalist Manu Dibango.

Curiously, in the UK, Walker received fewer plaudits than his Chicago-based counterparts such as Muddy Waters, Sonny Boy Williamson and Jimmy Reed, who had long been lionised by British groups like The Rolling Stones, John Mayall's Bluesbreakers and The Yardbirds. It was left to groups such as the Graham Bond Organisation and Georgie Fame & The Blue Flames to maintain his profile. Despite Walker's frequent dalliances with European operations, his stock in the US remained high, cutting albums such as *Stormy Monday Blues* (1967) and *Funky Town* (1968) for ABC's subsidiary Bluesway. In 1973, with Jerry Leiber and Mike Stoller at the controls, Walker recorded the presciently titled *Very Rare* for Reprise, featuring trumpeter Dizzy Gillespie, saxophonists Al Cohn, Zoot Sims and Gerry Mulligan and flautist Herbie Mann, among others. Today this particular waxing is indeed as rare as hen's teeth, but it marked another musical milestone. His last, in fact, because in 1974 Walker stopped touring as a result of a stroke, and the following year, on March 16th 1975, he died of bronchial pneumonia.

Although the influence of both Charlie Christian and T-Bone Walker was far-reaching in the long-term, impressing generations of young guitarists in later years, they also inspired near contemporaries such as Pee Wee Crayton. Crayton was a late starter, but he combined the lyrical and melodic flair of Christian with the smooth yet incisive economy of Walker. Desperately under-appreciated at first, Crayton's approach could well be the template for numerous guitarists who plied their trade as session musicians, including Cornell Dupree, Lee Ritenour, Robben Ford and Larry Carlton. Fortunately Pee Wee lived long enough to see his fortunes improve to some extent, when he came out of retirement in the late 1960s, and again in the early 1980s. He played at Antone's in Austin just weeks before his death in 1985. Still absurdly under-valued, Crayton was a key figure in the chain that started with Christian and Walker and culminated with a style of R&B that's totally distinct from its Chicagoan counterpart.

Born Connie Curtis Crayton on December 18th 1914, in Liberty Hill, which lies around 60 miles to the north east of Austin. He was raised in Austin and had been given his nickname even before he was born, as he later explained to Johnny Otis: "My daddy used to go to these things they hold in houses – they used to call them suppers – where they'd drink 'chock' homebrew. There was a piano player there that played very very good and his name was 'Pee Wee'. My daddy liked him so well that he said, 'I think I'll name my next child after him if he's a boy'." When he was ten he befriended a young chap called Elmore James who played ukelele (not to be confused with the slide guitarist of the same name). So Pee Wee, being an enterprising type, decided to make a ukelele for himself. That lasted for a spell, but unfortunately it was broken by his sister. Despite this temporary setback, his interest in music led him to go and see visiting musicians such as Duke Ellington and the Carolina Cotton Pickers.

In 1935, after his mother had moved out to the west coast, Pee Wee met a chap who was going to drive out to Los Angeles, so he offered to help out with the driving in return for a lift. Once in LA, Pee Wee secured a job selling cars, and then met and married his first wife, Anita Collins. While visiting his brother in Oakland, news began to come through that the Japanese had bombed Pearl Harbour. Pee Wee's response was to move to Oakland where he got a job in a munitions factory in Vallejo – one of his work colleagues there was Alexander Veliotes, whose son was the drummer and band-leader Johnny Otis.

Though the work in the factory was regular, diversions were few and far between; but when Pee Wee heard Charlie Christian playing 'Solo Flight' with Benny Goodman, his interest in music was rekindled. He bought an old National S12 guitar, but could not get to grips with it at all – even so he was taught chords and scales by another factory worker, Eddie Young, who could play guitar. Then T-Bone Walker came to Oakland to play a gig, and Pee Wee was sold. He went out and bought himself an Epiphone guitar, then he got in touch with T-Bone and prevailed upon him to teach him how to play. T-Bone agreed, in exchange for which he took up residence in the Crayton household for a spell. Then Crayton fell in with Nat King Cole's guitarist John Collins, "The greatest guitar player I ever heard," as Crayton described him to Ellen Blau in *Living Blues* magazine. "He taught me how to play with all four fingers," he explained. "That's the reason why I can play big chords."

By the time the war was over, Crayton was playing the local club circuit at places like Elk's and The Colny, first with the West Oakland House Rockers, before forming a trio with pianist Lee Dedman, soon replaced by David Lee Johnson, and bassist Gordon Jackson. This led to Pee Wee's recruitment by songwriter, pianist and vocalist Ivory Joe Hunter. Perhaps best known for his classic slow blues 'Since I Met You Baby', which fields tantalising triplets, Hunter was something of a maverick and an entrepreneur, sorting out publishing and his own record label long before such endeavours were the norm.

It was as a member of Hunter's band that Crayton made his recording debut, 'Seventh Street Boogie', on Ivory Joe's Pacific label. More sides were recorded but nothing emerged until he moved over to Slim Jenkins's Art Deco Club, where, with assistance from the house band of The Four Kings – featuring horn man Buddy Floyd and pianist David Lee Johnson – he cut a single for Gru-V-Tone. More moves to 4-Star and Gilt Edge ensued, but nothing was issued until he met Jules Bihari, who had flown up to LA at the behest of record distributor Tony Vallerio. After meeting Bihari, Pee Wee was signed to Modern, where he cut his first solo records.

At Modern he began to show his potential, cutting sides in a variety of styles from jump blues to ballads, and from slow blues to jazzy instrumentals. Initially Crayton was backed by just a rhythm section, but that was sufficient to show his mettle on 'Blues After Hours' and Walker's ballad 'I'm Still In Love With You'. At the same sessions he cut 'Rock Island Blues' and 'Bounce Pee Wee', augmented by a handful of session musicians. By the time the next sessions came around, Crayton was using Buddy Floyd to punctuate the rhythm, and in his solos on titles like 'Texas Hop', 'Central Avenue Blues' and 'I Love You So' he interpolated the harmonic inventiveness of Walker while adhering to the tried-and-tested formulae of R&B.

And they were successful. "Blues After Hours" became one of the Top Ten 'race' records (as the R&B charts were then known) of 1948, and 'I Love You So' spent three months on the same charts. Success did breed problems, though – notably in establishing a reliable working unit to accompany Crayton as he trekked back and forth across the country: he said once, "I went across the country with a band that could not play five songs all the way through." And another time: "I was playing a dance in Lubbock and [the band] was smoking dope on the bandstand, and the police told me about it. They didn't bust us because half of Lubbock is my people, my relatives."

Despite these now very familiar tribulations of life on the road, Pee Wee managed to keep things ticking over – which included deciding to forego the luxury of a full touring band in favour of a local pick-up group. But in 1951 he fell out with Modern and wanted a release from his contract. The sessions for Modern had all been very easy – he'd always had a free hand to go his own way – but the Biharis were not over over-generous with their payments, giving him just $3,000 for his troubles. He moved over to the Aladdin label, where he cut the prophetically titled 'When It Rains, It Pours', coupled with 'Daybreak'. This single sold, at least sketchily, but it seemed as if he antagonised somebody influential in LA's exceedingly nepotistic music industry, because he suddenly found himself out in the cold with no work coming in. It took him three years to get back on track, landing up at Imperial and working with Dave Bartholomew down in New Orleans.

Ultimately Pee Wee Crayton's efforts, with pumping New Orleans rhythm section, were overlooked in the turmoil of rock'n'roll

The Imperial sessions promised much, with songs such as 'Every Dog Has His Day', 'You Know Yeah' and 'Runnin' Wild' ranking among his best. The guitar was cranked up, over a characteristically pumping New Orleans rhythm section – as only they know how to confect in the Crescent City – with hornmen Alvin Tyler and Lee Allen providing a thrusting counterpoint. But ultimately these efforts were overlooked in the turmoil that was rock'n'roll. In 1956 Crayton moved to Detroit, cutting sessions in Chicago for the Fox and VeeJay labels, before returning to Los Angeles in 1960. Despite sessions with Kent, Edco and Smash, his career was well and truly in the doldrums and, after cutting *Sunset Blues Band* for Liberty's subsidiary Sunset in 1965, he retired from the music business to drive a truck and play golf.

By the end of the 1960s, with Europe and the US still in the grip of a rock-fuelled blues boom, Crayton re-emerged briefly to cut *Things I Used To Do* (1970) for Sam Charters' Vanguard label and to appear with the *Johnny Otis Show* at Monterey where he performed a scintillating reading of 'The Things I Used To Do', which showed he had not lost his touch. Ultimately it did little to stimulate interest in his career and more years passed in retirement. In 1980, although there was no blues boom, the market place had expanded sufficiently to allow independent specialist blues and roots labels such as Alligator and Rounder room to manoeuvre. As a consequence Johnny Otis established his Blues Spectrum label and suggested that Crayton should recut his best known tunes to form a part of a package that would include similar albums by Big Joe Turner and Jimmy Liggins, among others. Entitled *Great R&B Oldies Volume Five* (1982), and featuring a group of session musicians, Crayton's guitar work was as incisive as ever, while his vocals had acquired a patina of avuncular warmth.

This also encouraged Norman Granz at Pablo to cut Crayton with Turner on *Every Day I Have The Blues* (recorded in 1975, though not issued until 1982) alongside other collaborations with Turner such as *In The Evening* (1977) and *Nobody In Mind* (1982). In the late 1970s Crayton toured regularly – particularly on the festival circuits in North America and Europe – but somehow it was all a little too late, especially as it meant being away from his family and the beloved golf course.

Whereas Crayton adopted the jazzier influences of Walker and Christian, Johnny 'Guitar' Watson emulated Walker's natural stagecraft and flamboyance. Watson also possessed an extraordinary facility for penning appealing tunes with wryly witty lyrics. But he was such an iconoclast that for much of his career he failed to achieve the fame he deserved, because no-one seemed quite sure where he was coming from. Born on February 3rd 1935 in Houston, Texas, Watson moved to Los Angeles in 1950 – inspired by T-Bone and Clarence 'Gatemouth' Brown – and worked there with Big Jay Neely, Amos Milburn and Bumps Blackwell, among others. Around 1952 he joined the Chuck Higgins Band as pianist, making his vocal debut on 'Motor Head Blues' for the Combo label. Chart action for this waxing was negligible, but A&R man Ralph Bass detected potential in the young Watson and signed him to Federal, a subsidiary of the influential, independent King label. Almost immediately Young John Watson, as he was now called, drew attention to his guitar work with 'Highway 60' (1953) and 'You Can't Take It With

You' (1954), but it was the instrumental 'Space Guitar', with its liberal use of feedback and reverb, that caused jaws to hit the floor. Not surprisingly, perhaps, this all proved a little too much for his record company, and Watson was allowed to move on to the Bihari Brothers' RPM label.

Now answering to the name of Johnny 'Guitar' Watson, bestowed upon him by Joe Bihari, Watson proceeded to knock out a succession of singles such as 'Hot Little Mama' (1954), 'Too Tired', 'Those Lonely, Lonely Nights' and 'Oh Baby' (1955), and 'Three Hours Past Midnight' (1956). Of these, 'Those Lonely, Lonely Nights' was the most successful, reaching the R&B Top Ten. But it was his extravagant stage act that was generating most interest, and his solo career took a back seat when he was hired to tour with Little Richard and Don & Dewey, among others. In common with Guitar Slim – another ground-breaker, but one who passed away prematurely – Watson had a 150-foot cable for his guitar, which gave him the leeway to cavort around the stage, playing the guitar with his teeth and such like.

By 1961, with the first flush of rock'n'roll gradually losing its appeal, Watson revived his recording career when he was re-signed by the King label. This time his benefactor was the equally idiosyncratic and respected bandleader Johnny Otis. Although this proved to be a shortlived arrangement, he scored with 'Cuttin' In', a track that might have sounded anachronistic coming from anyone else, but Watson's jaunty style transcended trivial considerations such as fashion. On closer listening it reveals startling similarities to later disco-funk outings such as 'I Need It'. But it was the sly, almost mocking note to his delivery that him set apart: you were never quite sure whom he was deriding. This became even more noticeable with the follow-up, 'The Gangster Of Love' – which was nominally a 'novelty item', though the fluid, incisive guitar work belied such a damning description. Initially it sold well enough on the west coast, but it didn't reap its full rewards until it was covered by the Steve Miller Band on their second album *Sailor* (1968) – and it has remained an integral part of the Miller repertoire ever since. Miller himself was another honorary Texan, having moved there from Wisconsin and teamed up with Boz Scaggs to form the Steve Miller Band. He even adopted 'The Gangster Of Love' , alongside characters from his own songs such as 'The Joker' and 'Space Cowboy', into some kind of composite alter ego. Strange... and probably bizarre enough for Watson to have been extremely proud.

Johnny Guitar Watson's jaunty style and sly delivery transcended trivial considerations such as fashion

As the British beat group invasion gathered momentum Watson cut the curious *I Cried For*

You album, a suave and swanky affair that included such hoary old chestnuts as 'Witchcraft'. But then he was signed to the Columbia subsidiary Okeh by producer Larry Williams (of 'Short Fat Fannie' fame). The two of them started to tour and record together, most notably adding lyrics to Joe Zawinul's 'Mercy Mercy Mercy'. Although they probably could not compete with Sam & Dave as a duo, both were larger than life personalities Their shows, as captured on two live albums – *The Larry Williams Show* (1965) and *Two For The Price Of One* (1967) – sound as if they were a real hoot.

Returning to his roots as a pianist, Watson cut a tribute to Fats Waller, *In A Fats Bag* (1968). In the early 1970s, whether influenced by other noted eccentrics like Sly Stone and Funkadelic's George Clinton, Watson started to get funky, with albums such as *Listen* (1973) and *I Don't Want To Be Alone, Stranger* (1976). Then when disco arrived, Watson was on hand with such gems as 'I Need It' (1976) and 'A Real Mother For Ya' (1977). Although those two songs proved to be his final hits, he kept on knocking out albums with remarkable regularity and – this is bizarre as well – many of them managed to penetrate the lower reaches of the US album charts.

So, duly attired in his sequinned Lone Ranger outfit, and with a string of albums such as *Funk Beyond The Call Of Duty* (1977), *Giant* (1978), *What The Hell Is This?* (1979), *Love Jones* (1980), *Johnny 'Guitar' Watson & The Family Clone* (1981), *That's What Time It Is* (1982) and *Strike On Computers* (1986), Watson's popularity in the US and Japan never wavered right up to his death on May 17th 1996, after suffering a heart attack on-stage in Yokohama .

While Christian, Crayton and Walker joined the musicians' migration west to Los Angeles, others – such as guitarist and vocalist Clarence 'Gatemouth' Brown – decided to stay put, working the 'triangle' of Texas, Louisiana and Oklahoma. Brown was a seminal influence, embracing as many styles as took his fancy; he also typified the essential autonomy of the club scene in Texas at the beginning of the 1950s, being signed to the Peacock label, which had connections with the Bronze Peacock night club, owned by Don Robey. Robey, a flamboyant bear of a man, often accompanied by cavalcades of bouncers and minders, apparently only started the label to get the better of a business associate.

The story goes that T-Bone Walker, having just finished a stint at Robey's club, had recommended 'Gatemouth' Brown to Robey. As soon as he saw him, Robey was knocked out, and took Brown under his wing. He originally arranged sessions for him, accompanied by Maxwell Davis's band, for the Messner brothers at the Aladdin label in Los Angeles. But Aladdin's curious contract only called for two singles per year. Robey didn't feel this was enough.

"I wanted him to have a record out," Robey told Claude Hall of *Billboard*. "But Aladdin waited until the last day of the year before releasing Brown's second record. So I was mad."

Robey's response was to put Brown in the studio with Jack McVea's Band and cut six sides, which were then released by Robey on his own Peacock label. There was nothing altruistic about it, but Robey put Brown on the map.

Brown was born on April 18th 1924 in Vinton, Louisiana, but raised from the age of three in Orange, Texas. Learning the fiddle and guitar from his father (Fiddlin' Tom), Brown was influenced by Walker and Tampa Red and the big-bands – 'Take the 'A' Train' has always remained a centrepiece of Brown's repertoire. "I liked Ellington and Basie a lot," he later recalled, "but Ray Noble also impressed me, because he could really swing. What I heard most of, though, was country & western, and so Bob Wills & The Texas Playboys made a lasting impact. You see, my father played the fiddle, mandolin, accordion and lots of other things, and he would always be trying out these new tunes around the house – from Gene Autry and Roy Rogers through to Jimmie Rodgers. He had to have variety, you understand, 'cos he would be playing in a bluegrass band one night, and cajun band the next. He would travel right across Texas and into Louisiana. But he would never play zydeco, 'cos that was regarded as lower than the low." Robey would later echo those same sentiments about R&B, saying, "(It) was felt to be degrading, low, and not to be heard by respectable people."

For all Clarence Gatemouth Brown's eclecticism, his punchy no-frills attack has influenced many other musicians

While at high school, Brown was given the sobriquet 'Gatemouth' by a teacher who said Brown had a "mouth like a gate". Clarence's brother, James, also a guitarist, recorded 'Boogie Woogie Nighthawk' for Jax in 1951, and was known as 'Widemouth' – perhaps dubbed so by the same sensitive member of the teaching profession. Anyway, after touring as a drummer in Davis's band, Brown was drafted. On his discharge he returned to San Antonio where he developed his guitar style and ultimately started his association with Robey, which endured until 1961. From those first sessions with McVea, 'Mary's Fine' backed by 'Time's Expensive' sold well enough to encourage Robey to set up at the established ACA studios. At the next sessions in 1949, Brown cut two of the songs that would become staples in his repertoire, 'Boogie Rambler' and the slow blues 'I've Been Mistreated'.

Brown was in and out of the studios for the next five years, cutting at least four songs per session, which yielded more staples in the Brown canon – such as 'Midnight Hour', the classic instrumental 'Ain't That Dandy' where Brown's deft guitar work shows the influence of Walker, and 'Okie Dokie Stomp'. While Brown was settling into a rhythm of recording and touring, the broad-based range of influences from his upbringing ensured he was adaptable. Although he never attempted to embrace the rock'n'roll revolution, he started messing around with the formula, adding harmonica to 'Gate's Salty Blues' in 1956, and at his final session for Robey in 1960, three of the tunes recorded, including 'Just Before The Dawn', were instrumentals featuring Brown on fiddle.

By the end of his relationship with Peacock, Brown had shifted the emphasis more from R&B to country, though his cover of Little Jimmy Dickens' country novelty 'May The Bird Of Paradise Fly Up Your Nose' for the tiny Hermitage Records failed to make much impact. Even so, in 1966 he became the house bandleader for *The!!!! Beat*, an influential R&B television programme syndicated out of Dallas and hosted by DJ Bill 'Hoss' Allen of Nashville's WLAC.

In 1971 Brown toured the European festival circuit and started to cut a number of albums for the French label Black & Blue; these included *The Blues Ain't Nothin'* (1972) and *Cold Strange* (1973), as well as *Sings Louis Jordan* (1973). Featuring sidemen like Arnett Cobb, the big-blowing tenor from Texas, pianist Jay McShann and organist Milt Buckner, Brown sounds as sharp as ever on Peacock titles such as 'My Time Is Expensive' and 'She Winked Her Eye', alongside more recent material like 'Pressure Cooker' and 'Deep, Deep Water'. And the Jordan tribute sounds tailor-made, as Brown excels on gems like 'Ain't Nobody Here But Us Chickens'.

On July 1st 1973 he made a barnstorming appearance at the *Montreux Festival*. The consequence of this was more albums for the French Barclay label – *The Drifter Rides Again* (1973), *Down South In The Bayou Country* (1974) and *The Bogalusa Boogie Man* (1975). Again these seemed to demonstrate his eclecticism while underlining his enthusiasm for country and western swing. That was further emphasised by two more country-tinged sets, *Blackjack* (1975) and *Makin' Music* (1979), with country singer Roy Clark, percussionist Airto Moreira, drummer Jim Keltner and The Memphis Horns, among others. As Brown once commented to T-Bone Walker, "Variety is the spice of life".

The1980s started propitiously, with Brown picking up a Grammy for his debut on the Rounder label, *Alright Again*! (1981), which was followed by *One More Mile* (1982) and *Real Life (Live)* (1985). Then he shifted over to Alligator before fetching up at Verve for a series of glossy high-profile sets such as *The Man* (1995), *A Long Way From Home* (1996) – which features Eric Clapton, Ry Cooder and Leon Russell – and *Back To Bogalusa* (2001). For this last one he was shifted to the revived Blue Thumb label.

For all Brown's eclecticism, his punchy no-frills attack has influenced many other musicians, including Frank Zappa, Johnny 'Guitar' Watson, Albert Collins, Johnny Copeland, Long John Hunter and Smokin' Joe Kubek – not to mention, of course, Stevie Ray Vaughan.

CHAPTER 2

Blues Masters

"So powerful it was unbelievable – I never heard anybody play louder, not back then."

JIMMIE VAUGHAN ON FREDDIE KING

It was indicative of the enduring influence of Charlie Christian and T-Bone Walker that even as R&B and the blues were being supplanted in the public's affections by rock'n'roll in the late 1950s, guitarists such as Freddie King, Albert Collins and Johnny Copeland still kept the flame burning brightly – though they did have to wait until the blues-boom of the late 1960s and the emergence of an international festival circuit to achieve widespread appeal. Even then, a large percentage of their audiences were college-educated white kids.

Standing 6′ 3″ tall, Freddie King made a huge impression on a generation of British-born blues guitarists such as Peter Green, Eric Clapton, Stan Webb and Mick Taylor, to name just four. He was born Frederick Christian on September 3rd 1934 in Gilmer, Texas, and began to learn the guitar when he was five. At first he was influenced by the records of Blind Lemon Jefferson, Big Bill Broonzy and Louis Jordan, but on his move to Chicago in 1950 he fell under the spell of Muddy Waters and B.B. King.

Freddie's imposing physique also quickly secured him work in a steel mill. He recalled his

STEVIE RAY WITH ANOTHER TEXAN GREAT, ALBERT COLLINS, IN NEW YORK, 1988

time in Chicago to Bruce Iglauer in 1971: "When I finished high school I was 16, when I came from Texas. We were living right by the Zanzibar [club], so I started hanging around Muddy Waters. I'd sneak in the side-door – Muddy would sneak me in, you know, and I would sit there all night listening to these cats. There was Jimmy Rogers, Muddy Waters, Elgin and Little Walter – this was the band then." By this time he'd also changed his name from Christian to King.

In 1952 Freddie started sitting in with different bands at local nightclubs like the Kitty Cat Club until he formed his own band, The Every Hour Blues Boys, with Jimmy Lee Robinson. This was followed by session work with harmonica player Little Sonny Cooper and Earl Payton's Blues Cats, making his recording debut for the tiny Parrot label in the process. When Parrot went to the wall, one of the owners, 'Lawyer' John Burton, put together the El-Bee label and King made his solo recording debut in 1956 with 'Country Boy', backed by 'That's What You Think'. While this record set few hearts a-flutter, King had arrived. Sessions for Cobra and even a short stint doing session work at Chess followed; unfortunately the Cobra stuff never saw the light of day until after King's death in 1976, although he did appear on Howlin' Wolf's recording of Willie Dixon's 'Spoonful'.

Freddie's reputation was spreading like wildfire, and this led to a contract with King subsidiary Federal, where he remained for around six years. In that time he laid down some of his definitive sides: B.B. King's 'Have You Ever Loved A Woman' (1960) – which was to become a staple in the Clapton repertory for years – Freddie's own instrumental 'Hideaway' (1960), 'The Stumble' (1961), and 'Driving Sideways' (1962). Of these, 'Hideaway' even managed to hit the US charts, climbing to Number 29 – perhaps tapping into the contemporaneous popularity of instrumental groups like The Ventures. Yet King was far from happy with his output at Federal, especially when he had to record other instrumentals like 'The Bossa Nova Watusi Twist' or 'Surf Monkey'. When he eventually walked out in 1966, he did not record again for three years. But with his popularity in Europe and the UK on the up, he was still touring constantly – usually he would tour with a pick-up band, which at that time in the UK could perhaps be Fleetwood Mac or Chicken Shack.

When he resumed recording in 1969, it was with the Atlantic subsidiary Cotillion, though he only cut two albums for the label, *Freddie King Is A Bluesmaster* (1969) and *My Feeling For The Blues* (1970). With fellow Texan and tenor sax legend King Curtis producing, it should have been a perfect set-up, but King was unhappy with the mix, feeling that the studio band were drowning him out.

In 1970 he was signed to Leon Russell's Shelter label where his debut, *Gettin' Ready*, featured a combination of classic blues – such as Elmore James's 'Dust My Broom' and Big Bill

Broonzy's 'Key To The Highway' – alongside new material from Russell and Don Nix: Nix's 'Goin' Down' and 'Same Old Blues' enabled the heavy hand attack of King's guitar style to come into its own. Jimmie Vaughan's band Storm often accompanied King when he was on tour in Texas and he is quoted as saying that King was "so powerful it was unbelievable – I never heard anybody play louder, not back then."

The second Shelter album, *Texas Cannonball* (1972), took a comparable route with Lowell Fulson's 'Reconsider Baby' and Howlin' Wolf's 'How Many More Years' nestling comfortably alongside Russell's 'Big Legged Woman' and Isaac Hayes and David Porter's 'Can't Trust Your Neighbour'. The only slight surprise was the inclusion of Bill Withers' 'Ain't No Sunshine' – superficially it seems at odds with the remainder of the set, but King manages to give a touching vocal performance that more than complements his guitar work.

Woman Across The River completed the trilogy in 1973. Featuring two Willie Dixon compositions, 'I'm Ready' and 'Hoochie Coochie Man', both of which Freddie would have known from his early days listening to Muddy Waters back in Chicago, the highlight of the set is nonetheless the compelling reworking of 'Trouble In Mind', which Sister Rosetta Tharpe had recorded to such effect in the 1940s.

Moving on from Shelter, which was having legal troubles, Freddie King's new-found friend Eric Clapton persuaded him to sign with Robert Stigwood's label, RSO. His label debut, *Burglar* (1974), was produced by Mike Vernon, one of the most important individuals on the British blues scene, and it naturally enough featured Clapton as guest. The next set for the label was the live *Larger Than Life* (1975). In retrospect, neither of these albums do Freddie full justice, as both seem over-produced, allowing little scope for him to expand. *Larger Than Life* also proved to be an unfortunate title – at a Christmas evening concert in 1976 in Dallas (his home-town since 1963), he was taken ill and rushed to the Presbyterian Hospital, where he died three days later from a combination of heart failure, hepatitis and internal bleeding from ulcers.

In the years since his death, as during the later years of his career, Freddie King has continued to exert an enormous influence. If the albums he recorded sometimes sound patchy, it has to be remembered that for the last ten years of his career he worked consistently within a rock context, which was not really his natural element. But in 1995 tapes surfaced from a concert at the Electric Ballroom in Atlanta, Georgia, and this set – *Live At the Electric Ballroom, 1974* – on the Rounder subsidiary Black Top, gives a very good account of Freddie, especially on the long workout on 'Sweet Home Chicago'.

Apart from B.B. King, the guitarist who exerted the greatest influence on how the blues could work in the modern era was probably Albert Collins. Although aged 61 when he died,

Collins – known as The Master Of The Telecaster, The Iceman, and The Razor Blade – was beginning to pack a punch that was as lyrical yet incendiary in its impact as anyone's. Albert Collins was born on October 1st 1932 in Leona, Texas. His family moved to Houston when he was seven, and he grew up in the same neck of the woods as Johnny 'Guitar' Watson and Johnny 'Clyde' Copeland. Uncharacteristically, his first love was the piano, then he switched to the Hammond B3 – because of Jimmy McGriff – when he was in his his teens. But by the time he was 18 he had fallen under the spell of bluesmen such as Clarence Gatemouth Brown, John Lee Hooker, T-Bone Walker and his own cousin, Sam 'Lightnin'' Hopkins. From then on, for Collins, there was no alternative – especially as he not only got to see these guys, he also managed to hang out with them at local Houston clubs.

The competition was intense during the 1950s, but Collins honed a style of his own, using minor tunings and a capo. He was quick to recognise the need for little trademarks, and he started – with the help of some very long guitar cables – to wander around among the audience at gigs. This was not particularly novel, as both Watson and Guitar Slim had utilised long leads for various purposes, but when, much later in his career, Collins was playing principally to young white audiences, they went bananas when he went on a stroll-around.

Leading a ten-piece band, the Rhythm Rockers, Collins cut 'The Freeze', his first single, for the Houston-based Kangaroo label in 1958. This was followed by a number of other instrumental singles with such arctically allusive titles as 'Sno-Cone', 'Icy Blue', and 'Don't Lose Your Cool'. While these singles failed to take the national charts by storm they did enough to secure a solid regional base. 'De-Frost' coupled with 'Albert's Alley' for the Beaumont-based Hall-Way label kept up the momentum, and in 1962 Collins struck out with the million-seller 'Frosty' (still pushing the Iceman imagery). By way of a footnote, both Janis Joplin and Johnny Winter were hanging out at the studios at the time he recorded 'Frosty', and Jimi Hendrix would often cite Collins as a big influence.

Collins was quick to recognise the need for little trademarks ... he started to wander among the audience at gigs

After this brief flirtation with success Collins settled into a comfortable routine, working during the day and gigging at the weekends, or alternatively taking in short local tours. Curiously, despite the success of 'Frosty', he was still recording for small local labels like Great Scott, Brylen and TFC. That all changed, at least temporarily, in 1968 when vocalist Bob 'The Bear' Hite of Canned Heat (who at that time were one of the biggest concert attractions in the US) saw Collins playing live in Houston. Hite – an enthusiastic and knowledgeable devotee of the blues – took Collins to California, where he was immediately signed to Imperial Records. After moving his operations to Los Angeles, following the same route as T-Bone Walker, Collins' cult status developed – not harmed by opening for groups like The Allman Brothers. But after three albums, including *Love Can Be Found Anywhere (Even In A Guitar)* and *Trash Talkin'* (1969), Collins found himself out in the cold once again.

Collins had at first been purely an instrumentalist, armed with just his Fender Telecaster and a staccato, ringing guitar tone, but at Imperial that had changed, and he started to sing as well. After Imperial he moved to Blue Thumb and then to Tumbleweed, which was owned by The Eagles' producer Bill Szymczyk. Despite guitarist Joe Walsh producing several singles for him, Collins' appeal remained confined to the concert hall.

In 1977 he was signed by Bruce Iglauer at Alligator, and the following year *Ice Pickin'* was released to unanimous acclaim, and Collins was set. His band, now known as The Icebreakers, featured Larry Burton (guitar), A.C. Reed (tenor sax), Allen Batts (keyboards), Aron Burton (bass – later replaced by Johnny B. 'Good' Gayden), and Casey Jones (drums). Over the next eight years Collins recorded six further sets for the label, including *Frostbite* (1980), *Frozen Alive!* (1981), *Don't Lose Your Cool* (1981), *Live In Japan* (1984) and *Cold Snap* (1986) – on *Cold Snap* he secured the services of his former idol, organist Jimmy McGriff, and the album was duly nominated for a Grammy award.

Meanwhile, at *Live Aid* in 1985, Collins appeared with guitarist George Thorogood, making them the only blues artists to appear on the bill. The same year he collaborated with guitarists Johnny Copeland and Robert Cray on *Showdown!* for Alligator. (Interestingly, it was Collins' handling of the Telecaster that had inspired Cray to start playing the guitar: while he was still a teenager, Cray had even managed to get Collins to play at his high-school graduation, and then proceeded to go on the road with him.) *Showdown!* picked up a Grammy award for all three musicians. Perhaps the most significant element for Collins was the realisation that he was a reasonable vocalist, and this encouraged him, in partnership with his wife Gwynn, to assemble a bunch of self-written songs such as 'Mastercharge' and 'Conversation With Collins' that would keep the 'letterbox earnings' coming in.

In the late 1980s Collins shifted his base from Los Angeles to Las Vegas, and in 1989 he was signed to Virgin Records' Pointblank subsidiary. His debut for the label, *Iceman*, was released in 1991, but as is so often the case, his belated career was nipped in the bud by his death. He succumbed to liver cancer on November 24th 1993. Though Collins spent far too much time in relative obscurity, his performances – alongside those of The Fabulous Thunderbirds and Stevie Ray Vaughan – stimulated interest in the blues through the 1980s and into the 1990s.

Like Collins, with whom he was to collaborate on the Grammy award-winning *Showdown!*, Johnny Copeland had to wait many years to gain widespread acclaim. And like Collins, just as that acclaim was there for the taking, he died. Copeland first saw T-Bone Walker in Houston when he was 13 years old. Although he admitted his own style was a combination of New Orleans R&B and the swing and jump blues of Kansas City, after he moved to Houston as a teenager the spell of Walker was never far away.

Copeland was born on March 27th 1937 in Haynesville, Louisiana. Copeland's family were sharecroppers, but his parents soon separated, and then his father died within a few years. Copeland inherited his guitar. After moving to Houston, he became friends with Joe Hughes – who would soon earn the nickname 'Guitar' – and together they became known as The Dukes Of Rhythm. Throughout the 1950s Hughes and Copeland played in and around Houston – at the Eldorado Ballroom, and becoming the house band at Shady's Playhouse. Although Copeland accompanied such luminaries as Sonny Boy Williamson, Freddie King and Big Mama Thornton, he didn't make his own recording debut until 1958 when he cut 'Rock'n'Roll Lily' for Mercury, which was hardly a sign of things to come.

Throughout the 1960s he continued to label-hop, cutting 'Please Let Me Know' and 'Down On Bending Knees' for local Houston labels All Boy and Golden Eagle respectively. He even cut a version of Bob Dylan's 'Blowin' In The Wind' for Wand.

Despite these early forays into recording, his move to New York in 1974 did nothing to help his studio activities, even if it did mean an upsurge in his club work. His first album, *Copeland Special*, was issued by Rounder in 1981, and became the first of seven albums he would record for the label: *Make My Home Where I Hang My Hat* (1982); *Texas Twister* (1983), which features a cameo from Stevie Ray Vaughan; *Bringing It All Back Home* (1986); *Ain't Nothing But A Party* (1988), a live set that picked up a Grammy nomination; *When The Rain Starts A Fallin'* (1988); and *Boom Boom* (1990). These albums gave a good account of Copeland's tough guitar work and jump style vocals, and his songs highlighted his dry acerbic wit, echoing 'Guitar' Watson's propensity for drawing beyond the usual range of subjects deemed suitable for bluesmen. Also like Watson, Copeland managed to adapt enthusiastically to the fad for funk.

His deal with Polygram's Verve label, home of contemporaries like 'Gatemouth' Brown, gave him a free hand to continue putting out albums, such as *Flyin' High* (1992) and *Catch Up With The Blues* (1994). Copeland toured and gigged solidly until 1995-96. In late 1994, while on tour in Colorado, he'd discovered he had inherited a heart defect from his father – as Copeland was only six months old when his parents split up, he never knew his father's medical history. He was diagnosed with heart disease and spent the next few years in and out of hospital. Then on January 1st 1997, he underwent a heart transplant. At first this was successful, but complications arose and he died on July 3rd that year.

While Copeland has always been under-rated, his influence continues to grow. Now his daughter, singer Shemekia Copeland, shows every indication of keeping up the Copeland tradition. Perhaps the saddest thing is that Johnny did not live long enough to hear his daughter's Alligator label debut.

For all the major figures that have grafted away and eventually hit pay dirt, many others – like Joe Hughes, U.P. Wilson, Hop Wilson and Zuzu Bollin – spent most of their careers working the triangle. This may have been borne out of a reluctance to stray too far from their home territory: in any case the club circuits of each major town were self-sustaining. There were always going to be pockets of activity where individuals such as Hop Wilson or Zuzu Bollin or Joe Hughes could maintain a reasonable standard of living without being obliged to venture too far afield. These characters could be described as 'journeymen', but that term has always had slightly negative connotations, suggesting perhaps a parochial or uninspired attitude. Nothing could be further from the case here, as all these guys plied their trade with total conviction. It was their job; it was what they did, and in some cases still do. Hughes, for instance, will never be more than a competent professional, but to establish a footing in any of the major cities still required a level of commitment and accomplishment that these days seems unattainable, or even unreasonable.

Like Albert Collins, Johnny Copeland had to wait many years to gain widespread acclaim ... and then he died

Hughes was born in 1938 in Houston and was a neighbour of Johnny Guitar Watson. Thanks to his influence, and that of Gatemouth Brown and T-Bone Walker, by the time Hughes was 14 he was an accomplished guitarist. Then in 1953 Johnny Copeland moved to the same district of Houston, and he and Hughes teamed up in the Dukes Of Rhythm. Although Hughes cut the odd solo single along the way – 'I Can't Go On This Way', 'Ants In My Pants' and 'Shoe Shy' – he continued leading the Dukes Of Rhythm until 1963. After that he toured with The Upsetters, and toured and recorded with Bobby Bland – who at the time was one of the Duke label's biggest stars – and then with another local celebrity, Al 'TNT' Braggs.

During the 1970s and early 1980s, Hughes gigged around Houston, but generally it was a thin time for him musically. By the late 1980s the nationwide blues boom – kindled by, among others, the Vaughan brothers, Albert Collins and B.B.King – enabled journeymen like Hughes to cut albums on a fairly regular basis. He had added the sobriquet 'Guitar' to his name, in homage to his old friend Watson; and albums such as *If You Want To See These Blues* (1989) for Black Top and *Texas Guitar Slinger* (1996) for Bullseye Blues did more than enough to validate such a cognomen. Indeed, even when supplemented by a robust six-piece horn section, Hughes' brand of R&B and soul manages to sound timeless. He's still recording into the 21st century, and albums like *Down & Depressed: Dangerous* (1997) for Munich and *Stuff Like That* (2001) for Blues Express give no indication he is slowing down.

Fort Worth-based guitarist, singer and songwriter U.P. Wilson was born on September 4th 1935 in Shreveport, Louisiana. Although not out of the top drawer as a player, Wilson has evolved a highly individual style of soul-blues that seems to combine elements of country blues and gospel. Raised in west Dallas, Wilson learned his craft playing the bars and clubs that litter the region. Inspired by the likes of Gatemouth Brown, ZuZu Bollin and Frankie Lee Sims, Wilson moved from Dallas to Fort Worth and formed a band called the Boogie Chillen Boys with drummer and vocalist Robert Ealey. By the late 1970s Wilson and Ealey were playing every week at a Fort Worth club called the New Bluebird (which Ealey would eventually go on to buy).

Although both of them had acquired pretty large armies of admirers, neither Wilson nor Ealey began recording until comparatively late in their careers. But once Wilson got started, his work suggested a talent of quite formidable inventiveness and considerable originality – for instance albums like *Boogie Boy: Texas Guitar Returns* (1995) on the London-based JSP label, and the extraordinary live album, *Attack Of The Atomic Guitar* (1992) on another UK label, Red Lightnin', with tracks such as 'Enter The Tornado', 'Cold, Cold Feeling' and 'Johnny B. Goode' Like Ealey, Wilson has honed his skills as a songwriter and arranger, so at long last he's becoming better known beyond Texas.

Another Wilson – Harding Wilson, also known as Hop – was an impressive slide guitarist in the Elmore James mold, although Hop's playing possessed shadings and nuances James could only dream of – mainly because Hop's chosen instrument was an eight-string (non-pedal) steel guitar. Although Hop Wilson died well before his time, both Johnny Winter and Jimmie Vaughan have picked up enough tips from him to ensure his reputation can only continue to grow.

Born on April 27th 1927 in Grapeland, which lies around 120 miles to the north of Houston, Hop Wilson learned how to play guitar and harmonica as a child, inspired by local celebrities like Lightnin' Hopkins and Blind Lemon Jefferson. By the time he was 18, he received his first steel guitar and began playing it around Houston's thriving but low-key club circuit – though his career was interrupted by Pearl Harbour and the declaration of war. After his discharge from the army, he joined Ivory Semien's group, and eventually made his recording debut with this outfit in 1957. Recording for the Goldband label, based in Lake Charles, Louisiana, Wilson gives especially impressive accounts of himself on 'Chicken Stuff' and 'Rockin' In The Coconut Top' – both of which can be located on the admirable *Steel Guitar Flash!* (1988).

In 1960 Wilson was signed to the Ivory label and led a few sessions, but basically he loathed touring and was not prepared to put up with it. Consequently from 1961 until his death on August 27th 1975 he stayed put in Houston, playing the clubs and bars. Although his recording career was slight, he did crop up backing guitarist Fenton Robinson and bassist Larry Davis – yes, the same Larry Davis who wrote 'Texas Flood'.

The excellently named Zuzu Bollin – which seems to evoke the steamy swamps of the Bayous (though less exotically is derived from a brand of cookies called ZuZus that Bollin was particularly partial to) – had all the makings of a first-rate post-war axeman in the grand tradition of T-Bone Walker and Pee Wee Crayton. Unfortunately he recorded perhaps even less than the aforementioned Hop Wilson, but what he did was extremely influential.

A.D. Bollin was born in a little outcrop called Frisco, about 20 miles from Dallas, on September 5th 1922. Cast from the same mold as Jimmie Vaughan, albeit 30 years earlier, Bollin listened to anything he could lay his hands on, from Blind Lemon Jefferson and Lightnin' Hopkins to Joe Turner and Count Basie. He formed his first group in 1949, which numbered among its ranks a very youthful David 'Fathead' Newman (later to join the Ray Charles Band) on alto and tenor sax, before the band broke up and Bollin was recruited by songwriter and vocalist Percy Mayfield. That didn't last long either, but at least he made his recording debut with a couple of 78s, 'Why Don't You Eat Where You Slept Last Night' and 'Headlight Blues', and then 'Stavin' Chain' coupled with 'Cry, Cry, Cry' – on the latter he was accompanied by Jimmy McCracklin's group. And then that was that. He took part in a few tours with bandleaders Joe Morris and Ernie Fields, before leaving the music business and setting himself up in a dry cleaners' shop.

Unfortunately Zuzu Bollin recorded perhaps even less than Hop Wilson, but what he did was extremely influential

In 1987 the Dallas Blues Society coaxed him out of retirement, organising a handful of local gigs. Club owner Clifford Antone got into the act by setting up a serious of sessions for an album: produced by guitarist Duke Robillard – whom we shall return to later in the book – *Texas Bluesman* is a finely crafted effort giving full rein to Bollin's charismatic vocal style while allowing his very individual guitar work the opportunity to shine. It also included a number of cameos from some of Texas's finest, including Doug Sahm, drummers George Rains – erstwhile member of Sir Douglas Quintet and The Fabulous Thunderbirds – and Doyle Bramhall, David 'Fathead' Newman and Rocky Morales. Naturally enough the set included a splendid reworking of Bollin's most famous songs, 'Why Don't You Eat Where You Slept Last Night' and 'Headlight Blues', which imparted a sort of elegiac quality to the proceedings. In a curious way it was as if he was setting the record straight before he died. Almost predictably, he passed away on October 2nd 1990, about a year after the album's release.

In many respects guitarist Johnny Winter is the link between the pioneering black purveyors of R&B and the rock stars of the late 1960s and early 1970s. His striking appearance – albino complexion and long flowing white hair – made him noticeably different from his contemporaries, and he immediately struck a chord with fledgling rock audiences; but this should not disguise the authenticity of his roots in the blues. His style, based less on the lyrical, jazz-inflected approach of Walker et al than on the urban Chicago blues of Muddy Waters, had a major impact on younger generations of players like Stevie Ray, Eric Johnson and Smokin' Joe Kubek. Not to mention a couple generations of rock musicians who seemed to absorb the influence of blues and R&B by osmosis, and who played heavy stuff from the word go – Led Zeppelin and Iron Butterfly, to name just two.

Johnny Winter was born John Dawson Winter in Leland, Mississippi, on February 23rd 1944, then his family moved to Beaumont in Texas, where Winter's brother Edgar was born in 1946. Johnny formed his first band at 14, with Edgar, and made his recording debut with 'Schoolday Blues' in 1959 for the Dart label, under the name of Johnny & The Jammers. In 1962, after a spell in Chicago playing with such luminaries as guitarist Mike Bloomfield, he returned to Texas, where he recorded many demos for small labels and gigged around locally. It's a mark of how prolific he was during this period that the compilations of out-takes, live sets and the like seems endless.

In 1968, Winter recorded a one-off album for Imperial called The Progressive Blues Experiment, with Tommy Shannon on bass – later to fill the same role in Double Trouble with Stevie Ray – and John 'Red' Turner on drums. The album did not see the light of day until Winter had been signed to Columbia by Clive Davis for $300,000. This remarkable change in his circumstances had been prompted when Steve Paul, owner of the New York club Scene, read an article in *Rolling Stone* magazine about Winter's guitar work; Paul then recruited the band and took over management duties.

The following year, Winter's self-titled debut appeared and climbed up the charts, reaching Number 24. More than that, it placed Winter firmly on the map, and by the end of June 1969 he was playing gigs like Newport '69 and the Mile High Stadium in Denver, Colorado. *Second Winter* (1970) featured strong versions of Dylan's 'Highway 61 Revisited' and Chuck Berry's 'Johnny B Goode', but manager Paul was keen to link Winter to some of his other protégées: these turned out to be The McCoys who had scored a huge hit a few years earlier with 'Hang On Sloopy'. So Shannon and Turner were out, and bassist Randy Hobbs, drummer Randy Zehringer, and guitarist Rick Zehringer (who later changed his name to Derringer) were in.

The next set, *Johnny Winter And ...* (1970), showed Winter abandoning the blues for an acid-tinged brand of progressive rock. The follow-up, *Johnny Winter And/Live!* (1971), with substantially the same band, managed to be successful commercially, thanks in part to its collection of R&B covers and the Rolling Stones' 'Jumpin' Jack Flash' – but all was not well with Winter, and his growing heroin addiction sidelined him for a spell. In 1973 he re-emerged with the ironically titled Still Alive And Well: again this combination of classic rock'n'roll and R&B, cut through with covers of Stones' material such as 'Silver Train' and 'Let It Bleed', and a few group originals, showed that Winter, though not doing anything radically different from before, was still an abrasive and inventive guitarist capable of developing ideas from even the most humble riffs. One more album, *Saints And Sinners* (1974) followed for Columbia, then he moved over to the Blue Sky label, where he produced two albums for Muddy Waters. Although these records – *Hard Again* and *I'm Ready* – were fine efforts, confirming that Winter was as sympathetic a producer as he was an inventive guitarist, the six albums he cut for the label seemed to be marking time: even if *Together – Live!* (1976), with multi-instrumentalist brother Edgar, had plenty of zip and enthusiasm.

Johnny Winter is the link between the pioneering black purveyors of R&B and the rock stars of the late 1960s/early 1970s

Then in 1984 he signed to Alligator. The three albums he recorded for the label – *Guitar Slinger* (1984), *Serious Business* (1985) and *Third Degree* (1986) – showed him adopting a straightforward, no-frills approach. Accompanied by Albert Collins' rhythm section, Johnny B. 'Goode' Gayden on bass and Casy Jones on drums (except for a couple of tracks on *Third Degree* where he was joined by his former rhythm section of Tommy Shannon and John Turner), there was a sharpness in his delivery that had been lacking for a few years. In recent times Winter has continued to tour and record – there were three albums for Virgin in the 1990s – and he remains a pivotal influence in the great tradition of blues-based Texan axemen.

On the surface it may seem stretching a point to include here those three hirsute icons of the video-age, ZZ Top, but they do occupy a key position in the pantheon where the blues and R&B are vehicles for entertainment as much as for disseminating trials and tribulations. Like T-Bone Walker and Johnny Guitar Watson, ZZ Top seemed to know the value of showmanship from the word go. But the group's tongue-in-cheek, high-octane boogie can often disguise the considerable musicianship that drives them. They are, if you like, the template for every bar band you ever heard – though they themselves have long-since passed that point, and now in all probability the only bar you're likely to see them in is either on a movie set or one they own themselves. That does not alter the essential simplicity of the formula, nor the sophisticated vulgarity of the exposition.

Like T-Bone Walker and Johnny Guitar Watson, ZZ Top seemed to know the value of showmanship from the word go

Guitarist Billy Gibbons was born on December 12th 1949 in Houston. His father was conductor of the Houston Philharmonic Orchestra. When Billy was 14 he was given a Gibson Melody Maker guitar and a Fender Champ amplifier for his birthday; this largesse on the part of his parents encouraged him to form a string of bands, including The Saints, The Coachmen and The Ten Blue Flames. Around the same time, Joe Hill, born in 1949 in Dallas, was spending every spare minute in the local blues clubs where eventually he got to know Freddie King. Hill, with his older brother Rocky, decided to form a group, The Deadbeats. Meanwhile, over in Frankston, Frank Beard (also born in 1949) married his childhood sweetheart in 1964. When the marriage foundered, Beard – rather ominously – took up drumming, presumably as a form of sublimation.

By 1967 the Hill Brothers had become The Warlocks (not to be confused with an early incarnation of the Grateful Dead), and Beard soon joined them. Gibbons, however, had progressed and formed a psychedelic band, Moving Sidewalks. They enjoyed some limited celebrity when they had a local hit with '99th Floor' and then in 1968 they opened for Jimi Hendrix, who was typically generous enough to admit he was impressed by Gibbons' prowess. In June 1968 the group cut their first album, presciently titled *Flash*. The Warlocks had also been doing some recording, cutting a brace of albums for the local Paradise and Ara labels, before changing their name from The Warlocks to American Blues. As American Blues they would record another pair of albums, one for Karma in 1967 and one for MCA subsidiary Uni in 1969.

In 1969, as the Moving Sidewalks disbanded, Gibbons formed a new outfit with Lanier Greig and Dan Mitchell. Greig and Mitchell did not last long though, and Gibbons recruited first Beard and then Hill. At this point local promotion man Bill Ham entered the frame and the group, now called ZZ Top (alluding to blues artists like B.B. King and Texan singer Z.Z. Hill), cut the single 'Salt Lick' for Ham's Scat label. The group's first album, entitled *ZZ Top's First Album*, was recorded without label backing, but seemed to reflect their total confidence and their musical acuity. A blend of John Lee Hooker, Freddie and B.B. King, this first set was picked up by the London record label, who provided the band with the fuel to tour. They opened for Janis Joplin, Humble Pie, Ten Years After, and even Mott The Hoople. At first locally, throughout Texas, Louisiana and Mississippi, they built up a reputation that was consolidated by the release of *Rio Grande Mud* (1972), which led to an opening slot on The Rolling Stones' tour. This was followed by top-billing at *ZZ Top's First Annual Texas Size Rompin' Stompin' Barndance Bar B-Q* in Austin, which attracted an audience of over 100,000. This exposure and the constant touring made the difference the following year when *Tres Hombres* climbed up to Number Eight in the US charts. The single 'La Grange', about a Texan whorehouse, was based around Hooker's 'Boogie Chillen' and was a massive hit, while other tracks like 'Jesus Just Left Chicago' helped establish Gibbons's extraordinary guitar work.

By the time the group issued Fandango (1975) – half of which was cut in the studio, the other half live – the group was breaking attendance records set by Elvis and Led Zeppelin. This was to continue through 1976 and early 1977 when, in support of the album *Tejas*, they covered 100 US cities on *ZZ Top's Worldwide Texas Tour*. For this little outing they transported 75 tons of equipment, including a stage the shape of the state of Texas; and $140,000 worth of livestock – buffalos, steers and snakes – just to complete the illusion. Unfortunately quarantine laws meant that for the European, Australian and Japanese legs of the tour, the animals had to stay at home. Before that, even though they were clearly massive in the US, they'd only had a limited following elsewhere – but that changed after this 1977 tour, which grossed over ten million dollars.

Now signed to Warner Brothers, and after an extended break, they came up with the excellent *Deguello* (1979). Featuring Elmore James's 'Dust My Broom' and Sam & Dave's 'I Thank You', alongside the regular handful of new compositions such as 'Cheap Sunglasses', Deguello – and its follow-up *El Loco* (1981) – set the stage for *Eliminator* (1983). Gibbons had taken some time out to study synthesisers and their prospective application, and *Eliminator* and then *Afterburner* (1985) put that knowledge into action. With almost blanket coverage on MTV, the cheesy, sexist, glossy videos accompanying the singles 'Gimme All Your Lovin', 'Sharp Dressed Man' and 'Legs', from *Eliminator*, and 'Sleeping Bag', 'Rough Boy' and 'Velcro Fly' from *Afterburner*, made these unlikely individuals in trademark boiler suits and shades almost as familiar as cartoon characters.

Despite the group's success and their apparent distance from their early roots, they still seem to have their hearts in the right place. They still support the blues in different ways, though even here their slightly surreal approach is apparent. For example they were given a piece of wood from Muddy Waters' former home in Clarksdale, Mississippi, which they got made into a guitar. The guitar was named 'Muddywood', and used on tour to raise money for the Delta Blues Museum. Then in the early 1990s, under the name Das Combo, they accompanied the great slide guitarist Rainer Ptacek on *The Texas Tapes*, which was released by the German indie label Glitterhouse, after Rainer's premature death from a brain tumour.

Young blues musicians such as Stevie Ray Vaughan recognised that it wasn't just what you played, but how you played it

Throughout the 1990s, despite a move to RCA, their profile was perhaps not as high as it had been during the mid-1980s, even though albums such as *Recycler* (1990), *Antenna* (1994), *Rhythmeen* (1996) and *XXX* (1999) were still highly successful. And, of course, their consistent appeal as a live act has been untouched by changing fashions: they are arch-exponents of 'stadium rock' in all its dazzling spectacle, and have even surmounted the limitations of the trio format by using backing tapes.

ZZ Top's idiosyncratic approach struck a chord with kids across Texas from the start, imparting a charismatic flamboyance to the blues that gave it broader appeal, and certainly seemed worth emulating. Though Top were primarily a rock act with their feet in the traditions of the blues, young musicians such as Stevie Ray Vaughan saw them and recognised instinctively that when it came to the blues, it was precisely what you brought to it that was crucial. It wasn't just what you played, but how you played it. Presentation was one key element, but gut feeling was paramount.

CHAPTER 3

Groover's Paradise

"I was walking down the street and I heard this great guitar player. I went into the club and here's this little kid up there."

BASSIST TOMMY SHANNON ON HIS FIRST ENCOUNTER WITH THE YOUNG STEVIE RAY

When the tributes started rolling in after Stevie Ray Vaughan's death, one from Eric Clapton struck a particularly resonant chord: "The first time I heard Stevie Ray, I thought, 'Whoever this is, he is going to shake the world'. It's going to be a long time before anyone that brilliant will come along again." Eric hit the nail on the head because, in the tradition of all great performers, Stevie Ray was not just a groundbreaking musician in his own right, but more significantly he was a catalyst. It was largely thanks to the Stevie Ray effect that by the mid 1980s the blues was suddenly big business again, with bar bands crawling out of the woodwork and old timers like John Lee Hooker making comebacks with stellar casts of even more famous friends.

Stevie Ray may have been top of the heap, but his own biggest inspiration was his brother Jimmie. Music formed an important ingredient in the pair's upbringing – as it had done for both sides of the Vaughan family ever since their grandparents had moved to north-east Texas in the latter part of the 19th century. Robert Hodgen LaRue – a man blessed with profound convictions and an imposing air of authority (which wasn't harmed by his long white beard) – had gathered

KING OF THE ROADHOUSE, DISPLAYING SOME OF HIS JEWELS

Five, Under Fifteen, Or Free,
USIC EVERY NIGHT
FISH

his family and chattels together into a wagon and moved from Kentucky to Terrell, Texas, in 1890. Terrell in Rockwell County, was cotton country and, laying about 30 miles to the east of Dallas, was on the migratory route for those from the east and north who sought to improve their prospects by moving west or south west. This included James Robert Vaughan and his wife Sarah Catherine, originally from Fulton County up in Arkansas; and in the fullness of time, the paths of the two families crossed, when Robert LaRue's daughter, Laura Belle, met up with Vaughan's son, Thomas Lee.

They married on July 13th 1902, and moved to a small tract of land known as Griffith League, where they became sharecroppers. Although they were very poor, Laura Belle bore nine children, with only one dying in infancy; among the progeny were twins Jimmie Lee and Linnie Lee who arrived on September 6th 1921. But in 1928, just as the Depression was about to strike, Thomas Lee Vaughan succumbed to the kidney infection known as Bright's Disease, and Laura Belle was left with eight children to support alone. That number dropped to seven when Jimmie Lee enlisted in the navy just after the outbreak of war. When he returned from his tour of duty in the South Seas, Jimmie Lee could not face a return to sharecropping, and obtained employment in the local 7-Eleven store in downtown Dallas.

At first he seemed destined for a swift climb up the ladder, but this was curtailed mid-step by Martha Jean Cook. Martha was one of the regular customers, who not only looked sharp, but also drove her own car, and was therefore of independent means. Martha came from north-east Texas, where both sides of the family farmed cotton. Her father, Joseph Luther Cook, and her mother, Dora Ruth Deweese, were childhood sweethearts, and were married just before Joseph started to work for the Lonestar Gas Company in Eastland, an oil-rich area around 120 miles west of Dallas. Joe was soon promoted to foreman, and he and Dora Ruth, with their five children, settled at Cockrell Hill, close to the Oak Cliff district of Dallas, where they settled into a comfortable lifestyle. Martha, the eldest of the five children, graduated from Sunset High School, and became a secretary at a timber merchants in nearby Oak Cliff. As she travelled back and forth to work she began to stop off at the local 7-Eleven, where a certain young man had taken her eye.

Although diametrically opposite in many ways – Jimmie Lee liked a few drinks and could get rowdy, whereas Martha kept herself to herself – both liked music, especially the western swing of Hank Thompson's band, the Brazos Valley Boys. Despite their differences, Martha and Jimmie Lee were married on January 13th 1950.

Perhaps to take himself out of harm's way, or just to acknowledge his new-found responsibilities, Jimmie Lee secured a job as a member of the Asbestos Workers Union (Local 21) in Dallas. This was a long time before the hazards of asbestos became known, and for Jimmie Lee and Martha it represented a fine opportunity to obtain regular, sensible work – slightly different from working the cars at a convenience store. As Jimmie Vaughan later recalled to Margaret Moser in *Mojo* magazine, "He'd do what they called in the union 'sitting on the bench', literally waiting for a call to a job, wherever. 'November 22nd – Monroe, Louisiana. Next week'. And it would be like, 'OK, kids, let's go'. We'd stay however long the job was – one, two months, a week. All over the South." In the process, Jimmie Lee worked on construction – building power plants, office blocks and refineries, or insulating pipes and ventilation shafts.

Jimmie, their first child, was born Jimmie Lawrence Vaughan on March 20th 1951 at the Florence Baylor Medical Centre. Three-and-a-half years later, on October 3rd 1954, Stephen Ray was born at the Methodist Hospital in Dallas. Neither Jimmie nor Stevie Ray were big lads as babies, weighing just five pounds and three pounds nine ounces respectively. As children they lived a peripatetic existence, as the family trailed across the South in hot pursuit of Jimmy Lee's work assignments. Eventually Jimmie Lee managed to obtain jobs closer to Dallas, which enabled the family to abandon their nomadic lifestyle and settle back in Oak Cliff. While this new arrangement was a decisive improvement, Jimmie Lee could be volatile after a few drinks, and that did nothing to improve Stevie Ray's stability. Unlike his dark-haired elder brother Jimmie, who was considered handsome, Stevie Ray – with his spindly legs and skinny frame – always lacked self-confidence. The fact that his nose had been damaged in an operation to alleviate sinusitis when he was six only made things worse.

Stevie Ray only seemed to be genuinely comfortable when music was playing. Often their parents' friends and relations or work colleagues would stop by the Vaughan household in the evening for a game of dominoes, to the accompaniment of either the record player or someone messing around with a guitar. Both Martha's brothers, Joe and Jerrel, were good enough guitar players to pick out the recent country hits by the likes of Hank Williams, Merle Travis, Ray Price or Ernest Tubb; older cousins Sammy and 'Red' Klutts played in various western bands around Dallas. And Charles LaRue, albeit a distant relative, had played trombone in the famous Tommy Dorsey Orchestra.

Jimmie was the first to get a guitar when he was sidelined from football by an injury at the age of 12. Given to him by a family friend, the guitar was supposed to occupy him during his recuperation. And the ploy worked: from the moment Jimmie's fingers touched the fretboard, it was obvious he had a natural talent.

"It was like he played it all his life," Martha Vaughan later noted. Years afterwards Stevie Ray told how Jimmie had made up three songs the very first time he picked up a guitar. When the family friend came by a few days later to see how Jimmie was getting along he was so impressed by his progress that he took the guitar away to have it repaired and fitted with new strings – it only had three to start off with.

Now that Jimmie had a guitar, Stevie Ray wanted one as well, and his wish was granted at Christmas when he received a Sears toy guitar with a western motif. It might not have been a Stratocaster but it was good enough for Stevie Ray to learn 'Wine, Wine, Wine' and 'Thunderbird' by The Nightcaps. The die was cast.

Such was Stevie Ray's enthusiasm and dedication that when he bought a copy of Lonnie Mack's 'Wham', he played the record so much his father smashed it in a fit of pique. That made little difference to Stevie Ray – though perhaps more to Jimmie, who claimed later, "That was my record, the way I remember it."

Despite the sibling rivalry, Stevie Ray had a tutor of sorts in Jimmie, which was something Jimmie himself had always lacked – though of course with parents like Jimmie Lee and Martha offering encouragement at every turn (it's said that Jimmie Lee had a very good ear and could pick out anything on the piano) young Jimmie was never completely on his own. But Stevie Ray was in a perfect situation: nobody pestered him to play in front of family friends; he could pick up everything first-hand as Jimmie progressed; and best of all, whenever Jimmie acquired a new guitar, Stevie Ray usually managed to get his hands on the cast-off. As a matter of fact, Stevie Ray was not above borrowing Jimmie's guitar when he was not around: though if he was caught he got a good smacking for his pains.

Paul Ray, a friend of both brothers and leader of The Cobras, commented to Moser that the rivalry was a typical big brother/little brother thing, with common threats like "Don't touch my guitar or I'll break your thumbs". And yet, as is often the case with siblings, anybody else who tried to best Stevie Ray would have to deal with Jimmie, and was "dead meat". Paul Ray put the brothers' rivalry into perspective, saying, "He was Jimmie's little brother. He was treated accordingly. It was no big deal."

After Jimmie acquired a Gibson ES-300, Stevie Ray got the reject, a Gibson Messenger 125T – his first electric guitar. As well as their love of guitars, the radio was another source of inspiration. From the border station of XERF to Chicago's WLS and Nashville's WLAC Jimmie and Stevie Ray were exposed to a broad, eclectic mix that ranged from the Top 40 to the esoteric R&B of Muddy Waters, Howlin' Wolf, Jimmy Reed and Buddy Guy. And then there were the local stations, such as Dallas's WRR, which was more eclectic than the larger stations – so listeners could hear not only doo-wop and the latest rock'n'roll, but also everything from Clarence Gatemouth Brown and T-Bone Walker to Albert Collins and Freddie King, alongside the rural blues of Lightnin' Hopkins and the epic narratives of Mance Lipscomb.

All this exposure to R&B and rock'n'roll turned Jimmie Vaughan into an avid record collector, and Stevie Ray was naturally not far behind. So when British bands such as The Beatles, Rolling Stones, The Yardbirds and John Mayall's Bluesbreakers started making a mark, the interest of the Vaughan brothers was definitely fired. Jimmie was already set on a career in music, starting his first band, The Swinging Pendulums, in 1964. After their first gig at the Hob Nob Lounge in Dallas, they managed to pick up more gigs at places like The Fog, The Beachcomber, and The Loser's Club, and before long Jimmie was pulling in around $50 a week. It would have remained like that had it not been for another local group called The Chessmen.

The Chessmen were basically a covers band, their stock-in-trade being the works of The Beatles, the Stones, Chuck Berry and Bo Diddley. But things started to change for them when they were joined by a young drummer called Doyle Bramhall. Doyle was born on February 17th 1949, and had grown up listening to the likes of Jimmy Reed, Ray Charles and Bobby Bland on the local radio stations. He persuaded his father to turn their garage into a rehearsal room where he and his twin brother Dale could practise and jam with other local kids – some of whom, like Frank Beard and Dusty Hill, later of ZZ Top, would go on to greater things.

Jimmie was now keeping erratic hours, drinking too much and doing dope ... a fully fledged rock star in his own eyes

When Doyle joined The Chessmen they were very well established, often playing up to six gigs a week: Doyle was so busy that most of the time he was earning more than his father. But his father seemed to take this in pretty good part, driving Doyle to and from gigs, even helping transport the band's gear. Then when guitarist Robert Patton was drowned in a boating accident, the group needed to move fast to find a replacement, and Doyle suggested Jimmie, who went to the same school, Oak Cliff Christian Academy. At first Jimmie was reluctant to abandon his bandmates in The Swinging Pendulums, but common sense did prevail, and Jimmie joined The Chessmen.

While his parents had always been supportive, Jimmie was now keeping erratic hours, drinking too much and doing dope. The inevitable confrontation, when it came, caused Jimmie to drop out of school and move into an apartment with the rest of the group: he might have been a fully-fledged rock star in his own eyes – and his brother's, come to that – but to Jimmie Lee and Martha he was still a 16-year-old kid.

There were ramifications in this for Stevie Ray too, because, having seen what it had done to their eldest son, his parents were not keen on having two guitarists in the family. Still, Stevie Ray started showing more independence, even getting himself a part-time job at a local fast food joint – though this didn't last long, as one day he slipped and fell into a vat of grease. This was the rite of passage he had been waiting for: no-one was going to tell him what to do, and he was going to play the guitar irrespective of what others said and thought.

Jimmie's guitar playing, meanwhile, was becoming ever more accomplished; he had seen both Muddy Waters and Freddie King when they appeared in Dallas, and their influence had caused his style to become much cleaner and more economical, with rhythmic accents that relied on the power of his concise approach. This had paid dividends for the group, as they were now being booked to open for visiting dignitaries such as Jimi Hendrix. "I played on one show with him," Jimmie recalled to Dan Forte in *Guitar Player*. "We couldn't do our Hendrix songs, because Hendrix was there, so I think we came out and did a bunch of Cream stuff. They were amused. We were a copy band – as soon as a record came out, we'd be the first guys in town to know how to play it. Hendrix was amazing... I'll never forget it."

Jimmie and the other Chessmen were fast becoming victims of their own success. Certainly they were earning good wages, but the frustrations were all too plain. In order to counteract being just a covers band, they were drinking, smoking or ingesting anything they could lay their hands on. The net result was that Doyle contracted hepatitis, the bass player also became sick, and gradually the band fell to pieces.

After Doyle's recovery, he and Jimmie assembled Texas Storm, a group whose repertoire was much more to Jimmie's taste, as they played their own high-energy versions of Memphis soul and R&B classics by people like Sam & Dave, Wilson Pickett and Eddie Floyd. This made a lot more sense to Jimmie, but gigs and audiences were elusive. Things went from bad to worse as the bass player managed to rub the police up the wrong way and was rewarded with a spell in the slammer. His replacement was Stevie Ray – he didn't have a bass guitar, but he slackened his guitar strings enough to make it sound reasonably authentic.

For Stevie Ray this was another 'business as usual' type of gig. Since entering Justin F. Kimball High School he had played in a string of school bands with such extraordinary names as the Epileptic Marshmallows. He also played his first outdoor gig, which happened to be at Lee Park in Dallas, and had been good enough for drummer Billy Knight to persuade the owner of a local nightclub, End Of Cole, to give them a gig on the sidelines. When the spot with Texas Storm came along, Stevie Ray was more than ready for the role, if only on a temporary basis, and when the band was booked for a gig in Austin it must have seemed the big time was within his grasp.

But after Texas Storm's bass player got out of jail, Stevie Ray was on the loose once again.

So he auditioned as bass player for a group called Liberation. Led by lead guitarist Scott Phares, Liberation was an 11-piece outfit with horns and two vocalists, including Christian de Plicque. When Phares heard Stevie Ray playing around on the guitar, he took over bass playing duties himself so Stevie Ray could become the lead guitarist.

Around that time, soulful rock groups with horn sections – the likes of Blood, Sweat & Tears and Chicago – were enjoying some popularity, so it was slightly easier getting gigs, especially at clubs such as the Blackout and the Fog. One evening while Liberation were playing, Johnny Winter's rhythm section – bassist Tommy Shannon and drummer John Turner – came into the club: "It was at the same place I had met Johnny Winter," Shannon recalled years later to Dan Forte, "a club called the Fog in Dallas. I was walking down the street and I heard this great guitar player. I went in and here's this little kid up there." For Stevie Ray, who knew both men by reputation, this was another moment too good to be passed by, so he asked them both if they wanted to jam. Turner declined, but Shannon obliged, and a relationship started that would endure, off-and-on, until the end of Stevie Ray's life.

As it happened, Liberation did not last very long, but there were signs that Stevie Ray might be on the right track. One night the band was playing at Arthur's, which was situated in the seriously posh Adolphus hotel, when three guys walked in and asked if they might do a small set during Liberation's break. When they got up on stage and announced themselves, it transpired this was none other than Frank Beard, Dusty Hill and Billy Gibbons, by now calling themselves ZZ Top. With their debut album in the offing, and tenaciously managed by Bill Ham, ZZ Top's combination of Texas shuffles and hard-edged rock'n'roll was winning favour locally, though had yet to find success internationally. So when Stevie Ray asked Billy Gibbons if he would jam, there wasn't yet much of a reputation to jeopardise. Even so, Stevie Ray gave a good enough account of himself that Gibbons subsequently never seemed keen to repeat this kind of experience...

Stevie Ray was able to indulge his penchant for Hendrix, Cream and Otis Redding ... and the more he played, the better he got

Despite the adventure at Arthur's, Liberation began to drift apart, and soon Stevie Ray was looking for another group. After a few hiccups a new line-up emerged from the remnants of Liberation: Stevie Ray hooked up with vocalist Christian de Plicque and drummer Roddy Colonna to form Blackbird, with Kim Davis on guitar, Noel Deis on keyboards, David Frame on bass, and a second drummer, John Huff. This was probably the first time Stevie Ray had been the motivator, and so was able to determine the group's musical direction. For anyone else, that might have constituted a problem, but for Stevie Ray it was easy: night after night, from Dallas to Houston, and from Forth Worth to Austin, Stevie Ray was able to indulge his penchant for Hendrix, and Cream, as well as Otis Redding. And the more he played the better he got.

One of the group's regular gigs was a dubious sounding den of iniquity called The Cellars, whose main attractions, according to Joe Nick Patoski in *Caught In The Crossfire*, were "loud rock bands, fake alcoholic drinks and scantily clad waitresses who would perform impromptu stripteases when the mood struck them." The Cellars was also a regular home-from-home for many of the performers, of all musical persuasions, that gathered to play there – not least Jimmie Vaughan's Texas Storm.

Throughout all of this period, Stevie Ray was still attending high-school – though he was probably not what you might call a model student. All too often he was recovering from the after-effects of the night before. Despite his parents protestations, gaining a high-school diploma was a long way down Stevie Ray's list of priorities. Yet school did hold some attractions: one of the senior students, Stephen Tobolowsky, recruited Stevie Ray for his group Cast Of Thousands, who were contributing to a compilation album called *A New Hi*. This not only gave Stevie Ray the opportunity to record, he also contributed a couple of songs to the project. But he'd soon had enough of school generally, and he didn't bother returning for the spring semester in 1972.

News of this young hotshot guitarist spread like wildfire throughout Austin, and the bookings just flooded in from other clubs

Stevie Ray's next hurdle was to get out of Dallas. Dallas still had a reputation for being rather hard-bitten, a hang-over from the assassination of President Kennedy. What's more, his relationship with his father was fractious to say the least: it was not uncommon for Jimmie Lee to whack Stevie Ray without provocation. Stevie Ray would always be conciliatory, saying it was because his father, "didn't want him to turn out like Jimmie." So, early in 1972, Stevie Ray and his band moved to Austin. Not only was Austin jam-packed with students, musicians and all-round good eggs, but Jimmie had already moved there with his band Texas Storm, and so had a pretty good notion of the workings of the local club circuit.

Once there, Blackbird started to play regularly at the Rolling Hills Country Club, just outside of town. Set off the beaten track – literally quarter of a mile down a pitted pathway – it was run by a guy called Alex Napier, who also played guitar and bass. Definitely not the average club owner, Napier was a hippie at heart and allowed everyone to do pretty much as they liked. This was excellent news all round, because it meant they could all drink, smoke or ingest anything they liked, providing they were discreet. Within a very short period of time, news of this young hotshot guitarist spread like wildfire throughout Austin, and the bookings just flooded in from other clubs, such as the Black Queen, Mother Earth and the Waterloo Social Club. Although the group was still performing Hendrix and Cream covers most of the time, Stevie Ray's guitar work was becoming ever more intense. Consequently he and the rest of the group were locked into an extreme learning curve that would set them, and especially Stevie Ray, in good stead for the rest of their career.

Despite the importance of Blackbird, it was still, after all, only Stevie Ray's first proper band, and the longer he stayed with them the more he recognised he would have to move on sooner rather than later. That opportunity eventually arrived towards the end of the year, when he joined Krackerjack for a few months. No one could say Krackerjack was the be-all and end-all – it was just another bar band plying its trade around the Austin City limits – but it brought him into closer contact with bassist Tommy Shannon, known affectionately to his intimates as 'Slut', and drummer 'Uncle' John Turner, who had both been fired by Johnny Winter after a riotously disastrous European tour.

After leaving Winter, both Shannon and Turner had hooked up with Jesse Taylor. Taylor, a native of Lubbock, had joined them after moving up to Austin, but now with other offers to work with Joe Ely and Butch Hancock, among others, Taylor had decided to move on – leaving the way clear for Stevie Ray. Roddy Colonna from Blackbird joined as well, and with long-time chum and Stevie Ray's unofficial minder Robert 'Cutter' Brandenberg coming along to act as roadie, Krackerjack now looked as if Stevie Ray had taken over. But when Turner announced that perhaps they should start wearing make-up, like the New York Dolls, Stevie Ray was not keen, and he was fired. As it turned out, Krackerjack did not have to ponder the make-up option very long, as they were busted for possession of speed, heroin, and pills. Tommy was the only one taken into custody and, a few months later, was fined and given probation – one of the conditions of which was he should no longer play in Krackerjack.

None of this impacted on Stevie Ray because in the meantime he had been contacted by singer-songwriter and guitarist Marc Benno to work on an album he was about to record for A&M. Benno came from east Dallas and had moved to LA, where he'd hooked up with Leon Russell. Russell, in 1968/9, had one of the most impressive pedigrees in the business, having worked on many of the Phil Spector sessions at the Goldstar Studios in the early 1960s; he had arranged Ike & Tina Turner's 'River Deep, Mountain High'. This had turned him into one of LA's most high-profile session musicians, and so when he teamed up with Benno for an album entitled *The Asylum Choir*, Mercury duly signed them up. The first album bombed, and Russell moved over to A&M, taking Benno with him.

Russell's career at A&M was helped when he masterminded *Mad Dogs And Englishmen*, the travelling revue featuring Joe Cocker, before cutting a series of star-studded solo albums for his own record label Shelter. Apart from featuring such luminaries as George Harrison, Delaney & Bonnie and Eric Clapton, there was also a backing vocalist called Rita Coolidge, who had been signed to A&M as a solo artist, and whom Benno had provided with a couple of songs, 'Nice Feelin'' and 'Second Storey Window'. Although the three solo albums Benno had recorded for A&M – *Marc Benno* (1970), *Minnows* (1971) and *Ambush* (1972) – had evoked favourable comments from the critics, they'd not sold in any quantity. Still, A&M were keen to support him, even if all he wanted to do was make a blues album – a desire spurred by a visit to the home of venerated Texan songster Mance Lipscomb. After meeting Lipscomb, Benno returned to LA and convinced Jerry Moss at A&M that a blues album was the thing he should be doing. Extraordinarily, they complied with his suggestion and started throwing more cash at him.

First Benno contacted bassist Tommy McClure and guitarist Charlie Freeman – who were members of the Dixie Flyers, house band at Atlantic's Criteria Studios in Miami – telling them to come down to Austin. Four days after their arrival, Freeman – who was known for his reckless over-indulgences – was dead, having choked on his vomit. Undaunted by this tragic turn of events, Benno had to look elsewhere for a guitarist. First he turned to Jimmie Vaughan, who was completely unimpressed by the offer, though he grudgingly conceded that his brother Stevie Ray might oblige. Not surprisingly, Stevie Ray jumped at the offer. Calling themselves The Nightcrawlers, Benno recruited drummer Doyle Bramhall from Jimmie's group – by now called simply Storm – and Billy Etheridge, who had been a member of The Chessmen.

Once they arrived in LA, rehearsals started almost immediately in preparation for a round of gigs opening for Humble Pie and the J. Geils Band. Benno had been teamed with producer David Anderle, who had worked with Delaney & Bonnie, Frank Zappa and The Beach Boys. Anderle was sufficiently impressed by Stevie Ray to lend him Charlie Freeman's old white Stratocaster. The sessions themselves produced eight tracks, including 'Dirty Pool', which was sung by its author, Doyle Bramhall, 'Coffee Cup', 'Take Me Down Easy', and 'Love Is Turning Green'. But when Jerry Moss heard the tapes, he was not impressed and rejected them out of hand, telling Benno to go and try again. So that was the end of Stevie Ray's LA excursion, and The Nightcrawlers were on their way back to Austin, minus McClure.

Stevie Ray decided to keep the band going, recruiting Drew Pennington on harmonica and

Keith Ferguson from Storm – which probably didn't go down especially well with Jimmie. Rubbing just a little more salt in Jimmie's wounds, The Nightcrawlers were booked into a residency at the One Knite Dive & Tavern, one of the best venues in Austin for seeing and hearing good up-and-coming bands and performers. Not that it was the most salubrious of joints, but for Stevie Ray and The Nightcrawlers it was a part of their education. They also had a lot to learn about the business side of the music industry, and that proved to be a rather tougher lesson.

ZZ Top's manager Bill Ham had indicated an interest in Stevie Ray. He'd managed to turn ZZ Top into one of the biggest bands in the US, achieving this through the simple expedient of keeping them on the road for most of the year. Ham provided a truck and some amps for Stevie Ray and The Nightcrawlers, and he recorded a show at The Warehouse in New Orleans which he was going to hawk around as a demo. But the rigours of life on the road just proved a little too much too soon for the band, and they fell to pieces in Mississippi. Not only did Ham require the return of the truck and the amps, he also demanded over $10,000 which he had apparently invested in the band.

He came across an old sunburst-coloured Fender Strat ... a "raggedy looking thing"... but it seemed to speak to Stevie Ray

After The Nightcrawlers fell apart, the only ray of sunlight on the horizon for Stevie Ray appeared one day when visiting Ray Hennig's music store, Heart Of Texas Music. While he was browsing around, he came across an old sunburst-coloured Fender Stratocaster guitar, which was a "raggedy looking thing", according to Hennig, but it seemed to speak to Stevie Ray. It subsequently became his favourite guitar – known as 'Number One' – replacing the Barney Kessell guitar he had used for years. According to Rene Martinez, who looked after Stevie Ray's guitars from 1985 until his death in 1990, Number One "consisted of a neck from a '63 Strat, the body was from a '64, and the stamp on the pickups dated them as being from 1959. So we called it a '59." In due course, 'Number One' was modified to incorporate a left-hand tremolo arm.

Armed with this new guitar, Stevie Ray joined Paul Ray & The Cobras. To quote Margaret Moser, "it represented a steep learning curve" for Stevie Ray. As a member of The Cobras, playing up to three sets a night, the repertoire covered every facet of the blues, R&B and even soul. But it was not just about learning new songs, he also began to understand the dynamics of performance and how to pace himself, creating variety within the fairly orthodox conventions of the blues. These were essential disciplines that he never lost. He began appearing every Tuesday night at the Soap Creek Saloon, formerly known as The Rolling Hills Country Club, and from the middle of the following year at Antone's.

Paul Ray had been a member of Jimmie's band Texas Storm, and had made Stevie Ray's acquaintance when the young guitarist had been depping on bass. The Cobras didn't actually need a new guitarist because they had one already in Denny Freeman – another escapee from Dallas, who was known as The Professor due to his erudition and compendious knowledge of different guitar styles. The way Denny saw it, if Stevie Ray proved too dominant as a guitarist, he could always turn his own hand to keyboards. The rest of the band comprised Alex Napier on bass, drummer John Henry Alexander, who was followed by Robert Craig, and former Liberation man Jim Trimmier playing saxophones, until he too was replaced by Joe Sublett. While the repertoire was perhaps standard fare, with Bobby Bland and Junior Parker covers featuring prominently, there was a good smattering of more recent material by people like Wilson Pickett. And Stevie Ray was keen to show his chops – his high-volume flamboyance in marked contrast to Denny's eloquent lyricism.

While everything had been changing for Stevie Ray, Jimmie's determination to play only the blues had required considerable resolve in the face of adversity. In 1972 Waylon Jennings and Willie Nelson had abandoned Nashville and returned to Austin, sparking a rekindled interest in country music in the area – though not quite the country that Nashville was keen to foster. Instead it was fuelled by singer-songwriters such as Townes Van Zandt, Guy Clark, Butch Hancock, Jimmie Dale Gilmour, Joe Ely and Jerry Jeff Walker, and groups such as Asleep At The Wheel – led by Ray Benson – Commander Cody & His Lost Planet Airmen, and Doug Sahm. While both Asleep At The Wheel and Commander Cody were hybrids, besotted with, and based around, the western swing of Bob Wills, Doug Sahm had developed his own very singular approach over the years.

Jimmie's determination to play only the blues had required considerable resolve in the face of adversity

Sahm was born on November 6th 1941 in San Antonio, and from the mid 1950s had been creating his own very specific style that incorporated the blues, R&B, country and tejano (otherwise known as Tex-Mex). After recording a string of singles as Little Doug, including 'Real American Joe', for obscure labels such as Sarg and the Fort Worth-based Harlem, in 1965 he was encouraged by producer Huey Meaux to put together a group. Inspired by British groups like The Rolling Stones, The Beatles and The Small Faces, Sahm assembled The Sir Douglas Quintet, with Augie Meyers (organ), Jack Barber (bass), Johnny Perez (drums) and Frank Morin (horns).

Amazingly, they immediately hit paydirt with 'She's About A Mover', which climbed into the Top 20 in both the US and the UK. Meyers' very cheesy riffs on the Vox organ were so distinctive they became the group's trademark. But later singles such the 'The Tracker' and 'The Rains Came', and the debut album, *The Sir Douglas Quintet*, fared less well. The album was way ahead of its time – nobody at that juncture was combining country and rock so effectively. Compared to the bland fodder masquerading as country-rock in the late 1960s and early 1970s, The Sir Douglas Quintet album was totally anarchic. But after Sahm was busted for possession in 1966, he broke up the band and skipped out of Texas and headed to the West Coast, naturally enough gravitating to the Haight-Ashbury district of San Francisco. For the next couple of years Sahm remained pretty quiet – in all probability he was doing what everyone else was doing at that time: getting ripped on anything he could lay his hands on.

Sahm returned to the fray in 1968 with a new set, *The Sir Douglas Quintet + 2= (Honkey Blues)*, a new record label, Smash, a subsidiary of Mercury, and a bunch of session musicians. The album sleeve archly states that the recording took place "between St Patrick's Day and the first full moon in June of 1968". Sahm had very high standards, and these were implemented almost intuitively – something he managed throughout his career. The follow-up album, *Mendocino*, saw him returning to something approaching his top form. Equipped with a re-formed Sir Douglas Quintet – of the original line-up only Barber had resisted Sahm's advances, and was replaced by Harvey Kagan – *Mendocino* exudes a rough-edged warmth. As journalist Ed Ward asserts, "*Mendocino* is practically pure 'border pop' – with a different vocalist and Mexican-Spanish lyrics it could be something you'd hear drifting out of a cantina in Brownsville, Texas." Although it only went Top 30 in the US, that was an achievement in itself.

The next album, *Together After Five*, finds the group reunited with Sahm's original mentor and producer Huey Meaux: again the flavour and spirit is intoxicating, but closer scrutiny reveals a mixed bag. Two more albums, *1+1+1=4 (1970)* and *The Return Of Doug Saldana* (1971) followed, but Sahm had had enough of California for the time being. He packed his bags and headed back home – well not quite home, Austin, in fact – settling into a house not far from the Soap Creek Saloon. He was soon up in New York with producers Jerry Wexler and Arif Mardin recording *Doug Sahm & His Band* (1970); it was indicative of Sahm's cachet that 'His Band' included Bob Dylan, Dr John, Flaco Jimenez and guitarist David Bromberg. Then he returned to Austin to record with the Creedence Clearwater Revival rhythm section, Doug Clifford and Stu Cook. The result, *Groover's Paradise* (1974), was less impressive than its predecessor, but it effectively summed up Sahm's feelings about his new home, Austin – the "groover's paradise" in question.

CHAPTER 4

Double Trouble

"Stevie's style was based on Albert King, and Jimmie's was more on early-Fifties era B.B. King ... You listen to those old albums, that's the sound."

CLIFFORD ANTONE ON THE VAUGHAN BROTHERS AND THEIR INFLUENCES

When Clifford Antone opened his club on Sixth Street in downtown Austin on July 15th 1975, the blues was not especially well regarded in Texas. Consequently Antone's rapidly became a Mecca for anyone who did love the blues, as well as a welcome stop-over for veterans like John Lee Hooker and Jimmy Reed: "John Lee Hooker was begging for gigs," Antone recalled to Margaret Moser in Mojo; "Buddy Guy too – but no one wanted to hear them. It was even hard to get publicity when we brought Muddy Waters in … The blues community was like a bunch of immigrants from 1900. We had to stick together."

There were certainly other places where the blues were played, such as the Armadillo World Headquarters – though with Commander Cody & His Lost Planet Airmen as the house band (they recorded their album *Live From Deep In The Heart Of Texas* there in 1974), this had become more of an all-purpose venue, open to all styles. Indeed the Armadillo's profile was such that it was attracting performers of the calibre of Bruce Springsteen, Linda Ronstadt and Little Feat. And then there was Willie Nelson. Nelson's move to Austin, and his brace of albums for Atlantic – *Shotgun Willie* (1973) and *Phases And Stages* (1974) – had triggered a revival in his career. Not

STEVIE RAY WITH DOUBLE TROUBLE – TOMMY SHANNON AND CHRIS LAYTON

only that, his total commitment to the hippy ethos, including a more than passing fondness for copious amounts of marijuana, meant he was totally in his element in Austin, and revered there by all and sundry. In turn this meant country music was seen as a far better career option for younger, more liberal-minded musicians, and perhaps no longer a redneck preserve.

Meanwhile Doug Sahm, who tended to transcend all attempts at pigeon-holing, had established himself at the Soap Creek Saloon; the fact that he lived virtually next door to the place probably helped. Otherwise there was Alexander's, where the blues were always de rigueur. Presided over by a black family, it was also a place favoured by musicians as a regular source of gigs. No cash changed hands, but at least food was plentiful. And it was at Alexander's, one afternoon, that harmonica-playing singer Kim Wilson first met up with future fellow Thunderbird Jimmie Vaughan.

Kim Wilson was born on January 6th 1951 in Detroit, into a musical family. His parents were singers, who'd performed popular standards on the radio, and as a child Wilson took trombone and guitar lessons – though he didn't discover the blues, and the harmonica, until he was a senior in high-school. Wilson's father went on to work for General Motors, and brought the family up in Goleta, California: "We weren't rich, but we were all right," Wilson recalled in a 1994 interview. After dropping out of college he began playing blues full-time in 1970. Living a somewhat bohemian lifestyle in a rented room, Wilson honed his skills on the harmonica by playing with visiting bluesmen like guitarist Eddie Taylor, who for many years was Jimmy Reed's sidekick. Although Wilson had not been playing harmonica for long, he developed rapidly and soon got to know local bluesmen like Charlie Musselwhite and John Lee Hooker, both of whom were regular fixtures on the Bay area club circuit at that time. Kim had then moved over to Minnesota for a few months, until he was lured down to Austin by a blues fan called Shirley Dimmick Ratisseau, who'd started organising recording sessions on Sixth Street. He didn't need much more encouragement to relocate.

Kim's reputation as a blues musician preceded him, and he was soon sought out by impressionable schoolkid Stevie Ray and his friends. When Kim arrived at Alexander's that Sunday afternoon, Jimmie was on stage with Storm. Initially Jimmie was deaf to his kid brother's insistence that Kim be allowed to jam, but at the end of his set he relented and allowed Stevie Ray, Doyle Bramhall and Kim to do a few numbers. Jimmie was very impressed, but that was as far as it went at this point.

Despite Shirley's best efforts, she had not been able to place any of the Sixth Street demos with record labels, so Kim had to return to Minnesota. "Blues records don't sell," was the demoralising mantra. Clifford Antone didn't agree. He'd been born and raised, in a Lebanese family, in

Port Arthur, on the Texas-Louisiana border, where a blend of different styles – blues, R&B, rock and country – had coalesced and evolved into hybrids that were totally specific and unique to the region: there was cajun, usually acoustic, combining fiddles and accordion, with lyrics in a French-based patois; zydeco, a blend of R&B and cajun; and then more curiously, swamp rock, another mongrel, where the rhythm of the bayous was transposed to a rock context.

But Antone, who ran the Austin branch of the family grocery and liquor store business, was also a serious blues fan. He had no time for country or any of that sort of stuff; he preferred instead the more weighty figures of Lightnin' Hopkins, John Lee Hooker, Muddy Waters, Albert Collins, the three Kings and Buddy Guy. Behind his shop there was a large space that had been converted into a rehearsal room, and it was to here that Jimmie and Stevie Ray, Denny Freeman and Angela Strehli all gravitated. Angela was born on November 22nd 1945 in Lubbock, and was inspired by the mix of blues, country and rock'n'roll she heard on the radio in the early 1960s. After learning to play harmonica and bass she became a full-time vocalist, but it was her astuteness and keen assimilation of even the most arcane detail of the history of the blues that made her an almost matriarchal figure.

So it was natural that Clifford Antone turned to Angela when he decided opening a club was the obvious progression. Angela was asked to run the venue, having insisted that a state-of-the-art sound system be installed. All that was required now was to book the opening act. Through Antone's complex network of contacts, he arranged for Clifton Chenier & His Red Hot Louisiana Band, who had already played gigs at the Soap Creek Saloon, to do the honours. Chenier was a Creole, and the undisputed King Of Zydeco. His outré demeanour – set off by a gold tooth, and cape and crown – could not distract from his obvious mastery of the French and cajun two-steps and waltzes of southwest Louisiana, which he mixed with New Orleans R&B, Texas blues and big-band jazz. Chenier created the modern, dance-inspiring sounds of zydeco, and set the standard for all zydeco players who followed in his footsteps. This could not have been a better way for Antone's to get started. From day one, it was the Home Of The Blues.

Ever since Jimmie had seen Kim Wilson over at Alexander's he had wanted to move on from Storm and try something slightly different. He decided to form a new band, so he travelled up to Minnesota to talk Kim. They played and hung out together, and after three days Jimmie convinced Kim that moving to Austin was his best shot – he'd basically nothing to lose. Kim agreed, and moved in with Jimmie and his wife Connie. Connie wasn't thrilled with the arrangement, having one of Jimmie's bandmates around the place, but she at least knew him vaguely – Connie had been one of Stevie Ray's high-school friends and had already met Kim through him.

Getting the right line-up of the band took a bit longer to work out, but it eventually stabilised around Houston native and former Nightcrawler Keith Ferguson (born July 23rd 1946) on bass, Mike Buck (born in Texas on June 17th 1952) on drums, and vocalist Lou Ann Barton, who did not last long (but more of whom soon). They settled on the name The Fabulous Thunderbirds. In many ways this band became as influential in America as Dr Feelgood were in Britain: they represented a return to the basic tenets of rock'n'roll and R&B. Although bands such as ZZ Top and The Rolling Stones were packing stadiums, The Fabulous Thunderbirds, or T-Birds as they're affectionately known, demonstrated an enthusiasm that was conspicuously lacking in a progressively jaded and corporate music industry, where the quest for the next big thing (at this point 'disco', soon to be followed by 'new wave') negated even the most finely-tuned creative impulse.

Indeed had it not been for Antone's, the T-Birds might have had a rougher ride. "We could hardly get arrested when we started out," Jimmie recalled to Art Tipaldi in the book *Children Of The Blues*. "We didn't care – we were havin' too much fun, playing the music we loved, going out to clubs every night, and earning the money to pay our tab." Whether they cared or not, they quickly developed a formidable local reputation in their capacity as unofficial 'house band' at Antone's. In the same way that Stevie Ray's tenure with The Cobras taught him a lot of lessons about professionalism, Jimmie was also working through a comparable learning curve. The big difference was that the T-Birds, as well as playing their own sets, were often providing accompaniment for big-name touring musicians – such as Willie Dixon, Hound Dog Taylor, Jimmy Reed, Albert Collins, B.B. King, Freddie King, Otis Rush, Buddy Guy, Howlin' Wolf's former guitarist Hubert Sumlin, Koko Taylor, Sunnyland Slim, Luther Tucker, Junior Wells, Bobby Bland, Albert King and Muddy Waters. It was a rather remarkable apprenticeship. Kim later recalled the debt he owed to Muddy Waters in particular: "He was my biggest mentor. He really made my reputation for me ... it was a fantastic time of my life, being associated with that man,"

Stevie Ray had come a long way already ... The Cobras were no longer representing a serious challenge for him

For Jimmie, the effect of playing with artists whose records he had grown up with was just as important: "One time when we were playing Antone's, opening for Muddy, I thought, 'OK, I'm going to do this Muddy Waters-style slide thing and see if I can get a reaction from him.' And the next night I did it again. And he came out behind me and grabbed me around the neck, and said he liked it. And he told me, 'When I'm gone, I want you to do that, and show everybody that's what I did. I want you to do it for me'."

When he wasn't playing, Jimmie spent every spare moment at the side of the stage, watching. After Antone's closed in the evening the visiting bluesmen passed on little bits of information, held informal tutorials and so on. There was a knock-on benefit as well, because Muddy Waters was not slow in extolling the virtues of Jimmie and the rest of the band, and the word travelled fast. Buddy Guy was quick to chip in with his thoughts, saying to *Guitar Player* magazine, "That guy Jimmie pulled that slide out on me, and I just had to stand back in the corner and watch. I've never said no when I've been invited to play in Austin, ever since I've been going there, because of guys like Jimmie and his brother."

Club owner and blues devotee Clifford Antone once commented on how the Vaughan brothers' differing guitar style compared to particular blues legends: "Stevie's style was based on Albert King, and Jimmie's was more on early Fifties-era B.B. King. You go back and listen to those old albums, that's the sound. Stevie would not have been so good with Muddy Waters, but Jimmie was the perfect guitar player, and he could play slide. Stevie could sit in with Albert King, Albert Collins and Hubert Sumlin and really shine." On one occasion Antone asked Albert King if he would allow Stevie Ray to sit in with him, saying, "I wouldn't ask you if I didn't think he was good. You're his hero, man. He tunes his strings like you do and everything." King grudgingly conceded and invited Stevie Ray up.

Stevie Ray had come a long way already, but The Cobras were no longer representing a serious challenge for him. One clue to his frustration was his increased drug consumption: speed had been fine for a time, but now cocaine had taken over as the drug of choice. Apart from anything else The Cobras had made just one single – 'Other Days' coupled with 'Texas Clover', released on the Viper label in February 1977 – though that was enough to help them win Band Of The Year in the fortnightly *Austin-Sun*, as well as a Best Blues Band award. But Stevie Ray had done his learning, and was now keen to try something of his own.

By the time he left Paul Ray & The Cobras, he had acquired enough professional skills to set up his own band. Things had changed quite drastically since his last dalliance with leading a band, in Blackbird. Along with the concomitant professionalism, he'd also picked up a lot of bad habits – loads of drugs and as much alcohol as he could handle – which were in danger of pushing him out of control and nullifying his obvious natural talent. But for Stevie Ray it was all part of being a rock star. It was the same with girls: whether he was in a relationship or not, the number of groupies hanging around after a show seemed to him a barometer of how successful he was, or how well he had played. And this was still very important stuff, because while he was confident of his ability and talent as a guitarist, personally he was still inclined to be diffident – and so he tended to over-compensate.

Perhaps unwisely then, the motley collection of individuals he recruited for his new outfit, the Triple Threat Revue, were as temperamentally combustible as they come. Bassist W.C. Clark was the focal point of the band in Stevie Ray's mind – he'd been around the block and back again, in the process gaining the local sobriquet of 'the Godfather'.

Wesley Curley Clark was born on November 16th 1939, and raised in Austin. Clark's father was a guitarist and his mother and grandmother both sang in the choir at St John's College Baptist Church. By the time he was 16 he had played his first show at Victory Grill, where he got to know T.D. Bell and Erbie Bowser, both prominent figures on the local circuit. At first he played bass in Bell's band, in the meantime developing his skills on guitar. At this juncture – in the late 1950s and early 1960s – the club scene in Austin was becoming more established and Clark decided to become a full-time professional, having picked up a regular gig at Charlie's Playhouse. He stayed at the Playhouse for six years until meeting the great soul singer Joe Tex, who had made his mark with a bunch of hits such as 'Hold What You've Got', 'Show Me' and 'Skinny Legs And All' for Buddy Killen's Dial label. Tex invited Clark to join his band. After touring extensively with Tex, Clark left the band and returned to Austin where he formed Southern Feeling with Angela Strehli and Denny Freeman.

Although Clark was becoming a sophisticated and accomplished songwriter, record companies were resistant, so to make a living he was forced to work as a mechanic at a local Ford dealership. But Stevie Ray found out where he was working and started dropping by, pestering him to be part of the new band. Eventually Clark gave in and joined.

Triple Threat Review's keyboard player Mike Kindred had lived in Oak Cliff near Jimmie and Stevie Ray as a kid. Although they were not the greatest of friends, Kindred had earned considerable respect in Dallas for being a member of a group called The Mystics, who had a local hit with 'Didn't We Have A Good Time, Baby'. This had encouraged him early on to develop his skills as a songwriter.

Freddie Pharoah was engaged on drums. Another veteran of the Dallas circuit, Pharoah had once auditioned Stevie Ray for his own band, Dallas City Blues, and had turned him down on account of his youth – claiming that, as they would be playing night clubs, he could not be held responsible for a kid. In turn, when Stevie Ray hired Pharoah he wryly quipped that, as the drummer was so old, he might find it difficult keeping the late hours.

The coup-de-grace was vocalist Lou Ann Barton. Lou Ann was born in Fort Worth, Texas, on February 17th 1954, and had amassed a wealth of experience to complement her abilities. She could range from Patsy Cline to Koko Taylor, and Kitty Wells to Irma Thomas with absolutely no problem. She'd moved to Austin in the mid 1970s and played with Marc Benno's troop, as well as vocalist Robert Ealey, and when Stevie Ray hired her, her reputation was on the way up. But she was a real handful to work with: she liked to party hard and drink hard – and her spell with Jimmie and Kim in The Fabulous Thunderbirds had been more than they could handle. For Stevie Ray, though, her robust, earthy vocals would complement anything he could throw at her.

Despite the awesome potential of the individuals involved, by all accounts the musical synergy of the Triple Threat Review was always jeopardised by personal issues. Yet somehow they stayed together for almost a year – perhaps it lasted as long it did because there was an egalitarian spirit at work, and it was probably only the prevalence of artificial stimulants that distorted the broader picture.

Lou Ann had her moments, on songs like Barbara Lynn's 'You'll Lose A Good Thing', while Kindred, in collaboration with Clark, had penned 'Cold Shot', which Stevie Ray would record later with Double Trouble. Clark's vocals on 'Cold Shot' and other self-composed items provided a textured contrast to Barton's, suggesting the group possessed a much broader palette than was probably true. Stevie Ray was quite prepared to concentrate on playing his guitar, developing some of the ideas that guys like Denny Freeman had passed onto him; Kindred too, with his omnivorous tastes, had interested Stevie Ray in music from Africa and Asia. Working on his vocals could wait – there would be plenty of time for that later.

The recruits for his new outfit, The Triple Threat Revue, were as temperamentally combustible as they come

The opportunity came sooner than he perhaps anticipated. While the groups' reputation seemed to be on the up, the band had trouble keeping track. Gigs seemed to be abundant, with regular sorties into places like the Rome Inn, Antone's and The Soap Creek Saloon. There were even gigs beyond the Austin city limits in towns like Lubbock. Although a lot of water had passed under the bridge since Lubbock's most famous son, Buddy Holly, had been killed in a plane crash in 1959, the town still seemed to spawn musicians of a quite remarkable diversity – such as Delbert McClinton Joe Ely, Butch Hancock, Jimmie Dale Gilmour, Jesse Taylor and Terry Allen. The Triple Threat Revue seemed to fit right into this context, and enjoyed appreciative audiences: students from the Texas Technical University numbered in excess of 25,000 and were certainly not averse to cutting up rough if given the right encouragement.

But nobody was making any money. Clark had not abandoned a regular job as a mechanic just so he could earn 50 dollars every so often. He was also getting fed up with Lou Ann and

Stevie Ray's erratic behaviour. And of course Clark was a guitarist by inclination, and bassist by necessity – so he left the band to form his own group, with enviable results. After gigging around Austin, Clark eventually landed a deal with Black Top, cutting *Something For Everybody* (1986), *Heart Of Gold* (1994) and *Texas Soul* (1996) – on the last of which he was accompanied by Tommy Shannon and Chris Layton, by then both in Stevie Ray's band, and guitarist Derek O'Brien. But in March 1997, Clark and his band had an accident while returning to Austin in their van; Clark's fiancée and drummer were both killed. After spending a year recovering from the shock, Clark returned with *Lover's Plea* (1998) and *From Austin With Soul* (2002).

Mike Kindred was the next to leave Triple Threat Revue. His departure was triggered by Stevie Ray's decision to add a saxophone (Johnny Reno) to the line-up, but Kindred also wanted to concentrate on songwriting, and to play in a band that was not quite so erratic. Stevie Ray saw this as a good time to change the name of the group: the Triple Threat Revue had had its day, now it was the turn of Double Trouble – named after the Otis Rush song.

Stevie Ray could bide his time, accompanying whoever it may be, until it was his moment to move centre-stage

Clark's replacement on bass was Jackie Newhouse. Both Newhouse and sax player Reno had worked regularly in Robert Ealey's band at Fort Worth's New Blue Bird Nite Club – not such a bad gig, as Ealey had eventually bought the club and turned it into one of Fort Worth's most dependable institutions, with periodic appearances by Lou Ann and Mike Buck of The Fabulous Thunderbirds, as well as another Fort Worth native, guitarist Stephen Bruton. The addition of Reno to Double Trouble made a world of difference: the full-bodied honking of the saxophone seemed to punctuate Stevie Ray's guitar work, thrusting it further into relief. But for both Reno and Newhouse it was like walking into a madhouse.

Newhouse later observed to Joe Nick Patoski that, "He [Stevie Ray] absorbed a lot of styles, but I don't think he played like anyone else". In much the same way that the Triple Threat Revue had organised their sets to accommodate the individual demands of each player – everyone had a solo spot – so too did Double Trouble. That was always one of Stevie Ray's greatest qualities: he could bide his time, accompanying whoever it may be, until it was his moment to move centre-stage. He learned that lesson when he was very young: many never learn it. For Stevie Ray, every gig was an education. Some, like *Juneteenth*, an annual festival staged to commemorate the emancipation of the slaves – General Gordon Granger read the proclamation in 1865 –

were more demanding than others. Staged in the Miller Amphitheatre in Houston, with Lightnin' Hopkins and Koko Taylor sharing the bill, in front of an audience of over 30,000, this was the type of set-up where no prisoners would be taken. Naturally everyone was dazzled by Stevie Ray's abilities, but it was a big test nonetheless.

Eventually, after getting too wired up with amphetamines, Pharoah turned and high-tailed it back to Dallas. There was a brief stop-gap – in the shape of Roomful Of Blues' alumnus Jack Moore – but Pharoah's long-term replacement was former Greezy Wheels' drummer Chris Layton. Rumour has it that Stevie Ray originally discovered Layton – better known as 'Whipper' – drumming to a Donny Hathaway record in the kitchen of Cobras' saxophonist Joe Sublett. More to the point, Layton was looking for a fresh challenge. Greezy Wheels were a rocking combo who, if they'd ever had a day, had seen it disappearing down the turnpike in the opposite direction some years earlier. So Chris required little cajoling to make the move.

Despite the reputation that drummers seem to have for being totally inept in everything other than their chosen sphere (or rather semi-circle) of activity, Layton was in fact Mr Organised. He sorted out PA sound equipment and was generally a very useful guy to have around. And he fitted into the band immediately. In hindsight some of the pithiest comments about Stevie Ray also came from Chris. "Stevie was a very observant person," he recalled to Margaret Moser in *Mojo* magazine. "So much of what he learned came from Jimmie's records. But when I met Stevie he already knew most of the bluesmen, and they knew who he was, from Buddy Guy to Muddy Waters to Albert King."

Chris also understood exactly what it was that Stevie Ray was doing, or sometimes attempting to do. After all, he had been raised on Chick Webb 78s (Webb led one of the swing era's most incisive big-bands, which famously featured a very youthful Ella Fitzgerald in its ranks), and his inspirations had been Mitch Mitchell in the Jimi Hendrix Experience, Mike Shrieve in Santana, former Miles Davis prodigy Tony Williams, and Frank Beard in ZZ Top. This may have been an eclectic set of influences, but it meant that both Chris and Jackie Newhouse kept Stevie Ray on his toes. And vice versa... For instance, Stevie Ray tended not to announce what the group would play next – they were expected to pick it up after two or three bars.

But the hard economics of being in a band run on a shoestring tempted the resolve of each group member – apart, that is, from Stevie Ray himself, who seemed to be under the impression you could live on fresh air. In May of 1979, Johnny Reno, who had fallen into debt, gave up the struggle and returned to Fort Worth. Stevie Ray might have felt let down, but Reno asserted, "By playing with someone of his ability and calibre, I got better".

Now that the group was down to a three-piece, plus Lou Ann out front, the pacing of each set was very gradually altered, and Lou Ann perhaps had more opportunity to sing ballads, while the group reverted to a more straightforward 12-bar blues format.

If these enforced changes represented a problem, there was at least the incentive provided by the comparative success of Jimmie's Thunderbirds. They had been gigging solidly for four years, up and down the country and coast to coast, and they had at last been rewarded with a recording contract. While the label, Takoma – home to legendary folk-blues guitarist John Fahey – was only a small independent, it showed someone at least had some faith in them. The resulting album, *The Fabulous Thunderbirds*, with its blend of original material and slightly esoteric covers, proved a more than fitting memento for those that had seen the band live.

Kim's songs – such as 'Wait On Time', 'Pocket Rocket', 'Walkin' To My Baby', 'Rock With Me' and 'Let Me In' – displayed a command of the blues vernacular without resorting to the stock clichés. And the reworking of Slim Harpo's 'Scratch My Back' was incendiary. Jimmie's guitar work was measured and abrasive, while retaining a breath of lyricism and a willingness to experiment. Both Keith and Mike did everything that could have been expected of them in the noble tradition of the well-oiled rhythm section.

It wasn't the best record they would ever make, but it was a start. In a sense it was a triumph of tenacity over substance: as Stevie Ray recalled to Larry Coryell in *Musician* magazine: "When they [The Fabulous Thunderbirds] got together, there were a lot of us just doing local club gigs in Austin and every once in a while going into Dallas or Houston or San Antonio and playing a club with only five or ten people in it." But after The T-Birds got their deal the feeling was, "if they can do that, we can do that too".

On reflection, perhaps the only disappointment with the T-Birds debut was that Lou Ann Barton hadn't stayed long enough to record with them. But she was with Double Trouble now, where things were about to take another turn.

Double Trouble's first flirtation with the big time came in 1979, one evening in spring. They were playing a gig at the Rome Inn when Joe Gracey, a former DJ from one of the Austin country stations, KOKE-FM, dropped by to see what was happening. Gracey had retired from DJing after being diagnosed with throat cancer, but his interest in music had not abated, and he had taken to recording impromptu sessions in the basement of the radio station. Gracey was impressed enough by Double Trouble to suggest they come round to the station to do some sessions, which they did.

While the equipment was pretty rudimentary, Stevie Ray was absolutely fascinated by the whole process, which Gracey in turn found very endearing. Lou Ann had plenty of scope on songs such as 'Hip Hip Baby', Irma Thomas's 'You Can Have My Husband (But Leave My Man Alone)' and Lazy Lester's 'Sugar Coated Love', though she only turned up when she was required to put some vocals down. And Stevie Ray had been working on his songwriting and had come up with two compositions, 'Love Struck Baby' and 'Pride And Joy'. These two songs gave a much clearer view of Stevie Ray's potential, and showed how seriously he took his role as a musician: he was no longer just a kid infatuated with guitars and the idea of being a rock star, he was a musician with the ability to translate potential into achievement. He was working on his vocals too. With Lou Ann up-front, the need to sing had never been a major issue but even in his early days he had sung a little bit, and now as his songwriting took shape, so did the desire to sing the words he had written.

After the sessions in the basement, local entrepreneur John Dyer offered to invest $7,000 in Stevie Ray's career. In November 1979 Gracey and Stevie Ray decided to go down to Nashville to recut some of the tracks for an album at Jack Clement's 24-track Nashville Studio. It probably wasn't a great idea going to Nashville at that point because 'the Nashville Sound' was inclined to be rather thin and colourless, with the rhythm pushed so far back into the mix you needed a stethoscope to detect the pulse. (To be honest it wasn't much better in Los Angeles either.) The resulting tapes were, to put it bluntly, a travesty. They returned to Austin to do some more recording, but Gracey, who had spent some of his own money as well, was keen to recoup his investment. Dyer tried to intimidate Stevie Ray into signing a contract that would enable him to put the record out, but Stevie Ray refused. Dyer started turning up at gigs, issuing threats and imprecations. Still Stevie Ray would not let the tapes be released. Eventually Gracey offered the tapes to Rounder – the largest independent record label in the US, who specialised in folk, R&B, blues and gospel – but they turned them down as well.

He was no longer just a kid infatuated with guitars and the idea of being a star – he was a serious musician

Despite this, Double Trouble had acquired a new booking agent, Joe Priesnitz, who was securing them gigs all over the place. Two shows at the Lone Star Café in New York City were especially memorable, for very different reasons. First of all, veteran songwriter Doc Pomus was bowled over by Lou Ann's performance; then, after the second show, Lou Ann got completely wrecked and started trashing the place, hurling glasses and abuse at waitresses. Before the next gig, at Lupo's Heartbreak Hotel in Providence, Rhode Island, Lou Ann told the rest of the band she was leaving, and was joining Roomful Of Blues. Nobody was entirely put out by the news.

As it turned out, Lou Ann did not stay long with Roomful Of Blues. She had always seemed destined for great things, and had her finger on the pulse of what was going on in Austin – still does, come to that. So there was a certain justice when she secured a solo deal with Asylum. The resulting album, *Old Enough* – produced by the legendary Jerry Wexler, who'd produced Aretha Franklin in the 1960s, and erstwhile Eagle Glenn Frey – is one of the great undiscovered gems of our time. Featuring a cast of regulars, such as Jimmie and various members of Roomful Of Blues, it was cut at Muscle Shoals studios in Alabama with the classic rhythm section of Jimmy Johnson (guitar), Barry Beckett (keyboards), David Hood (bass) and Roger Hawkins (drums), with Harrison Calloway leading and arranging the horns. It's not faultless, but there's enough to warrant investigation – especially Marshall Crenshaw's 'Brand New Lover', which is cunningly transformed into a rich, full-on barnstormer.

Unfortunately *Old Enough* sank from sight, despite winning a glowing review in *Rolling Stone*. Barton, far too much of a trouper to be hoodwinked by the sweet promises of record companies, resumed her career in Austin as if nothing had happened. She has subsequently cut the odd album here and there, such as *Read My Lips* (1986) and *Dreams Come True* (1990), with fellow songsters Marcia Ball and Angela Strehli. To some extent her reputation precedes her, and she has become an awe-inspiring figure on the Austin session circuit, working with Jimmie Vaughan, Stephen Bruton, Marcia Ball, Angela Strehli and Alejandro Escovedo, among others. But like Strehli, Barton remains something of an enigma, whose potential is still largely unfulfilled – though somehow you can't help thinking she could not care less.

When asked, 'Who's going to front the band?', Stevie Ray gave the response, 'I am' – a clear sign of his growing confidence

With Lou Ann's departure, Stevie Ray and Double Trouble were now down to a trio. Although this was not to last indefinitely, it naturally provoked the odd raised eyebrow and knowing nod whenever the name Jimi Hendrix was mentioned. Stevie Ray seemed to take any such comparisons in his stride. More significantly, when asked the question "Who's going to front the band?", Stevie Ray gave the straight-faced response, "I am". A clear indication of how his confidence had grown.

Indeed the only cloud on the horizon was his consumption of alcohol and drugs. Muddy Waters observed that, "Stevie could perhaps be the greatest guitar player that ever lived, but he won't live to get 40 years old if he doesn't leave that white powder alone". It was a valid point, made even more persuasive when Stevie Ray and his girlfriend, Lenny Bailey, were busted by an off-duty policeman in Houston, who by all accounts spotted them doing coke near an open window. Priesnitz had to bail them out of jail, because Stevie Ray and Double Trouble were in town for a gig – ironically enough opening for Muddy Waters at the Palace.

On December 23rd 1979 Stevie Ray asked Lenny to marry him. He had asked other girlfriends the same question in the past, but had been turned down. Lenny accepted. The two of them were as erratic as each other. The setting for the marriage was hardly a romantic idyll either, taking place in the offices upstairs at the Rome Inn, in front of a motley collection of family and friends. And the wedding reception – for want of a better word – was just another excuse for them to party. Marriage changed nothing for Stevie Ray, or for Lenny.

But the club circuit around Austin was changing. Lots of places had been pulled down to make way for new developments: some, like the Armadillo World Headquarters, would never reappear, while others such as Antone's and the Soap Creek Saloon merely opened up elsewhere. The intimacy of a small, rather seedy club and bar circuit was disappearing, to be replaced by larger venues where the audiences were commensurately bigger. Consequently the type of performer appearing at these venues tended to command larger fees. This had a knock-on effect for Stevie Ray and Double Trouble, especially as they had settled into a comfortable groove as a trio and were constantly touring nationwide, often appearing alongside such venerated figures as Willie Dixon and Buddy Guy.

On April 1st 1980 Stevie Ray and the band were captured live in a broadcast on KLBJ-FM from the Steamboat 1874 venue on Sixth Street in Austin. Although the resulting album was released in 1992, after Stevie Ray's death, under the title *In The Beginning*, this is more than just a record of a young wannabe in the early stages of his career. It is a fully realised statement of where Stevie Ray and Double Trouble were at that point. Naturally they were learning all the time, but the material was set, the pacing of the performance was organised, and the sheer ebullience and confidence of the performers was inescapable.

From the first bars of Freddie King's 'In the Open' to the dying notes of Stevie Ray's 'Live Another Day', the momentum is breathtaking in its rawness. Perhaps some of that can be attributed to the fact that it was recorded on two-track and has not been messed around with, but 'Tin Pan Alley (AKA The Roughest Place In Town)' is still remarkable for the total conviction and assurance of Stevie Ray's guitar work, while Guitar Slim's 'They Call Me Guitar Hurricane' displays a wit and lyricism that's often obscured in the quest for effect. As for the rest of the band, Jackie Newhouse and Chris Layton are thoroughly convincing. But changes were in the offing, even though no one knew it at the time.

In the weeks after the gig at the Steamboat 1874, Stevie Ray and Lenny were required to return to Houston to face charges of drug possession. They were both fined and put on probation, Lenny for five years, and Stevie Ray for two – and he was not allowed to travel beyond the state line. This was a huge blow, and it underlined the need for him to rationalise the business side of the operation. Chris Layton had been shouldering much of the burden of management – and been successful in securing bigger fees for appearances – but he couldn't be expected to look after everything. Things came to a head when Denny Bruce at Takoma, the Fabulous Thunderbirds' record label, offered Stevie Ray and Double Trouble a deal. Stevie Ray knew then they needed a proper manager to negotiate such contracts. He asked several people, but it wasn't until he came into contact with Chesley Millikin that he found somebody he felt could do the job.

Millikin had run a club, The Magic Mushroom, in North Hollywood, and he shared an apartment with Steve LaVere (now legal guardian of the estate of blues legend Robert Johnson). Millikin had also been a salesmen and, after running The Magic Mushroom, had inveigled his way into the music industry, rising the corporate ladder to become European label manager for Epic, a subsidiary of Columbia. Millikin became interested in band management, and after seeing Double Trouble at the Steamboat 1874, he popped the timely question.

Stevie Ray's career seemed to have its own momentum, evidenced by the importance and scale of the gigs he was now being offered

His first task was to put the band on salaries of $225 a week, plus per diems (a nominal amount paid to cover daily expenses). For Stevie Ray this was the first time he had ever had a regular wage as a musician, and so he immediately put his old chum Robert 'Cutter' Brandenberg on salary as the group's roadie. Millikin's next decision was to offer a swift rejection to the Takoma deal. Then with Priesnitz he worked out a schedule for Stevie Ray and the band that would see them touring the East Coast. The only problem was Stevie Ray's probation – and he had a parole officer who was not remotely helpful. But Millikin and the lawyers intervened, and the parole officer was replaced by one who was much more sympathetic to Stevie Ray's dilemma.

Despite the fact that Millikin was well-organised, he was inclined to treat Stevie Ray as if he needed to be protected, and he would often refer to the 25-year-old guitarist as 'Junior'. At one point he even tried to get Stevie Ray to turn the volume down – but Stevie Ray wasn't going to have any of that.

Double Trouble was now working out fine, but there was still a missing ingredient – an ingredient that made his presence felt one evening in August at Fitzgerald's in Houston. Bass player Tommy Shannon had of course known Stevie Ray for years, since they'd jammed together back at the Fog in Dallas, and as well as working with Johnny Winter he'd shared the stage with Jerry Garcia and Elvin Bishop. But at the time he turned up to see Double Trouble play at Fitzgerald's, he was working as a bricklayer: "It was the trio – Chris and Stevie and Jackie Newhouse," Shannon recalled to Dan Forte, "and it was like a revelation – that's where I wanted to be, right there. I didn't hold back; I just told Stevie and Chris I really wanted to play with them." Of course Double Trouble already had a bass player, but for several months Tommy would call by and jam with the band – and he fitted in perfectly. At length there was no alternative but to fire Jack Newhouse. "There was no animosity," Newhouse remembered later. "It was just getting pretty bizarre." On January 2nd 1981, Tommy Shannon became a member of Double Trouble. "That was one of the happiest days of my life," Shannon said later.

Ordinarily the arrival of a new bass player might signify a dramatic stylistic shift. To take an obvious analogy, Noel Redding and Billy Cox were in completely different stylistic map squares, and the Jimi Hendrix albums with Billy Cox are so different that Hendrix sounds like a completely different player. But for Stevie Ray, a new bass player made little overt difference; perhaps Tommy was a little sharper and perhaps the empathy with Chris Layton seemed more clearly defined. But at this juncture in their career, with no album available, it was like starting afresh. And again it was almost as if it were a part of a carefully conceived plan – it seemed as though Stevie Ray's career had its own momentum, evidenced by the importance and scale of the gigs he was now being invited to attend. And it was all happening very fast...

CHAPTER 5

Texas Flood

"He brought back a style that had died, and he brought it back at exactly the right time."

JOHN HAMMOND ON STEVIE RAY VAUGHAN

While Double Trouble were still rock stars waiting in the wings, Jimmie and The Fabulous Thunderbirds seemed to be doing very well. Just doing a gig could often pull in up to $15,000 – which was pretty good considering the blues was still a specialist market. Then in 1980 they were signed by Chrysalis (the British label founded by Chris Wright to record the blues-based progressive band Jethro Tull), who were keen for The Fabulous Thunderbirds to go into the studio and record a follow-up to their eponymous debut. For some second albums, especially those recorded hot on the the heels of the debut, finding material can be difficult. The T-Birds had no such worries, because although Kim had penned half the tracks for the debut, the second set featured songs from both Jimmie and Keith.

This immediately gave *What's The Word?* (1980) a contrasting flavour to its predecessor. It meant Kim now had prospective collaborators too. Kim himself contributed 'Low Down Woman', 'Learn To Treat Me Right', 'I'm A Good Man (If You Give Me A Chance)', 'Dirty Work' and ' That's Enough Of That Stuff', and he worked with Jimmie on ' Last Call For Alcohol' and 'Jumpin' Bad',

while Jimmie and Keith turned out 'Extra Jimmies'. The remainder of the album was fleshed out with covers, like the traditional 'Runnin' Shoes', still a staple in the T-Birds' live show. Again the maturity is evident, as the group demonstrate a palette of styles and influences that gives plenty of scope for the individual talents to shine, while never betraying the origins of the enthusiasms. But years of touring was beginning to take its toll, and drummer Mike Buck left midway through the sessions (and promptly formed The LeRoi Brothers). His replacement for the remainder of the album was Fran Christina from Roomful Of Blues.

Christina – born February 1st 1951 in Westerly, Rhode Island – heralded a very subtle change in emphasis for the group's third outing, *Butt Rockin'* (1981). Christina also strengthened the links between the Thunderbirds and the Roomful Of Blues by recruiting the horn section of Greg Piccolo on tenor and Doug James on baritone saxes, with Al Copley on piano for a few of the tracks, alongside young Dallas-based guitarist Anson Funderburgh.

Although T-Birds' manager Denny Bruce was again handling the production, somehow *Butt Rockin'* seemed stilted. There were still echoes of the blues (Slim Harpo's 'Tip On In') and New Orleans R&B ('I Hear You Knockin', which had been a hit for Smiley Lewis and then revived by Dave Edmonds in 1970), but the profusion of Kim's compositions made the set sound less varied. Two instrumentals, though, compensate for any deficiencies elsewhere: the quirky revival of Perez Prado's hit 'Cherry Pink And Apple Blossom White' and 'In Orbit', on which Kim's harmonica playing proves that all those hours listening to Little Walter had not been wasted. Perhaps the biggest clue to what might happen next was the collaboration between Kim and English bassist, songwriter and producer Nick Lowe on 'One's Too Many'. More of him later.

For Stevie Ray and Double Trouble, meanwhile, there were still some false dawns – one of which turned out to be the Chicago-based Alligator label. Alligator was founded and run by blues enthusiast Bruce Iglauer, a white guy who made a point of signing authentic blues men and women that had been languishing in the shadows, on the point of retirement, or working the chitlin circuit. Consequently Iglauer had a roster that included Koko Taylor, Fenton Robinson, Albert Collins, Son Seals and Lonnie Brooks, among many others. For Iglauer, though, Stevie Ray was not quite 'authentic' enough – even if within months of passing over Stevie Ray he had signed Johnny Winter to the label.

A better break came when Lou Ann Barton's album, *Old Enough*, was launched at the Continental early in 1982. The album's co producer Jerry Wexler was in town to see the show-case. The whole performance turned into an on-stage jam featuring Stevie Ray and Jimmie Vaughan, Doug Sahm and Charlie Sexton, who was another Austin born and bred axeman of some repute. Wexler was so impressed with Stevie Ray that he stayed in town an extra day to see

Double Trouble the following night at the same venue. After watching them perform, Wexler cornered Millikin, saying he would recommend Stevie Ray and the band to Claude Nobs, who controlled the booking for the prestigious *Montreux International Jazz Festival* on the shores of Lake Geneva in Switzerland. Stevie Ray and the band were not especially impressed with this offer, as it meant they would have to fork out around $10,000 in plane fares and hotel accommodation to attend – all of which would be set against future earnings. But they decided to go anyway.

Millikin had always bragged about his contacts with the Rolling Stones, but thus far this had not paid any dividends – until Mick Jagger and Jerry Hall turned up at a place called Manor Farms. You see, before getting bitten by the rock'n'roll bug, Millikin had been involved in equestrianism and horse breeding. Indeed Classic management, the company that handled Stevie Ray, was funded by bloodstock interests. When Mick and Jerry turned up they were actually looking for horses; but when Mick mentioned to Millikin in passing that he had not seen any new young guitarists on the blues scene, Millikin quickly disabused him of the notion, thrusting a video of Stevie Ray and the band upon him, which had been filmed the previous summer when they performed at a festival at Manor Farms. Jagger in turn passed the video on to Stones drummer Charlie Watts.

After watching the video, Watts contacted Millikin to arrange to see the band playing live. It was duly contrived that the band should play a showcase for the Rolling Stones at Manhattan's Danceteria on April 22nd, just to see if perhaps they were suitable for the Stones' own label. By all accounts, despite a few setbacks, Double Trouble took no prisoners that evening, and when the club manager tried to tell them to finish for the night, Jagger told him he would buy the place if necessary to keep them going. The band played on. Contemporary reports suggest that everyone who attended was completely wiped out from all the cocaine and alcohol floating around. So Stevie Ray and friends were in their element. There was even a photo opportunity featuring Stevie Ray and Jagger, which was published in *Rolling Stone* magazine's 'Random Notes' section.

Within the month, Stevie Ray and Double Trouble had been booked to appear at the *Montreux Jazz Festival*. This was unprecedented for an unsigned band – and helped to assuage some of the disappointment felt when the Rolling Stones decided against signing Double Trouble to their label. Ostensibly the reason was that the blues did not sell records in the volume required. This may have been undeniable, but perhaps there was also an element of competition – Stevie Ray and Double Trouble seemed to have the potential to blow most bands off any stage whenever they liked, which could have reflected badly on the Stones.

Preparations for going to Montreux were hardly auspicious: Priesnitz had booked the band into two opening slots for punk band The Clash at the City Coliseum in Austin. The Clash patently did not have a comparable fan base to that of Double Trouble, and the net result was predictable: Double Trouble were pelted with beer cans and widely booed.

When they arrived on-stage in Montreux on July 17th 1982 and started to play, the audience was initially thunderstruck, then some of them were again moved to boo, this time because Stevie Ray and the boys were a little louder than was customary for a jazz festival performance. But Stevie Ray did not let a few spoilsports rattle him – he just got stuck in, and, as Patoski says in *Caught In The Crossfire*, "performed as if he was having an out-of-body experience". By the end of the gig the doubters had been quelled, and everyone else was totally drained. (The following year the band picked up a Grammy award for their live version of 'Texas Flood' at the festival.)

After the group's appearance on the main stage at the Casino, Millikin arranged for them to play at the after-hours sessions in the Casino's basement bar. It was here that both David Bowie and Jackson Browne came up with bright, constructive suggestions. On the first night, David Bowie cornered Stevie Ray and talked him into taking part in a music video he was making. On the second night, Millikin met Jackson Browne and persuaded him to bring his band around to the after-hours' session later that evening. Millikin had known Browne since the late 1960s when they were both hanging around in LA, and had actually worked with Browne's guitarist David Lindley, at that time a member of a very superior band called Kaleidoscope. Browne and his band were so impressed with Double Trouble that they all jammed together, then he suggested they should come up to Los Angeles to lay down some tracks at his studio, Downtown, free of charge.

On the group's return to Austin Stevie Ray's exploits in Switzerland had been widely noted, and they were rewarded with several very well-attended gigs, including two packed-out nights at Fitzgerald's in Houston. Double Trouble took time out to accept Jackson Browne's offer. As it happened Browne had suddenly become very busy, but he did not renege, offering them three days over Thanksgiving, The tracks they put down over those three days were to form the core of Stevie Ray's debut album, *Texas Flood* – which we'll return to shortly. While in Los Angeles they took the opportunity of playing some club dates before returning to Texas for a couple of high-profile gigs at Antone's.

In the meantime, David Bowie had been in touch saying that the music video idea was off, but he'd like Stevie Ray to be on the album he was cutting – which would become *Let's Dance* – at the Power Station in New York. For Stevie Ray, playing with Bowie was not quite the enticement it might have been for other axemen. Certainly it was a prestigious gig, but their styles were diametrically opposed to one another. Bowie had always managed to fashion his albums to tie in with the expectations of the beau-monde; now studio techniques and the application of electronic effects had become so widespread that Bowie was endeavouring to revamp his image. Using

Nile Rodgers from Chic as producer along with a blues guitarist from Texas, Bowie intended to keep himself ahead in a notoriously fickle market place.

When Stevie Ray arrived in New York, the basic rhythm tracks had been laid down already, and Bowie only needed to add the finishing touches to the vocal tracks. Then Stevie Ray had to record the guitar parts. It may not be true to say that Stevie Ray re-shaped the Bowie sound, but his muscular contributions added depth and texture to the album that would be emblematic of Bowie in the 1980s. The three singles from the album – 'Let's Dance', 'China Girl' and 'Modern Love' – seem with hindsight to capture the zeitgeist of Thatcher's Britain in the 1980s. But then Bowie's forte had always been assessing moods with great accuracy.

For Stevie Ray it was all right, but that was as far as it went: "I had no idea at all what to play," Stevie Ray commented to the *Dallas Times-Herald*, "even though he'd already shown me on the rehearsal tape what he wanted. But I finally realized just to go in there and play like I play and it would fit. I'd never played on anything like that before, but I just played like I play and it worked."

It really hurt him that he was going to have to leave the band for what he thought would be a year

Such was his confidence now that when Johnny Copeland invited him to add guitar to his next album, *Texas Twister*, Stevie Ray jumped at the chance. But *Let's Dance* and Bowie had placed Stevie Ray in something of a quandary. The album went on to sell over five million copies, making it Bowie's single most successful album commercially, and Bowie had invited Stevie Ray to join him on the the upcoming worldwide *Serious Moonlight* tour. Expected to last at least a year, this was Bowie's opportunity to move into the major league of stadium performers, something he'd only achieved to a limited extent thus far – especially in the US, where he hadn't had a big hit since the mid 1970s. And as *Let's Dance* was geared specifically to US audiences, the presence of a guitar-toting young gunslinger was potentially a vital ingredient to the success of the tour. Stevie Ray, though, was unhappy at the prospect of mothballing Double Trouble for a year.

"For years, for his whole life, he wanted to get to a point where he had a band," Chris Layton explained later. "And he knew he had that with us ... Even management and other people were saying, 'Go on the Bowie tour; it'll only be a year', and 'This is a great thing for your career.' Finally, he said, 'Well, OK.' But it really hurt him that he was going to have to leave the band for what he thought would be a year. He said, 'Well, what are they gonna do?' We said, 'We'll find something to do'.

"I think it was the night before he was supposed to go on tour, he just couldn't do it, he couldn't sell out. Stevie could not turn his back on what he thought was right. A lot of people would have said, 'Wow, David Bowie – see you later, guys'."

The full facts behind Stevie Ray's dramatic departure from the Bowie camp were more complex. It's true he had agreed to go with some reluctance, but he recognised this was a rare chance to crack the rock'n'roll super league big-time. So he turned up when rehearsals commenced at the beginning of March on a soundstage at Las Colinas studios outside of Dallas. But there were problems from the outset, before Bowie even arrived.

For Stevie Ray, as fans clustered around at every opportunity, easy access to drugs was the hallmark of success

Bowie's musical director and bandleader Carlos Alomar – also a guitarist of some note – started getting irritated by the presence of Stevie Ray's wife, Lenny. When she and Stevie Ray had married there was perhaps the unspoken expectation that, as Stevie Ray was going to hit the big time, the cocaine and the partying would be non-stop. It was a reasonable assumption. But Bowie, like many performers of his generation, had done his share of drugs and wild-living, and had survived to tell the tale. Now making and playing music was what he did. So touring was a serious business, not just an excuse to get wrecked for a year. Alomar knew this, everyone else in the band knew it – except Stevie Ray. For Stevie Ray, as fans clustered around at every opportunity, easy access to drugs was the hallmark of success.

So when Bowie turned up to take charge of the rehearsals, Alomar complained bitterly to him that Lenny was being a pain and creating all sorts of mayhem. Bowie responded by barring her from rehearsals. Stevie Ray was furious – though he was slightly mollified when Bowie suggested it might be a good idea if Double Trouble were to open some of the dates on the tour. But then, not stopping to consider whether he needed Bowie's official sanction, Chesley Millikin saw a chance to capitalise on the Bowie association, lining up an appearance for Stevie Ray Vaughan on the German television programme *Musicladen*. When Bowie found out, he apparently went ballistic – whether worried about loss of control, or perhaps even that Stevie Ray and Double Trouble were trying to steal his thunder, or at least cash in on the tour behind his back. Whatever the reason, Bowie demanded that Millikin should cease managing Stevie Ray while the guitarist was on the tour. Now it was Millikin's turn to be incensed. He responded by simply demanding an increase in the $300 per night appearance fee, and sent the contract over to high-profile music business lawyer Lee Eastman (Linda McCartney's father). But when Millikin and Stevie Ray went to see Eastman, it seems he simply denied all knowledge of the contract. This was the last straw, and Stevie Ray immediately pulled out of the tour.

Although it was a decision that could have had damning repercussions for Stevie Ray, Millikin had a 'Plan B'. With Stevie Ray's name in the limelight, Millikin had been quietly working away trying to sort out a recording deal, which he was close to finalising. And with an album already recorded, the timing was right, and the sky was the limit. As Tommy Shannon pointed out later, "It was a big risk, commercially, to turn the tour down, but it paid off. It was the smartest thing he could have done."

No one suspected that *Texas Flood*, Double Trouble's debut album, would generate quite as much interest as it eventually did, but there was already a buzz of anticipation in the air before it was released. This was enthusiastically captured in the New York Post on May 9th 1983, in a review of one of the band's gigs at the Bottom Line, which stated that the stage had been, "rendered to cinders by some of the most explosively original showmanship to grace the New York stage in quite some time." And of course in Texas, where Stevie Ray was something of a hero already, it was bound to cut deep. But nobody expected it to cross over into the national charts, where it climbed into the Top 40 and remained there for about six months.

On top of that, *Texas Flood* kick-started a blues boom in the States, the like of which had not been witnessed since the mid-1960s when groups like the Jimi Hendrix Experience, Cream, The Paul Butterfield Blues Band, and John Mayall's Bluesbreakers had been in their pomp. The fact that it sold consistently well was a novelty in itself for a blues album, and it vindicated John Hammond's decision to sign the band. Not that Hammond required vindication.

Hammond, the scion of a wealthy New England dynasty, was born in 1910, an heir to the Vanderbilt fortune. He had been educated at The Hotchkiss School in Connecticut and Yale, and now resided in Manhattan. After leaving Yale, Hammond started to indulge his passion for music, becoming one of the most astute and enthusiastic monitors of trends in contemporary music. He discovered the teenage Billie Holiday when she was working the Harlem club circuit, and then set up the *Spirituals To Swing* concert at Carnegie Hall in 1938 with Big Joe Turner, Pete Johnson, Count Basie, Big Bill Broonzy, Sonny Terry, and The Golden Gate Quartet – a gospel group who had been crucial in the crossover of African-American performers to the 'mainstream', not just in terms of their acceptance as entertainers, but more significantly a recognition that blues, jazz and gospel were fundamental components of contemporaneous American culture.

Hammond didn't rest there. As we saw in Chapter One, he helped change the future of the electric guitar when he introduced young Texan guitarist Charlie Christian to Benny Goodman (whose racially integrated orchestra Hammond had already been partly responsible for). Then over the next 30-odd years he signed, and often produced, the likes of Aretha Franklin, Bob Dylan and Bruce Springsteen. So John Hammond was no fool.

But it had taken Millikin a long time to persuade him of Stevie Ray's merit. Two years, to be precise, during which time he sent him tapes, reviews and general stuff about the band. In the end it was his son, John Hammond Jr, who made the difference: he had been in Montreux and had got hold of a copy of the Double Trouble sessions recorded at Jackson Browne's studio. Hammond Jr was no mug either. Although born with a full set of silver spoons in his mouth, he was (is) a superb guitarist with a great sensitivity for Afro-American styles. Yet for all Hammond Jr's contacts and influence he had steadfastly resisted the temptation to rely on his father – indeed his parents had separated when he was very young – so he understood exactly how difficult it was for a young (white) blues guitarist to gain the necessary introductions. Hammond Sr also loved the tapes, saying Stevie Ray, "brought back a style that had died, and he brought it back at exactly the right time".

While Stevie Ray's stagecraft had improved over the years, there's still a sense of him playing by the seat of his pants

As for Stevie Ray, he knew Hammond Sr's track record, and did not need any arm-twisting. They both seemed to understand one another intuitively. Although Hammond had wanted to sign Stevie Ray to his own record label, HME (Hammond Music Enterprises), which was distributed by CBS, there was not enough cash to do the deal. So Hammond ensured that Stevie Ray went to another CBS label, Epic, whose A&R vice president, Gregg Geller, was an old friend of Hammond's. News of Stevie Ray signing to Epic – admittedly not for a huge amount of money, just $65,000 – became the talk of the New York headquarters. As well as the moderate advance, the recording of the album had been largely free of charge (based as it was on the sessions at Jackson Browne's studio), so Epic were not significantly out of pocket on the deal. In view of this, Millikin managed to extract several further undertakings from them: firstly that they would commission a couple of music videos to be made; and they would promote the album for six months, rather than the normal six weeks.

After the deal with Epic was done, Hammond Sr was installed as executive producer. The tapes were then taken into Media Sound Studios in New York to be remixed for release. The tracks themselves had been recorded in just a couple of days – it was almost like a live album. All the preparation had been worked out over the years, playing night after night, across Texas, and latterly across the US. The energy and conviction of the performance was more important to all concerned than any studio trickery or production gloss. One of the key reasons why Stevie Ray and John Hammond got on so well together was that they both understood that emotion was a far stronger commodity than technical brilliance. And Hammond, for his part, had no need to impress anyone – he didn't need to leave his mark on the resulting album.

Of course there were some drawbacks: John Dyer, who had invested $7,000 in the inferior Nashville sessions, crawled out of woodwork, agitating for his money and threatening to release a 'spoiler' album unless he was remunerated in full immediately. He was paid off.

Though not perfect, *Texas Flood* was a very assured album, with very strong material. Also, while Stevie Ray's stagecraft had improved immeasurably over the years, and the timing and pace of his sets had their own drive, there was still the sense of him playing by the seat of his pants throughout. The formula, if that's what it was, had vitality and potency – and nothing will ever be a substitute for that.

The album opens with two of Stevie Ray's compositions, 'Love Struck Baby' and 'Pride And Joy'. The former is a jump-style blues with a steady slow-burning fuse, which sets the pace for the album, while the latter swaggered. 'Pride And Joy' became the track favoured by radio stations, and was accompanied by a video on the fledgling MTV.

The title track, though, had everything. It had been passed onto Stevie Ray by Angela Strehli: "I remember Angela Strehli teaching him 'Texas Flood'," Clifford Antone recalled to Margaret Moser. "I can still see us sitting on the stage [at Antone's] in the afternoon – Angela, Stevie and me, going over that song. Like coaching a little brother who was gonna be in the school play." The song 'Texas Flood' was credited to a young protégé of Albert King called Larry Davis (though as it turns out the writing credit was erroneous, and it was more likely composed by Davis's bandmate Fenton Robinson). Chris Layton recalls, "Albert had brought Larry down to the Sixth Street club several times. 'Texas Flood' was just the right song for Stevie. It was a great song, with a cool guitar part. The songs he was attracted to – where he'd go, 'You gotta hear this' – always had intriguing guitar parts, not just your typical blues."

On Howlin' Wolf's 'Tell Me', Stevie Ray used an old yellow Strat which had formerly belonged to a member of Sixties proto-heavy-rock band Vanilla Fudge. Customised with a stock Fender treble pickup, the crystal clear tone imparted authority to the track. Similarly George Clinton's 'Testify' was turned on its head, allowing Stevie Ray the chance to create subtle changes to the harmonic structure alongside a superficially simple, repetitive melody.

Another Stevie Ray composition, 'Rude Mood', was followed by a strong re-working of Buddy Guy's 'Mary Had A Little Lamb'. Although not one of Guy's best compositions, it becomes another opportunity for Stevie Ray to demonstrate the vast array of different stylistic tricks he now had at his disposal.

Looking into the future at this point in Stevie Ray's career, it's doubtful whether anyone would have concluded that the most telling and decisive track on the album would be 'Dirty Pool'. Written in collaboration with Doyle Bramhall, and therefore a leftover from the Nightcrawlers' days, 'Dirty Pool' has a melodic fluency that enables it to function on different levels and in different circumstances. The set was completed with two more original compositions, 'I'm Crying' and 'Lenny' – the latter a melodic, languorous tribute to his wife, which Kurt Loder described in *Rolling Stone* as a "delicately detailed Hendrix-like landscape".

Sometimes Stevie Ray's vocals seemed over-stretched and perhaps a little insubstantial, but this pales into insignificance when juxtaposed with the accomplished lyricism and economy of his guitar work – more about which in Chapter Nine. Most importantly, with *Texas Flood* Stevie Ray managed to allude overtly to his influences while making his own very personal statement.

When *Texas Flood* was released in June 1983, reaction was strong enough to encourage Millikin, presumably because there was now a major label behind the band, to contact Joe Priesnitz and tell him they were going to obtain the services of another booking agent. Millikin lined up a new booker, Rick Alter, who worked out of the Empire Agency in Marietta, Georgia. This agency was presided over by Alex Hodges, who had been around since the 1960s and had worked with Otis Redding in Macon. When Redding was killed in a plane crash in 1967, Hodges left the music industry until he was contacted by Phil Walden, Redding's former manager, about a group he was planning to manage. They were called The Allman Brothers Band. Working with Phil Walden, who had set up the Capricorn label, Hodges established the Paragon booking agency to look after the Allmans, though in later years they booked a plethora of other Southern rock bands, such as Wet Willie and The Marshall Tucker Band.

Stevie Ray's only indication of having made the big time was that he now always kept $5000 in cash in his boot

Initially things had gone well, until two members of the The Allman Brothers Band, guitarist Duane Allman and bass player Berry Oakley, died in motor bike accidents within 13 months of one another. Very gradually everything started to unravel, culminating in them filing for bankruptcy, and the dissolution of Capricorn at the end of the 1970s. Hodges then set up the rather more conservative operation Empire, where he started to book the roots country band Asleep At The Wheel. Now based in Austin and playing over 250 gigs a year, Asleep At The Wheel, like

Commander Cody & His Lost Planet Airmen, had perfected a country-based hybrid that drew on western swing, blues, jazz and tejano. Although they sold relatively few records, and had worked their way through several record labels, the group's driving force, Ray Benson, was widely held to be the fount of all knowledge – a bit like Willie Nelson. So when Benson suggested to Hodges that Stevie Ray and Double Trouble were worth checking out, Hodges didn't argue.

Hodges' contacts in the rock'n'roll world immediately paid dividends, and the group was booked onto the Stadium circuit, opening for the likes of The Police and Huey Lewis & The News. The downside to this success was that Stevie Ray now had carte blanche to do as he chose, when he chose – and in Tommy Shannon he had a very willing crony. At least Shannon, a real survivor, seemed to possess enough savoir faire to know when to try and rein in Stevie Ray and his self-destructive proclivities. It was particularly difficult at gigs, though, where many of the fans wishing to express their admiration for Stevie Ray were inclined to demonstrate this by providing him with an endless supply of cocaine or booze.

Stevie Ray's old chum Cutter Brandenberg did his utmost to protect him, often resorting to violence to keep the fans out of the backstage areas. Cutter had been with Stevie Ray on-and-off for around 15 years now, but everything came to a head during a brief European tour, which included another appearance at the *Monterey International Jazz Festival*, following the triumphant debut there the previous year. Cutter went completely over the top in his hotel room, trashing it perhaps more thoroughly than anyone ever managed before or since. What's more, Cutter's wife had had a baby earlier that year. All in all, it was time for him to go back to Texas.

Cutter's departure was symptomatic of the barely concealed chaos that seemed to dominate the running of Stevie Ray's career. Millikin reckoned that keeping them out of Texas and on the road was the route to stardom, but the management was haemorrhaging money to keep the band afloat. And, of course, as the band was always on the road, they had no idea how much money they were earning, or how much was being spent. For Stevie Ray the only real indication of having made the big time was that now he always kept $5000 in cash in his boot, and he got exactly what he wanted from promoters.

It was all a far cry from the fate Jimmie was suffering in the The Fabulous Thunderbirds... Their record label, Chrysalis, was beginning to get a little fed up with bank-rolling a band who just did not sell in any quantity. Their albums were efficient rather than ground-breaking. So when the band took a break from their gruelling day-to-day routine of cross-country touring to record the follow-up to *Butt Rockin'*, there was a make-or-break atmosphere to the proceedings.

This was partially alleviated by the sunny, jocular presence of Nick Lowe as producer. In the late 1960s Lowe had been a member of influential British country-rock band Brinsley Schwartz

– whose management made the famous mistake of flying a plane-load of journalists to New York for the group's album launch: a plan which backfired in spectacular fashion when they all proceeded to slate the album mercilessly on their return. Lowe had then played in a number of bar bands, not totally dissimilar in style and quality to The Fabulous Thunderbirds, before hooking up with Dave Edmunds in Rockpile. His credentials had not been harmed either by his marriage to Johnny Cash's stepdaughter, Carlene Carter.

It was an inspired choice of producer, especially as Lowe and Kim Wilson had written a song together for the *Butt Rockin'* album. On the new album, *T-Bird Rhythm*, Lowe managed to rekindle some of the fire that had been lacking on *Butt Rockin'* – the sound was in fact stylistically closer to the first album, with no horns or keyboards this time. But Lowe was clearly more sympathetic to what the band were doing than to the commercial requirements of a large record label, as *T-Bird Rhythm* failed to stimulate sales significantly.

Jimmie began to reap some benefits of his years on the road – but as with Stevie Ray there was a cost

Once again there were a few esoteric R&B covers like 'How Do You Spell Love' (which had been a hit for the soul singer Margie Joseph in the early 1970s), the Dave Bartholomew and Earl King chestnut 'Monkey', and Huey Meaux's 'Neighbour Tend To Your Business'. Then there was a brace of R&B classics: 'My Babe', which harmonica ace Little Walter had taken to the top of the R&B charts in the mid 1950s, and 'Diddy Wah Diddy', a Willie Dixon and Bo Diddley tune that had been given an extraordinary reworking by Captain Beefheart in the early days of his career. The rest of the tracks – 'Can't Tear It Up Enuff', 'Lover's Crime' and 'Poor Boy' – all came from the pen of Kim Wilson. All things considered, *T-Bird Rhythm* should have done better than it did.

But Chrysalis did not hang about: they dropped the T-Birds as quickly as possible. It seemed almost as if they had made up their minds before the album was even released – they certainly did not over-burden the promotional budget. Despite not having a record label, the T-Birds continued working coast-to-coast, even undertaking some low-key tours of Europe. But cracks were appearing, and bassist Keith Ferguson left to try his luck elsewhere – the suggestion is there was some animosity involved. Once back in Austin, he formed The Tail Gators, who would end up making a couple of albums before gradually sinking into the anonymity of the club circuit.

A similar fate almost befell the T-Birds – though when they were finally signed by Epic/Associated in 1985, the recording drought ended, and at last Jimmie began to reap some of the benefits of all his years on the road. But as with Stevie Ray, there was a personal cost...

CHAPTER 6

Entertainer Of The Year

"Now we're gonna be Serious Trouble."

STEVIE RAY, ON THE ADDITION OF ORGANIST REESE WYNANS TO DOUBLE TROUBLE

The aftermath of *Texas Flood* saw Stevie Ray picking up three awards from *Guitar Player* magazine – Best New Talent, Best Electric Blues Guitar Player, and Best Guitar Album for *Texas Flood* itself – the first triple-award winner since British guitarist Jeff Beck in 1976. His workload was still intensive, but the burden could always be alleviated by the ubiquitous booze or a line of coke. It was against this backdrop that Stevie Ray and Double Trouble went into the studios to cut their follow-up album, which featured almost exactly the same recording team of John Hammond Sr and engineer Richard Mullen, who were credited as co-producers, alongside Stevie Ray, Layton and Shannon.

This time Hammond, who had only officiated during the final mix-down of *Texas Flood* ,was on-hand throughout, offering encouragement and constructive observations. Neither confrontational nor disciplinarian, he always sought to elicit the best performances from his charges, and the fact that he abstained from drink and drugs (without criticising others' indulgence) enhanced his objectivity. The only real changes on this album were the additions of drummer Fran

NOW AND AGAIN STEVIE RAY'S SHOWMANSHIP DISTRACTED FROM HIS MUSICIANSHIP

SRV

Christina and Jimmie Vaughan from The Fabulous Thunderbirds, and Stan Harrison on tenor sax.

Considering the brouhaha attending the release of *Texas Flood* and its consequent success, *Couldn't Stand The Weather* was a pretty good stab at a second album, though it did lack the edge of its predecessor. The recording circumstances might have been a contributory factor: the band spent 19 days at the Power Station in New York (where *Let's Dance* had been cut), but as they had only booked daytime sessions, they were obliged to pack up their gear every evening to allow someone else to use the studio at night, and reassemble everything again next morning. After this, Stevie Ray vowed he would only record if the studio was block-booked. Despite the difficulties, the vastly improved sales of *Couldn't Stand The Weather* confirmed that *Texas Flood* was no fluke, and Stevie Ray's ascendancy in the major league was now unchallenged.

It was also notable that Stevie Ray's vocals had improved out of all recognition – though there was still plenty of scope for development in other areas. His writing on *Couldn't Stand The Weather* lacks the rough-hewn authenticity and calibre of 'Love Struck Baby' or 'Pride And Joy'. In general he was not a fluent or especially assured composer. 'Scuttle Buttin'' was an affectionate nod in the direction of Lonnie Mack, one his earliest influences; 'Stang's Swang', like 'Lenny' on *Texas Flood*, showed Stevie Ray in a jazzier vein, doing his utmost to illustrate the breadth of his ability; while 'Honey Bee' was just another derivative blues-based riff.

It falls again to the covers to make the big statements. Guitar Slim's 'The Things That I Used To Do' features Jimmie, playing great rhythm, alongside Stevie Ray, and gives a good account of the brothers' stylistic differences. Both 'Cold Shot' – penned by Mike Kindred and W.C. Clark, his former colleagues in the Triple Threat Revue – and 'Tin Pan Alley (AKA The Roughest Place In Town)' had been in the group's repertoire for many years, and are consequently executed with the minimum of fuss and boundless vitality.

When asked once whether he wanted to play like Hendrix, Stevie Ray retorted, 'No, I want to *be* Hendrix' ... He was his own worst enemy in that regard

The decision to cover Hendrix's 'Voodoo Chile (Slight Return)' was perhaps understandable, but it was too obvious. The spectre of Hendrix had always loomed large. It wasn't because Steve Ray was stylistically an imitator – far from it, he had developed his own style using heavy-gauge strings, tuned low and played hard. But he often invited this comparison, so was his own worst enemy in that regard: when asked once whether he wanted to play like Hendrix, his retort was, "No, I want to *be* Hendrix".

For Stevie Ray's detractors (and there were some), the Hendrix analogy only provided ammunition, and so actually covering one of the cornerstones of the Hendrix catalogue was tantamount to throwing down the gauntlet. On the other hand, Stevie Ray asserted that he was simply introducing a new generation of fans to Hendrix's music – after all nobody jumped to the same conclusions when he covered Jimmy Reed, Albert King or Guitar Slim's material. A trifle disingenuous, perhaps – but the bottom line was that Stevie Ray's interpretation in this case was immaculate. Hammond was so impressed that he actually suggested calling the whole album *Voodoo Chile*. Thankfully they plumped for the less burdensome *Couldn't Stand The Weather*.

After the album's completion, the group was booked into the Volunteer Jam in Nashville, a regular event that fiddler and country singer Charlie Daniels had started in 1974. This was followed by more touring taking in the south-east and mid-west before heading out to Honolulu to open for The Police. After that it was a short haul through Scandinavia, stopping off in Norway, Sweden and Finland. Despite the difficulty in procuring drugs in Scandinavia, the enthusiastic audiences were perhaps some compensation. On their return to the US, the group was due to appear at the Grammy Awards, for which they'd received four nominations. In the event they picked up just the one award which, as mentioned earlier, was in the Best Traditional Blues category for their performance of 'Texas Flood' at Montreux in 1982 – the recording had recently been issued on a compilation album, *Blues Explosion Montreux '82*, on the Atlantic label. Then it was down to Austin for an appearance at the *Austin Music Awards* where *Couldn't Stand The Weather* was due to be previewed. During the lay-off in Austin, two videos were filmed – for 'Couldn't Stand The Weather' and 'Cold Shot' – to accompany the album's release.

Couldn't Stand The Weather hit the shops much harder than was expected, selling almost 250,000 copies in the first three weeks. The videos surprised many people too, running on heavy rotation on MTV throughout the summer that year. In the end *Couldn't Stand The Weather* went platinum, despite peaking at only Number 31 in the US album charts. Better than that – better even than sharing the stage with Albert King in Mississippi for the Delta Blues Festival – Stevie Ray had been booked to appear at New York's famed Carnegie Hall on October 4th 1984, the day after his 30th birthday. He was accompanied by a host of guests, including brother Jimmie, vocalist Angela Strehli, the legendary Dr John on piano, drummer George Rains, who had been in the Sir Douglas Quintet at one point, plus Bob Enos (trumpet), Porky Cohen (trombone), Doug James (baritone sax) and Greg Piccolo (tenor sax) from Roomful Of Blues. While the idea of such a big line-up had been to cast a nod in the direction of T-Bone Walker and all the other great R&B bands, it didn't quite work. It wasn't that it was sloppy, exactly, just that it would have been improved if it were sharper... As well as the prestige of the gig itself, the presence in the audience of Stevie Ray's parents, Jim and Martha, provided him with the perfect opportunity to prove that all those years fiddling around with guitars had finally paid off. He had hit the big time.

The plaudits and awards did not stop there. During November he was compelled to interrupt a tour of Australia and New Zealand to return to the US to pick up two W.C. Handy National Blues Awards, for Entertainer Of The Year and Blues Instrumentalist Of The Year – making him the first white recipient of either award.

While his stock as a musician was high, even with idols such as Albert and B.B. King and Eric Clapton, few could miss the tell-tale signs that he was, in Sly Stone's immortal words, "not so much burning the candle at both ends, more using a blow-torch on the middle". Clapton's comment to Stevie Ray, when they met in New Zealand, was "sometimes you gotta go through that".

Naturally, while Stevie Ray was completely messed up on cocaine and alcohol, and often away touring, he was in no position to monitor how well his interests were being protected. It's clear that his manager, Chesley Millikin, had no feelings for Stevie Ray other than as a meal ticket. They were not friends. Business was business. But despite the fog that permanently seemed to blur Stevie Ray's vision, he was getting fed up with Millikin's interference, and had actually asked around for a loan to buy himself out of Classic Management, though this didn't materialise. Quite apart from Stevie Ray's own dissatisfaction, sound engineer Richard Mullen and former roadie Cutter Brandenberg had been obliged to file law suits for failure to honour financial commitments.

Despite his gullibility and the chinks in his armour, Stevie Ray remained accessible and amenable, always prepared to help out where he was able to – and still the quintessential music fan. For instance he was invited to guest on Marcia Ball's album, *Soulful Dress*. Born in Orange, just over the border in Texas, Ball was a colleague of Angela Strehli and Lou Ann Barton, and had been working the Texas Triangle for years – though she had to wait until her mid-thirties before cutting her solo debut. When the album emerged, on the Rounder label, Ball's robust piano playing brought with it elements of Chicagoans such as Otis Spann and Sunnyland Slim, while retaining the rolling, loose-limbed style of Doctor John.

Potentially of even greater interest to Stevie Ray was his commitment to produce an album for Lonnie Mack. Ever since the days when he had driven his father crazy playing Lonnie Mack's 'Wham' incessantly, Stevie Ray had been a major fan. The only downside was that Mack had been signed to Alligator, the same label that had turned Stevie Ray down. But Alligator boss Bruce Iglauer recognised that Stevie Ray's involvement might galvanise interest in Mack, who at best had a very modest fan-base. And there was no sense of recrimination over past slights from Iglauer – as far as Stevie Ray was concerned, Mack was such a hero that anything he could offer was fine by him. As he observed to *Guitar World*, "They were his tunes, and I just tried to help him by doing the best I could... Most of us got a lot from him. Nobody else can play a whammy bar like him." Though Stevie Ray didn't go as far as changing his wayward lifestyle when working on Mack's album, titled *Strike Like Lightning*, he fastidiously made sure his contributions were completely spot-on.

In the meantime his relationship with Lenny wasn't being helped by his prolonged absences. Although Stevie Ray himself was not averse to tangling with groupies, he was possessive about Lenny. So at the end of the Lonnie Mack sessions, Stevie Ray and Lenny went off together to the Virgin Islands to try to work out their accrued problems. On their return, in an attempt to provide a more stable living environment, Lenny moved the family home away from central Austin to the much quieter Volente, on Lake Travis, 30 miles outside of the city. It was a ploy that didn't work, because Stevie Ray, if he was in town, was just as likely to sleep over at any one of a number of friends' houses, or else invite numerous visitors to crash at their new house.

Apart from anything else, the road beckoned once again, and Double Trouble were soon back on a tour of Japan. But the trio format that had once worked so well was now getting threadbare. There was no doubt the band were now going through the motions. On their return from Japan, with the prospect of another album to record, one suggestion mooted to forestall the decline was to expand the line-up by adding another guitarist. Derek O'Brien, a long-time figure on the Austin circuit and an erstwhile member of the Antone's house band, was duly recruited and installed to play four dates. But Millikin made it clear to O'Brien that he disapproved, and wanted no part in his involvement with Double Trouble. Eventually Stevie Ray got his extra musician, but Millikin insisted it had to someone who played a different instrument. The person Stevie Ray chose to hire was Hammond B3 specialist Reese Wynans. Stevie Ray had always been fond of organists, such as Big John Patton, Richard 'Groove' Holmes, and Jimmy McGriff. Reese Wynans, though, had the great virtue of having played around Austin in the bands of Jerry Jeff Walker, Joe Ely and Delbert McClinton, among others. In other words, he knew the ropes.

The trio format that had once worked so well was getting threadbare. There was no doubt the band were now going through the motions

"I was working with Delbert McClinton in Dallas," Wynans recalled to *Guitar Player*'s Dan Forte, "and I had given him my notice because I thought it was time for me to get out of the touring business for a while and try to be a family man. Stevie was in town recording *Soul To Soul*, and Chris came over to our gig and told me about this song they wanted to put some piano on, 'Look At Little Sister'. When Delbert's show was over, I went to the studio, and ended up playing all night – 'Change It' and 'Soul To Soul.' I was a big fan of Stevie and the trio. I thought they were a great trio – a definitive trio. They were a band that had their business together, so it was a real pleasure for me to sit in with them that night. Things were really clicking. He liked the way I played with him, and I didn't have any problem with the intonation on his guitar, because he tuned everything down to E-flat. It was easy for me to play in E-flat and A-flat, instead of E and A – at least I told him it was. We seemed to be on the same wavelength, musically. The next night we came back to the studio, and apparently the three of them had gotten together and talked, and he asked me if I wanted to join the band."

In addition to Wynans, Joe Sublett, Stevie Ray's former bandmate from The Cobras, was brought in on saxophone for the new album. John Hammond was not around for these sessions, although he was still credited as executive producer: production credits went to engineer Richard Mullen and Double Trouble. Recorded at the 48-track Sound Labs in Dallas, *Soul To Soul* was assembled over three-and-a-half weeks on a block booking, so that valuable time wouldn't be wasted setting up the equipment for every session. The studios had been re-equipped with every kind of amplifier Stevie Ray might require. They didn't wear headphones during the sessions, theoretically to create a mood of playing 'live'.

The work ethic was hardly impressive ... and when inspiration was short, the stock response was to have another line of coke

Despite all the special arrangements to make their job easier, the work ethic was hardly impressive. The routine on arrival at the studios was to do some dope and then play ping-pong before getting down to business. While they were playing, there was the usual endless drip-feed of alcohol. Not surprisingly, the actual recording of the album was a little like pulling teeth. Inspiration was hard to come by, and when inspiration was short, the stock response was to have another line of coke.

As a consequence the resulting album was patchy, and Stevie Ray's writing – despite some excellent touches along the way – exemplified this. 'Say What!', with a splendid opening salvo on the wah-wah, and the way-down deep 'Ain't Gone 'N' Give Up On Love' seemed destined to slide into the Vaughan songbook. 'Life Without You' was dedicated to Charlie Wirz, the Dallas guitar dealer who had died recently; curiously, it had the enigmatic ring of Curtis Mayfield about it, and was to become the fulcrum of Stevie Ray's live performance, where he would launch into reflective raps about anything that was on his mind at that particular moment.

Of far greater significance was the inclusion of two Doyle Bramhall compositions, 'Lookin' Out The Window' and 'Change It'. Bramhall had undergone some radical changes since the disintegration of The Nightcrawlers. After his marriage had broken down he had moved back to the environs of Dallas, stopped doing dope and drinking, and taken up with Barbara Logan. When he received the call from Stevie Ray for material, his lyrics seemed to be apposite.

Now a four-piece unit, Double Trouble had far more dynamic options, and could practically rebuild the stage act

The cover versions, from wildly disparate sources, merely underlined Stevie Ray's impeccable taste. Hank Ballard's 'Look At Little Sister', Earl King's 'Come On' and Willie Dixon's 'You'll Be Mine' provided sharp stylistic contrasts to Bramhall's contributions. But overall there is the abiding sense that, like a re-touched picture, the use of overdubs detracts from the album's natural flow.

When the album was finished it was time to get back on the road. Now a four-piece unit, Double Trouble had far more dynamic options, and could practically rebuild the stage act. As Stevie Ray commented after Reese joined the band, "Now we're gonna be Serious Trouble".

Ironically, by joining Double Trouble, Wynans was unlikely to fulfil his original intention of spending more time with his family. But at least whereas most 'new-boys' are made to pay their dues, irrespective of how experienced they are, Wynans instantly became an equal partner in the band. "That's just kind of the way Stevie was," Reese said. "I was surprised when they wanted to make me a full-time member; I would have been happy just playing on one song on the record. They treated me great, right from the beginning ... And Stevie continually urged me to stretch out as much as I desired, to become more of a member of the band. I was a big fan, and I figured the people came mainly to hear him play, so I had a tendency to lay back at first, but he encouraged me to get out of that shell. He really felt that on-stage we were presenting a total thing, a band."

Having a new bandmember should have been a great opportunity for Double Trouble. In fact it had the reverse effect, because the addition of Wynans' keyboards meant that now Stevie Ray had someone to cover over his errors. Also, Wynans was quite capable of looking after business affairs, and as a full member of the band he started asking questions about the group's financial arrangements. He even questioned Millikin, saying that if the group was earning up to $25,000 a night, how could they be losing $30,000 a month? It was the same gripe – albeit from a very different standpoint – that Lenny had been repeating for years. Millikin's riposte was along the lines of, "That's what happens when you keep the band on salaries when you're not touring." It was a valid point, and even when two different sets of accountants went through the books, nothing was resolved.

When *Soul To Soul* was released in August 1985, it was pretty successful, reaching Number 34 in the charts. But as Jimmy Guterman asserted in *Rolling Stone*: "There's enough evidence on *Soul To Soul* to suggest that there's some life left in their blues-rock pastiche; it's also possible that they've run out of gas." It was a comment that had also been levelled at The Fabulous Thunderbirds; though at least Double Trouble sold records, whereas the T-Birds' sales figures were notably erratic. But that was about to change.

Since being dropped by Chrysalis, and the subsequent departure of bassist Keith Ferguson, the T-Birds had just continued doing what they had always done: gigging, and touring, and more gigging. Ferguson's replacement was another former member of Roomful Of Blues, Preston Hubbard (born March 15th 1953 in Providence, Rhode Island). Over the years The Fabulous Thunderbirds and Roomful Of Blues had developed a synergistic rapport, enabling members of the latter to migrate in a south-westerly direction and find work through the extensive network of contacts of the former. Although it was one-way traffic, both groups were committed, roughly, to the blues, in its myriad manifestations. During Hubbard's tenure with Roomful Of Blues he had accompanied the late Big Joe Turner on *Blues Train* for Muse – one of Turner's final recordings – so his credentials were unimpeachable. Armed with a new deal from Epic/Associated the T-Birds were packed off to London to record their fifth album.

Apart from Hubbard's arrival and a new record label, they also had a new producer in Dave Edmunds. Edmunds was a scary figure in the music industry of the mid-1980s because he was totally unpredictable. His talent in the studio was matched only by his penchant for the bizarre. Starting with a blues band called Love Sculpture in the late 1960s, he had found fleeting fame with a curious reworking (for guitar) of 'Sabre Dance', composed by the Russian conductor Khachaturian. That had been followed by re-workings of the Smiley Lewis gem 'I Hear You Knocking' and The Ronettes' 'Baby I Love You'. Then he had teamed up with Nick Lowe in Rockpile, while issuing a series of quirky solo albums that were as much pastiche as they were lovingly fashioned tributes to rock'n roll's golden age. But Edmunds was a dab hand in the studio, able to employ any amount of trickery in order to create an effect. What the T-Birds required was a fresh pair of ears, and with Edmunds they could not have made a better choice; Edmunds' knowledge of R&B exotica was on a par with that of Jimmie and Kim.

The resulting album, *Tuff Enuff*, hit the stores in the spring of 1986 and, to everyone's astonishment, became a major crossover success. The title track, 'Tuff Enuff', was released as a single and its accompanying video received heavy airplay on MTV, which helped the song reach Number Ten on the national charts; and the success of the single sent the album to Number 13, in the end shifting over a million units. Why it should have achieved such success, when it was substantially no different from its predecessors, was an enigma. Edmunds' production was clean, and surprisingly devoid of technological gimmickry. There were a number of guests on hand, including David Hidalgo and Cesar Rosas from Los Lobos, Al Copley from Roomful Of Blues on keyboards, Chuck Leavell, formerly of The Allman Brothers Band, on piano, and Geraint Watkins – a compadre of Edmunds and Lowe's from days gone by – on piano and accordion.

Still there was the tried-and-tested formula of juxtaposing standards with new material, but with Kim writing five of the tracks – 'Tuff Enuff', 'Two Time My Lovin', 'Amnesia', 'True Love' and 'I Don't Care' – and two group compositions – 'Look At That, Look At That' and 'Down At Antone's' – there seemed a much greater desire to become more rock oriented while retaining the strong R&B influence. The second single, 'Wrap It Up' – an Isaac Hayes and David Porter composition which had been recorded by Sam & Dave – only managed to climb to Number 50 in the Billboard charts. Despite mutterings from hardcore fans that the T-Birds had sold out, later that year they picked up the prestigious W.C. Handy Award for Best Blues Band: certainly not an award routinely handed out just for commercial success.

Jimmie would join Stevie Ray on-stage for the encore, 'Love Struck Baby', which they would play together on a twin-necked guitar

Prior to the album's launch in the spring, The Fabulous Thunderbirds had undertaken a tour of Australia and New Zealand with Double Trouble. Although this might have inspired a fresh tidal wave of comment over Jimmie and Stevie Ray's alleged competitiveness, the reality was demonstrably something different: Jimmie would join Stevie Ray on-stage for the encore, 'Love Struck Baby', which they would play together on a twin-necked guitar.

There were other developments on that tour too. While in Auckland Stevie Ray became besotted with a young New Zealand model called Janna Lapidus. Although Janna was only 17,

Stevie Ray was a not especially worldly 31-year-old. Apart from anything else, his relationship with Lenny was still running downhill rapidly, so meeting Janna seemed to offer the possibility of starting afresh.

Someone else who wanted to start afresh was Chesley Millikin's, who announced that as of June 1st 1986, Classic Management would no longer represent Stevie Ray Vaughan and Double Trouble. On their return from Australia the split with the manager was ratified and a list of prospective replacements drawn up by Alex Hodges, the group's booking agent. Hodges had shut down his Empire agency the previous year and moved over to International Creative Management (ICM), one of the most prestigious agencies in the world.

> **Although Stevie Ray told him the band needed time off, Hodges maintained that the only way to get themselves out of debt was by gigging to as many people as possible**

Stevie Ray eventually persuaded Hodges to take on the role of manager himself – it was something he was eminently suited for, as he'd toured extensively during the 1970s with The Allman Brothers and other bands, and there was surely nothing Stevie Ray and Double Trouble could throw at him that he'd not marshalled many times before.

The biggest problem, apart from Stevie Ray's prodigious cocaine habit, was the debt of $100,000 owed to Millikin and Classic Management. Although Stevie Ray had told Hodges that the group needed more time off the road, Hodges maintained the only way to get themselves out of debt was by gigging to as many people as possible. Hodges was right, of course, in theory – but the way Stevie Ray was behaving, it seemed clear he was heading for a major fall.

CHAPTER 7

Live Alive (Just)

"He had that hollow look in his eyes ... like if you've ever seen a dead animal – like looking into a dead deer's eye ... Vacant."

CHRIS LAYTON ON STEVIE RAY'S LOWEST EBB

After the Australian tour with The Fabulous Thunderbirds, and yet more touring in the US, Stevie Ray returned to Austin to find that his apartment in Travis Heights was locked up, and had no electricity. Lenny had done a bunk with the cash he had been sending while on tour. Chastened and aggrieved at this situation, he went to Los Angeles, where Alex Hodges was based. While there he hooked up with Tim Duckworth, an old acquaintance from Austin who'd told him there would always be a place to stay if he was ever in LA. Duckworth was not only a guitarist and songwriter, he also had the stamina to cope with the band's lifestyle, and Hodges was soon prevailed upon to add Tim's name to the payroll as Stevie Ray's personal assistant. Hodges was not especially keen, but he recognised the need to have someone around who could get Stevie Ray from A to B on time.

The other looming problem was the need to provide Epic with a new album. It was decided it would be a live one – which should have been like shelling peas for someone of Stevie Ray's calibre. Always a great way to sneak through contractual obligations, live albums had the added

AT THE HEIGHT OF HIS EXCESS, STEVIE RAY'S FAVOURED ON-STAGE TIPPLE WAS COCAINE DISSOLVED IN WHISKEY

virtue of being cheap to produce. In the meantime Stevie Ray occupied himself by doing a spot of session work in Los Angeles – though this was presumably more to mollify the powers-that-be at Epic, as his contributions to actor Don Johnson's solo album, *Heartbeat*, and Teena Marie's *Emerald City*, were hardly the stuff that dreams are made of. At least on Heartbeat he was joined by Ronnie Wood of The Rolling Stones, Bonnie Raitt and Dickey Betts of The Allman Brothers Band (so he was obviously not the only performer happy to take advantage of a quick session fee). Then he contributed guitar to James Brown's 'Living In America', which later popped up on the soundtrack of the Sylvester Stallone film *Rocky 4*.

The logistics for the live album still needed to be worked out. Initially it was thought that the show at Montreux earlier that year might make up the bulk of the set. On closer listening the Montreux recording was irreparably flawed, and no amount of overdubbing would remedy the shortcomings. So it was decided they would return to Austin and Dallas to record some shows there; the thinking was that on home territory the band would presumably be relaxed and at their best. Given Stevie Ray's physical condition at the time, this was a hopelessly optimistic view.

Hanging around in Los Angeles should have presented him with an ideal opportunity to recharge his batteries, but when they got back to Austin for the two shows, Stevie Ray was so far gone that much of his guitar work lacked the sparkle of years gone by, and his rap during 'Life Without You' was little more than an incoherent ramble which seemed to be about Africa, for some reason. In Dallas it was the same story.

As Tommy Shannon later told Dan Forte in *Guitar Player*, "It was supposed to be a live record, but we ended up overdubbing just about everything, from studio to studio, all over America." As they were still booked for gigs, making the live album had to be done at the same time. Chris Layton explained: "We proceeded to go back on the road, taking the tapes with us. At Stevie Wonder's studio in Los Angeles, I tried to overdub an entire drum track to a live track … We'd wanted to do a live record for a long time, but I'd always wanted it to be much more than what Live Alive turned out to be. Out of necessity, *Live Alive* became something we did at that time because we were so fucked up we couldn't have gotten it together to do a serious, good studio album. It served a lot of purposes, because a lot of fans had been asking for a live album, but after we'd done the recordings we really couldn't escape this monster after all."

In the end, considering the truly appalling circumstances under which the record was made, they wound up with a set that some fans found quite appealing. Even Stevie Ray, according to Layton, changed his mind later and didn't think it was the clinker it's sometimes made out to be: "Stevie and I would talk about it, and he'd get pissed off at me because I'd say, 'That record really kind of sucked.' He'd say, 'It didn't. There's some brilliant moments on it.' So I'd drop it."

Live Alive offers a very good cross-section of the strongest material from the first three albums, though more recent additions, such as 'Willie The Wimp', written by Bill Carter and Ruth Ellsworth, and Howlin' Wolf's 'I'm Leaving You (Commit A Crime)' also seem fully integrated into the group's canon. And there's an inspired version of Stevie Wonder's 'Superstition' – which seems appropriate as they were using his Wonderland studios in Los Angeles for some of the overdubbing. Later on Wonder himself appeared in a video for Double Trouble's version of 'Superstition'.

The most interesting facet of *Live Alive* is the addition of Reese Wynans' keyboards to tracks like 'Mary Had A Little Lamb' and 'Texas Flood', but it was probably the extended work-outs on Hendrix's 'Voodoo Chile (Slight Return)' and 'Ain't Gone 'N' Give Up On Love' which won the hearts of the fans. On the whole, Double Trouble are not on top form – they don't quite plod, but there's certainly not much of a spring in the step.

After spending much of July in Wonderland and at the Record Plant, at the end of the month they played two nights at the Greek Theatre in Los Angeles. At one of the shows, Hank Ballard, composer of 'Look At Little Sister', was persuaded to join the band on-stage, and Hendrix's former drummer Mitch Miller came up to help out on 'Voodoo Chile'. But the road beckoned once again and, with Bonnie Raitt as opening act, they set off on a short haul up and down the Pacific seaboard, stopping off at places like San Diego, Santa Cruz and Salem (Oregon), before heading over to Memphis to work with Lonnie Mack on a pilot TV showcase, *American Caravan*, for the Public Broadcasting Service (PBS). Then Stevie Ray heard that his father had become very ill.

The death of his father from a heart attack caused Stevie Ray to do some fairly immediate re-evaluating of his own life

The relationship between father and youngest son had sometimes been acrimonious, and this had not been helped by his father's medical condition, which often made him cantankerous and abusive to anyone who came to see him. Exactly what it was he suffered from is open to question: asbestosis is perhaps the most common diagnosis, although Parkinson's Disease has also been cited. Whatever the history, his death from a heart attack on August 27th 1986 caused Stevie Ray to do some fairly immediate re-evaluating of his own life – which as often as not came out when he was playing 'Life Without You' on-stage.

Despite his father's death, Stevie Ray still had professional commitments, and within minutes of the burial at Laurel Land cemetery, Stevie Ray was on the way to the airport to pick up a flight that would take him off to play at the *Miller Beer Festival* in Montreal. This was followed by another stint mixing at the studios in Los Angeles before he and the rest of the band were due to start a 28-date tour of Europe, starting in Scandinavia on September 12th.

As his substance dependencies had increased, Stevie Ray had become ever more inventive when it came to having a mid-set livener

The tour was scheduled to begin in Denmark, before moving on across Europe. Playing before sell-out crowds, he and the group were treated like conquering heroes returning from the front. Stevie Ray, though, was seriously battle-scarred. As his substance dependencies had increased, he had become ever more inventive when it came to having a little mid-set livener. One method was having cocaine dissolved in his favourite brand of whiskey, Crown Royal, thereby avoiding any tell-tale residues on the upper lip. It could also be described as killing two birds with one stone, so to speak. But he'd been doing this for so long now that his physical reserves were exhausted, and matters were soon to come to a head

After two nights at the Paris Olympia, the tour moved on to Munich, where they were due play the Circus Krone. ZZ Top were appearing on the bill that evening, but they were not around when Stevie Ray showed up so, for some reason – presumably thinking he was being helpful – he decided he'd do ZZ Top's soundcheck for them. This was not the done thing, and did little to endear him to ZZ Top and their management. Bill Ham, like many people, was aware of Stevie Ray's increasingly erratic behaviour and self-destructive lifestyle. He later told Joe Nick Patoski in *Caught In The Crossfire* that he'd taken Stevie Ray aside after this gig and warned him he was "killing himself": "I remember being appalled," the Top manager said, "that whoever was responsible for Stevie's life and career had not intervened to rescue this talented young man from what appeared to be a downward spiral."

On September 28th Double Trouble moved on to Ludwigshafen in Germany. After the show Stevie Ray and the rest of the group were walking over to a restaurant when Stevie Ray collapsed, throwing up and going into convulsions. Chris Layton related the story to Dan Forte in *Guitar Player*: "We'd stop for a minute and he'd vomit – throwing up bile, almost like dry-heaving, and a little bit of blood. In the course of a few blocks this happened several times. He said, 'I need a drink.' I said, 'You can't drink like this,' and he said, 'I know. I need one, though.' He looked up at me, and I could see the look in his eyes – like, 'I'm really tucked up [sic]. How can I physically be in this state and think that I need a drink?'

"We went back to the hotel room, and that's where it really happened. He started gasping for breath .... I think as much as anything he was thinking, 'I've got to do something' ... He had that hollow look in his eyes: like if you've ever seen a dead animal – like looking into a dead deer's eye, like nothing's there. Vacant. I saw that happen, then I could see the life come back to him, and he said, 'I need help. I need help.' We called the ambulance, and it was like five German paramedics in white suits, and they started sticking needles in his arms – glucose and saline for dehydration – trying to stabilize him, because he was real borderline. We went to the hospital, and they looked him over and let him check out."

For Stevie Ray this was perhaps the writing on the wall he had been waiting for: "I finally hit rock bottom when I collapsed," he recalled in 1988 to *Guitarist* magazine. "I could no longer carry on the schedule we had. ... As long as I kept going, anaesthetising my feelings, and doing things that would give me enough energy ... we would just play right through it. If I'd had the time to stop and think about it, I would have seen it was going to lead nowhere real quick. ... It was mainly cocaine, because ... somehow along the line I got the idea it was safer than other drugs, and that's a lie. It's one of the more distorting drugs, it can really lead to problems, as I found out the hard way. ... I got to the point where I was completely wrecked in my thinking, in my heart, and physically. Most of my values were gone. ... I finally gave up fighting this whole deal, and then it dawned on me that now I can get some help."

I was completely wrecked – physically, in my heart, and in my thinking. Most of my values were gone

It wasn't quite as easy as that, though, because the group still had a schedule to keep to. "The next day we went to Zurich," said Chris, taking up the story again, "and then there were a few days off before the London shows. I called our manager, Alex Hodges, and said, 'Stevie needs help. We've got to stop this thing. He's said he needs help. Who's that doctor in London who helped Clapton and everybody get off heroin?' Alex called Eric's manager and got in touch with Dr Bloom, and Stevie checked into the clinic."

"I went to Doctor Victor Bloom, here in London," Stevie Ray himself explained, "and he put me in hospital to detox and to observe my stomach – because I'd torn my stomach up real bad." More specifically, there was severe internal bleeding. Alcohol was eating holes in his stomach wall, and the cocaine – which of course he'd dissolved first in whiskey – was crystallising again, and eating into his intestines.

But there was still the small matter of a London gig to do. The show was scheduled to take place at the Hammersmith Palais in west London and Stevie Ray was dead set on doing it. He'd even asked his mother Martha and his new girlfriend Janna Lapidus, the model from New Zealand, to come over to London – perhaps for much-needed moral support.

"He got out of the clinic to do the first London show, and that's when he stepped off the back of the stage," Chris recalled to Dan Forte. "It was a real funky staging at the Hammersmith Palais. There was this drop-off between the backstage area and the stage, with a tiny gangplank only about two feet wide. When we came off-stage, they turned all the lights off, and Stevie just took a step and missed the gangplank. First he went with one leg down, knocking the shit out of his leg, and then he hit his head on the floor. The press said, 'Stevie Ray Vaughan collapses on-stage from drug addiction and alcohol abuse,' when actually he just tripped. But at that point, we said, 'This is it.' It was kind of symbolic. 'The show's over'." Chris was right. There was a simple choice for Stevie Ray – clean up or check out.

The press said, 'Stevie Ray collapses on-stage from drug addiction and alcohol abuse,' when actually he just tripped ... but it was kind of symbolic

Perhaps the most damning indictment of all – which Stevie Ray himself had come to recognise while going through two years-worth of tapes for the *Live Alive* album – was how often his playing had been just plain sloppy. It was nearly always necessary to add overdubs or redo parts in the studio to tidy things up.

But it wasn't just Stevie Ray who had a problem. Double Trouble bassist Tommy Shannon – who shared Stevie Ray's indulgent tastes – knew he too had to change everything, from top to bottom. And the rest of the band made the effort at the same time. "Chris and Reese weren't really of an addictive nature," Shannon told Dan Forte, "but I've seen them change their lives as much as we did. It was like a change of the whole band. Everybody was real supportive – the crew and the whole organisation."

In fact, of all their immediate intimates, Stevie Ray's brother Jimmie was the only one who did not clean up – at least not for the moment. Despite the success of *Tuff Enuff*, not everything was entirely up to the mark with The Fabulous Thunderbirds. They had toured solidly for years, but had yet to consolidate themselves in the wider marketplace. The new album, *Hot Number*, was supposed to do that.

Once again it had a slick, radio-friendly veneer of sophistication. It almost seemed as if Kim Wilson was trying to do the impossible – to develop a formula that would achieve the essential commercial acceptance (they undoubtedly needed to sell more records), but at the same time wouldn't offend the individual members, most notably die-hard Jimmie, or indeed alienate the existing fan base. This was a tricky balancing act. In an attempt to achieve it they retained essentially the same personnel as on *Tuff Enuff*, with Dave Edmunds producing and adding some guitar, and Chuck Leavell on keyboards and piano. But the addition of the Memphis Horns, instead of the Roomful Of Blues horn section, suggested that Epic were prepared to spend just a little bit more money.

The Memphis Horns had been around since the late 1960s, appearing on many of the classic sides from the Stax and Atlantic labels with such luminaries as Aretha Franklin and Eddie Floyd. Though basically just two guys, Wayne Jackson and Andrew Love, they augmented the line-up as required; for the T-Birds' sessions Jack Hale came in on trombone and another veteran, Jim Horn, turned up to add baritone.

The treatment centre gave me the tools to live without using these things ... to not need to get loaded. I have a choice now

Instead of the usual raft of blues obscurities and R&B classics, most of the material was very contemporary. Kim Wilson wrote approximately half the album, including 'Stand Back', which became a big turntable hit that summer; Duke Robillard, erstwhile guitarist with Roomful Of Blues, contributed 'Don't Bother Trying To Steal Your Love'; and Al Anderson, guitarist from NRBQ (not surprisingly the acronym is more interesting than the full name, New Rhythm & Blues Quartet), provided 'It Comes To Me Naturally'. Indeed the only track that might have had some claim to being a soul or R&B classic was 'How Do You Spell Love?' – but they had recorded this before, so they were not exactly breaking fresh ground.

Despite what anyone may think or say about *Hot Number*, there is enough variety to make it stand up fairly well, reflecting the group's total professionalism. Initially it sold OK – peaking at Number 49 on the charts – but that did not last, and in general it merely succeeded in further alienating some of the T-Birds' long-time fans.

Stevie Ray, meanwhile, had taken to heart the admonitions of Doctor Bloom in London.

Bloom had suggested a course of treatment, the Charter programme, at the Peachford Hospital in Atlanta, Georgia. This was a programme that required total withdrawal – and total commitment as well. "The treatment centre gave me the tools to live without using these things ... to not need to get loaded," Stevie Ray told *Guitarist* magazine in 1988, "and also to have more inspiration, more faith in life and myself. I have a choice now: instead of 'I'll do this because I have to', I have a choice ... I choose to be healthier, and I choose to grow spiritually, and I choose not to use any drugs or alcohol – because I know what kind of thinking goes on in my head when I do. If I was to have a drink, I wouldn't just have a drink, I'd have a lot of drinks, and it might be that I would die, because the disease of alcoholism is very progressive. Now I wake up in the morning and it's neat, real neat."

Despite the fees for the treatment (which could vary from $12,000 to $20,000) there was no guarantee that the chemical – as well as psychological – dependency would be beaten in the long term. Many people had undertaken the programme, only to capitulate within months and be back where they started. After completing his 30 days he was discharged with the message, "It's up to you now". While at Peachford Stevie Ray had enrolled with Alcoholics Anonymous – although AA is independent of any official institutions, they work in co-operation with local hospital authorities. So he had some back-up.

Enrolling at the local Alcoholics Anonymous centre, he found he knew many of those attending, from different bands around Dallas

He was not alone, in any case. One of his cousins had gone into treatment, and Tommy Shannon had entered a facility in Austin the same day as Stevie Ray started his treatment at Peachford. What's more, after moving his things back to Dallas from Austin and enrolling at the local AA centre, he found he knew many of those attending, from different bands around Dallas.

At this point Stevie Ray also filed for divorce from Lenny, and moved Janna into his new apartment in north Dallas. He was at least endeavouring to start anew – even Tabasco sauce had been kicked out of his diet (it contains alcohol), and he started frequenting health food stores and restaurants. Being off the road also enabled him to dig deep into the record collection that had inspired him in the first place, listening to albums by people like Bobby 'Blue' Bland, Johnny 'Guitar' Watson, and even jazz guitarist Grant Green. Although he wasn't gigging in his own right he still found time to appear alongside Lonnie Mack at the Fox Theatre in Atlanta for a New

Year's Eve radio broadcast; then he appeared at Dallas's Redux Theatre with Robert Cray for another two shows that were being taped for future broadcast.

But on January 30th 1987 he returned to the fray, performing at the huge Fair Park Coliseum in Dallas. It was back to business again – yet even the maudlin rap on 'Life Without You' had been replaced by a homily, speaking of the need to "quit tearing our bodies apart", which was altogether far more in keeping with the redeemed Stevie Ray. This was followed by a short haul up the east coast, playing gigs that had been cancelled due to his indisposition; including a show at New York's Radio City Music Hall. Then it was back to Hollywood to attend the premiere of the movie *Back To The Beach*, in which Stevie Ray and Dick Dale, the undisputed supremo of the surf guitar, duetted on the old 1960s Chantays hit 'Pipeline'.

Other notable appearances included a B.B. King 'tribute' show, on video, alongside Eric Clapton, Albert King, Gladys Knight, Chaka Khan and Paul Butterfield and others. Butterfield, as a harmonica player and as leader of the Paul Butterfield Blues Band, had been a huge influence on the embryonic blues scene in the early 1960s – so his death a few days after this show might well have caused Stevie Ray some moments of reflection.

Although he had managed to clean up and resist all temptations – and there were still many – this desire to start afresh helped him sort out other trying details, such as the divorce settlement with Lenny and his financial obligations to Chesley Millikin and Classic Management. In Lenny's case, in addition to $130,000 lawyers' fees, he had to pay her $50,000 as a lump sum, and then 25 percent of all future royalties on each of the first four albums. The divorce became final on June 1st 1988. As for Millikin and Classic Management, they were reimbursed a significant percentage of accrued expenses, still pending settlement; Millikin and Classic were not thrilled with the outcome, as they felt they were owed more.

As well as the domestic changes that had been taking place in Stevie Ray's life, there were other developments that needed to be considered – most notably at his record label, Epic, which had just been taken over by electronics giant Sony. As Stevie Ray was itching to get back into the studio, it was time for manager Alex Hodges to approach the new record company bosses on his behalf.

CHAPTER 8

Musician Of The Decade

"Stevie was really afraid of not being able to make a good record sober, but it's my favourite of all the albums."

TOMMY SHANNON ON DOUBLE TROUBLE'S FINAL RELEASE, *IN STEP*

"Since the live album there's been a lot of changes going on, changes in my life as well as other people in the band, and we're trying to take things at a more sensible pace." This is how Stevie Ray described his born-again attitude in *Guitarist* magazine in 1988, when he was starting work on the *In Step* album. "You know, this record will be the first one I've ever done sober, completely sober, so things are a lot different now, and there's a lot more to see and be thankful for."

But during Stevie Ray's lay-off, the world had kept on spinning, and not everything revolved around his new healthy lifestyle. Take the sale of Columbia (CBS), the parent company of Epic Records, to the Japanese electronics and media empire Sony. For Sony, Stevie Ray Vaughan and Double Trouble were definitely small potatoes compared to someone of the stature of Michael Jackson or Barbra Streisand. Even so, Alex Hodges felt this was the precise moment to go to the new 'head honchos' to work out a new deal for Stevie and the band. It took a certain amount of chutzpah to do this, since not only had his client(s) been out of sight for a chunk of time, but it

BROTHERS IN ARMS – JIMMIE AND STEVIE RAY DURING THEIR ON-STAGE DOUBLE-NECK GUITAR DUEL

was undeniable that Stevie Ray had never been the best-behaved artist on their books – in truth he'd been a malefactor of fairly gargantuan proportions. Hodges worked out a plan, citing Stevie Ray's achievements thus far.

Whatever the backbiters may have thought, there was little doubt that, since his renaissance, Stevie Ray had taken to the road anew, sparkling with confidence and glistening with health. Above all he was playing out of his skin. Many people had speculated that perhaps the new slimline Vaughan would have lost some of his ardour, and perhaps without the stimulants (or depressants) the fire would be quenched. This was not the case – indeed many long-term fans asserted they had never seen him play better. His stagecraft, something he had studied assiduously while working with people like Paul Ray in The Cobras, had always been good, and his pacing and song selection for each set always been impressive. But now, no longer off his face, he was able to bring a coherence and professionalism to each gig that amplified the latent power of his performance.

Hodges may not have been able to point to sales figures that would bear much scrutiny alongside those of, say, Michael Jackson, but the demand for the group's albums and merchandising was growing incrementally – sales remained buoyant for the rest of Stevie Ray's life, and beyond. And it didn't do any harm that the group had headlined prestigious gigs such as the *New Orleans Jazz & Heritage Festival*. In the face of such persuasive evidence, Sony had little alternative but to renew the deal, giving Stevie Ray and the band three months or so to put together a new album, which would eventually become *In Step*.

The plan was to go into the studios – Sound Castle and Summa Studios in Los Angeles, Kiva Studios in Memphis – and try to eradicate the woeful memory of *Live Alive*. To achieve this end, Stevie Ray almost had to start from scratch. John Hammond, who had died in 1987, was replaced by producer Jim Gaines. Gaines was an astute choice, having worked as an engineer with groups like the Steve Miller Band, Carlos Santana, Huey Lewis & The News, The Doobie Brothers, Bruce Hornsby & The Range, Tower Of Power and Van Morrison (on *St Dominic's Preview*). Although his career as a producer had yet to pick up momentum, his work on *In Step* helped him become one of the most in-demand blues producers of the 1990s, working with people like John Lee Hooker, Luther Allison, Deborah Coleman, Albert Collins, Walter Trout and Lonnie Brooks.

As mentioned already, both Chris Layton and Reese Wynans had to make some changes, to one extent or another, to facilitate Stevie Ray's new approach. "It was a little bit edgy and scary," Layton told *Guitar Player*'s Dan Forte in 1991. "I know Stevie had fears about his first sober record. It was kind of a struggle on that level, but musically, when we went in to play something, we were clear. We were either finding things we had lost or discovering things we didn't know were there before. It was like a whole new band cutting our first record." Tommy Shannon – so often Stevie Ray's partner in crime – had to agree, adding, "Stevie was really afraid of not being able to make a good record sober, but it's my favourite of all of the albums."

The other thing Stevie Ray wanted to address was his own songwriting. It had never come easily before, but now he was keen to write about his recent experiences – he wanted his songs to reflect his life. The problem was putting this into practice. He turned once again for help to his old bandmate from The Nightcrawlers, Doyle Bramhall. They had already collaborated before, of course, on 'Change It' from *Soul To Soul*, and Doyle had contributed 'Dirty Pool' to *Texas Flood*, but what was required now was something far more specific which would reflect Stevie Ray's new-found peace of mind. Bramhall knew what was wanted – he had been down the same road as Stevie Ray at the end of the 1970s, and had been teetotal and 'clean' ever since.

On both 'Tightrope' and 'Wall Of Denial', Bramhall came up with ideas that accurately described Stevie Ray's perspective. But both men were mindful of the fact that this was still a rock'n'roll band, and the fans would expect them to comport themselves accordingly. So Bramhall and Stevie Ray wrote two more songs, 'The House Is Rockin'' and 'Scratch-N-Sniff' (which became the album's opener). 'Crossfire', with lyrics by Ruth Ellsworth and Bill Carter, was issued as a single, and was yet another take on Stevie Ray's past experiences. There's none so zealous as a convert. It's also the only full-group composition in the entire Double Trouble canon, crediting Shannon, Layton and Wynans as well as Stevie Ray. "We wrote about five or six songs with Bill and Ruth," Reese told *Guitar Player*, "and I'm still interested in doing more of that."

Songwriting had never come easily before, but now he was keen to write about his recent experiences – he wanted his songs to reflect his life

In addition to the Bramhall co-writes, there was a brace of Stevie Ray originals: 'Travis Walk', an instrumental, was an overt tribute to the great country guitarist Merle Travis, whose lightning finger-picking style had inspired generations of acoustic guitarists across the world for many years. It was also further confirmation of Stevie Ray's growth, not just as a technically proficient and exciting guitarist, but as an innovative musician able to transcend genres with little effort – it manages to show off various facets of Stevie Ray's expertise, with its deft finger-picking and the loose-limbed jauntiness of the melody.

'Riviera Paradise', another instrumental, reminiscent of 'Lenny' on *Texas Flood*, was recorded under particularly informal circumstances: "We didn't really think of it being a take," Tommy Shannon recalled. "It was weird, because we just sat down and they turned on the machine, and we played it ... We were real relaxed, and it just came out – the best one. I don't think we could have done that song any better." Chris Layton expanded: "It was our first pass at the song – and we hadn't done it in months. We played it completely by instinct. We'd just done something else, like 'House Is Rockin'' or something, and we had a whole different cue [headphone] mix set up. Stevie was in a room just to the side of me, with a window between us, but he turned his lights down, so I couldn't see him. The song before, he was playing so loud I had the cue mix adjusted down, so when he played real quiet on 'Riviera Paradise' I couldn't even hear him. I could just barely catch things once in a while."

Once again this track demonstrates Stevie Ray's eclecticism, allied with an omnivorous appetite – he was able to draw inspiration from such diverse sources: from jazz guitarists like Kenny Burrell and Grant Green, to T-Bone Walker and Jimi Hendrix.

It's also worth emphasising that the two instrumentals here are far more than just exercises in technical expertise – you could say they irradiate Stevie Ray's total pleasure and delight in his own abilities. By the same token, the covers on *In Step* are well-chosen, providing resonant contrast to the Vaughan originals. Take for instance Willie Dixon's 'Let Me Love You Baby'. Dixon, bassist and house arranger and composer at Chicago's legendary Chess studios, had composed dozens of songs such as 'Hoochie Coochie Man' for Muddy Waters, 'My Babe' for Little Walter, and 'Evil' for Howlin' Wolf , and these had provided a small part of the soundtrack to Stevie Ray's youth, via Jimmie's record collection. But 'Let Me Love You Baby' had been popularised by another denizen of the Windy City, Buddy Guy. Guy had always been one of Stevie Ray's most vocal champions, ever since they'd met and played together at Antone's in the late 1970s – and Stevie Ray had always jumped at any opportunity to play at Guy's Chicago nightclub, Legends. So covering Guy's 'Leave My Girl Alone' on the same album was another quixotic gesture on Stevie Ray's part.

Stevie Ray had an omnivorous appetite, able to draw inspiration from diverse sources ... from jazz to Jimi Hendrix

Howlin' Wolf had been another big influence during Stevie Ray's adolescence. His death in 1976 meant they never got to play together, but Stevie Ray had often played with Wolf's foil and guitarist Hubert Sumlin. Wolf's 'Love Me Darlin'' shows Stevie Ray in typically expansive form, while Shannon and Layton maintain their challenge as one of the best rock'n'roll rhythm sections on the planet. "Our role was to play the best we could for Stevie," Shannon stated to Art Tipaldi in *Children Of The Blues*. "Stevie never played anything the same way twice, unless it was the main riff of the song. But he would just all of a sudden go to a change, knowing we'd be there. He wouldn't turn around and tell anybody. Sometimes I'd do a bassline running down, and get it to go right down with him. It was like this intuitive thing we were doing ... ultimately that's a bass player's role, to be the bridge between the drums and Stevie."

By the time the sessions were completed, there was more than enough material in the can. "We didn't get to finish all of them," Chris said, "but we cut some stuff that there wasn't room for on the album: 'I Wrote The Book', 'Boot Hill', a Little Willie John song called 'Take My Love' and a Dyke & The Blazers song, 'Let A Woman Be A Woman, Let A Man Be A Man'."

Stevie never played anything the same twice, unless it was the main riff of the song ... he would all of a sudden go to a change, knowing we'd be there

After finishing *In Step*, Stevie Ray and Double Trouble appeared at the White House at one of the inaugural parties for President George Bush (senior) before embarking on a tour with The Jeff Beck Group. Entitled *The Fire Meets The Fury Tour*, it might have been a testing situation, for those with less resilience, to be confronted by the sight of Beck and his entourage regularly indulging in all that hotel bars have to offer without a moment's hesitation. But for Stevie Ray it was just an enormous thrill to be touring with someone he had idolised ever since Beck was with The Yardbirds in the mid-1960s: "Everybody would play 'Jeff's Boogie'," Stevie Ray recalled. "You'd play it part of the way, then double-time it and double-time it again. Chuck Berry's was a lot more tame, but Jeff Beck took it and it had wild guitars and echo and the whole bit."

As neither Beck nor Stevie Ray was prepared to top the bill, this was done on rotation, with Beck opening the first show, as decided by the flip of a coin. Then each evening of the 28-day tour, Beck and Vaughan duetted on Don Nix's 'Goin' Down', which had also been a particular favourite of Freddy King's. The fact that Jeff and Stevie Ray got on so well with each other wasn't particularly surprising, but the degree to which they were able to play together was unexpected, in view of the alleged rivalry that's supposed to exist between guitarists. Indeed, in Chicago, Stevie Ray stopped by Buddy Guy's club and jammed on stage with Guy and Beck: "I was terrified," Beck recalled, "but I went along, because I couldn't resist seeing [Stevie Ray] and

Buddy playing. Seeing Buddy in his element, I didn't mind getting up there, because that's as close as you come to the heart of the blues, as I know it. And the man will suddenly smile, and say something, so there's no way you can not do it. I found my legs just carried me on-stage."

Beck and Stevie Ray even managed to sell out New York City's Madison Square Garden, but the zenith of the tour was the concert in Austin at the Frank Erwin Center. Forget about rivalry, but there was no way that Stevie Ray, back on his old stamping ground, was ever likely to take a hiding – even from someone he held in such high esteem.

When *In Step* appeared in June 1989 it became Stevie Ray's most successful album, peaking at Number 33 on the US charts (and putting him in the UK charts for the first time), earning a Grammy for Best Contemporary Blues Recording, and going gold just over six months after its release, and then platinum not long after that. Despite being garlanded with honours, he had other projects on his mind, most notably with his brother Jimmie. For over 15 years now Jimmie had criss-crossed the country with The Fabulous Thunderbirds, but the novelty had definitely worn thin, and Kim Wilson was becoming ever more dominant in the band. Personality clashes between the two of them had been occurring more frequently, and the albums were gradually turning out less blues-based, more rock-orientated with the passage of time

In Step became Stevie Ray's most successful album, peaking at Number 33 in the US charts, and putting him in the UK charts for the first time

On the most recent album, *Powerful Stuff*, the group appeared to be just marking time. The title track was another big radio hit, mainly due to its use on the soundtrack of the Tom Cruise movie *Cocktail*, but otherwise the band did not seem to be trying very hard. Even Kim, who had always written the lion's share of the band's original material, seemed disinterested, contributing just two songs, 'Emergency' and 'She's Hot'. The covers too – which included Jerry 'Swamp Dog' Williams' 'Rock This Place', the Isaac Hayes and David Porter collaboration 'Now Loosen Up Baby', and Slim Harpo's 'Rainin' In My Heart' – although varied enough, were somehow rather tepid and lacklustre. Apart from anything else, Jimmie had been experimenting with steel guitars and jazz, and all sorts of other things, and so it really was time to move on. "Early days with the T-Birds was a blast," Jimmie recalled to Art Tipaldi. "We started the same time as Antone's opened. That was perfect because it gave us a place to play ... We had a great time going all over the world. We did everything I dreamed about and more – I never really expected to do any of it." But he'd gone as far as he felt he could go in that set-up. "I was tired, drinkin' too much and everything that goes with it. I just wanted to get off the bus and go home. I didn't feel like we were going anywhere."

By the time *Powerful Stuff* was released, Jimmie and Stevie Ray had already worked together on Bob Dylan's album *Under The Red Sky*, alongside the likes of George Harrison, Elton John, David Lindley (from Jackson Browne's Band), Al Kooper, Bruce Hornsby, Slash and Robben Ford. The brothers also appeared – with Angela Strehli, Lou Ann Barton, Denny Freeman, George Rains and Derek O'Brien – on *Austin City Limits*, a PBS TV tribute to Stevie Ray's former bandmate, W.C. Clark. Then came Stevie Ray's suggestion that he and Jimmie cut an album together. But if that were going to happen, Jimmie needed to 'clean up' his own act as well.

Family Style was far removed from the chunky riffing of The T-Birds' albums, or the spiky soloing of Stevie Ray's

Once they had made the decision to go ahead and make a joint album, Stevie Ray and Jimmie did what they had done when they were kids. They dug deep into the record collection, listening to all the old stuff they had cut their teeth on: from Bob Wills & His Texas Cowboys to Charlie Christian, from T-Bone Walker to U.P. Wilson; from B.B. King to Albert King; and from Booker T & The MGs to Richard 'Groove' Holmes. And that was just the start of it. They then began to rehearse in the garage at Jimmie's house in south Austin, before going over to Ardent Studios in Memphis where the basic tracks were going to be hammered into shape.

Credited to the Vaughan Brothers, the resulting album, *Family Style*, was another turnaround, this time for both Stevie Ray and Jimmie. Possessed of considerable warmth, *Family Style* was far removed from the chunky riffing that characterised the Fabulous Thunderbirds' albums, or the spiky soloing of Stevie Ray's albums. John Swenson in *Rolling Stone* magazine described it as, "a witty, understated dialogue in which both players come up with new sounds for the occasion." More than that, though – and this is very significant – it laid bare the influences from their past. This was not paying homage, this was re-interpreting those sources, and how they affected each of them at that particular point. So they were not trying to best one another. According to Swenson, "They play all the way through with an exhilarating sense of abandon and discovery ... the happiness that pours out is irresistible." At the start of the opening track, 'Hard to Be', Jimmie's voice can be heard saying to the tape engineer, "Roll 'em and I'll just ... *feel* something."

Family Style was the brothers' first official album together, even though they'd always worked with each other whenever they could, going right back to the beginning of their respective careers. This project meant a lot to both of them. As Stevie Ray put it: "We've probably gotten closer making this record than we have been since we were little kids at home. And I can honestly say I needed it." Always eager to sing the other's praises, the two had a mutual admiration society that was part family pride and part genuine awe of one another's talent. In his July 1986 cover interview Jimmie told Guitar Player: "I'm very proud to say that Stevie gets plugged into his soul's emotions. He wails and he's mellow, all at the same time, without ever playing it the same way once, much less twice."

In a 1989 *Off The Record* radio interview for Westwood One, Stevie Ray summed up his feelings about Jimmie. "He's still my favourite guitar player in the world," he said. "Having him as a mentor, watching him play, and watching him learn to play – it was almost like he didn't learn to play ... As soon as he picked up a guitar, it was like he knew more about it than he should have. Ever since I can remember he was, if not the hottest guitar player in Texas, then about to be known as the hottest. Having a big brother like that gives you a lot of incentive, to put it lightly. He knows a lot more than a lot of people realize, and he plays about a tenth of what he knows, because he doesn't have to try to prove what he knows. I end up trying to play everything I can think of."

Jimmie knows a lot more than people realise ... he plays about a tenth of what he knows. I end up trying to play everything I can think of

But *Family Style* – with its relaxed, non-riff-dominated, simpler approach – wasn't typical of what was going on at the time. The blues boom had settled into a groove where great players such as Johnny Copeland, Clarence 'Gatemouth' Brown, Buddy Guy, Luther Allison, Hubert Sumlin, and whoever else you care to think of, had resurrected their careers and were now gigging and recording on a regular basis. Young players such as Anson Funderburgh, Mike Morgan, Long John Hunter, Smokin' Joe Kubek, Charlie Sexton and Eric Johnson had emerged as well, but there was a sea change taking place, caused by singer-songwriters such as Steve Earle. Although Earle had been feted when he first appeared in Nashville – after his family had relocated to San Antonio from Fort Monroe in Virginia when he was a child – Earle had never been a thorough-going country act. His whole demeanour was far too rock'n'roll for the good burghers of Nashville's Music Row. His album *Guitar Town* caused an upset: songs like the title track and 'Someday' seemed to have more in common with Bruce Springsteen's *Born In The USA*. But it had a big, big heart as well. It was, in conventional terms, a hybrid – *Guitar Town* caused a blurring of the edges between what was perceived as country and what was perceived as rock'n'roll .

Family Style raised similar questions. It embraced the broadest of churches, accommodating not just rural blues and R&B, but also jazz, country and to some extent western swing. It was a different kind of hybrid. Sophisticated but relaxed, warm but technically acute, and organised but never over-produced. Jimmie told Dan Forte in *Guitar Player* in 1991, "I had a lot of things I'd been wanting to do for a long time – just my version of the way I want to hear things. Everybody thought we were just going to do a jam blues record – try to outdo each other – and neither one of us were really into that, musically. That's OK for some things, and I even like hearing that sometimes – like Speedy West and Jimmy Bryant, sort of trick guitar, or Chuck Berry and Bo Diddley – because it's just fun. But we wanted to do songs, and do our style in a way that had our roots but was contemporary. We wanted to do everything we could on the guitar, instead of, 'We need some horns here' or 'We need some synths here'."

As if to give themselves more chance of creating something beyond their usual brief, Jimmie and Stevie Ray engaged producer Nile Rodgers, whom Stevie Ray had worked with on David Bowie's *Let's Dance* album. Although Rodgers' reputation still revolved around his work in Chic, since working with Bowie in 1983 he had gone on to work with icons such as Diana Ross, Debbie Harry and Madonna, but he had also worked with bands like INXS and The B52s – and he produced *Flash* for Jeff Beck in 1985. He was also, as often as not, hired as a guitarist in his own right – by people like Steve Winwood, Bryan Ferry and Peter Gabriel – so he could contribute to the Vaughan brothers' project not just as a producer, but also as a fellow guitarist who knew his chops as well as anyone. It was this empathy that enabled Rodgers to elicit such comfortable, natural performances from Jimmie and Stevie Ray. Bearing in mind what Jimmie said about the guitar orientation of the album, Rodgers was also able to use occasional samples and synths sympathetically, which helped create the textured homogeneity of styles, without compromising the overall natural effect.

At one point Jimmie and Stevie Ray seriously considered playing all the instruments themselves, but Rodgers put his foot down, saying he didn't want them to be distracted by anything other than just getting their performances right. "[He] helped us a lot with getting our thoughts together," Jimmie explained in *Guitar Player*. "Neither one of us were really good at explaining how it would sound, because we didn't like to use examples – like other people's names. But once we got going, it really didn't take very long. It was a relatively short time from when we said, 'OK, we're gonna do it,' to when we got a date and started looking at producers. We went to New York and saw Nile, and he was great. We liked him. I'd never met him before, but Stevie had worked with him on that David Bowie thing. And I liked his records and everything. Great musician. He helped us put it together, as far as getting specific, and a lot of it was left open to, you know, what happened."

The chosen rhythm section of Al Berry on bass and Larry Aberman on drums was ideal too, as both knew and understood what was expected of them. "[They] are really great, and they were into it," Jimmie told Dan Forte. "We'd never met them, but we went to Memphis and played them the songs, and – Nile said this several times, too – there was just this great feeling when we started making the record in the studio."

Doyle Bramhall on drums and Preston Hubbard on bass (from The Fabulous Thunderbirds) were the only contributors from the Vaughan brothers' inner circle. Doyle also co-wrote three of the songs with Stevie Ray – 'Hard To Be', 'Long Way From Home' and 'Telephone Song'. Much of the other material was purpose-built for the occasion. "Once we decided we were going to do it at a certain time," Jimmie continued, "Stevie and I got together a lot on the phone and out in the garage here, just fartin' around, throwing ideas back and forth. But a lot of the songs were finished in the studio."

Indeed such was the ad hoc nature of the sessions that Rodgers helped out on two songs, 'Good Texan' and 'Tick Tock'. The two instrumentals – 'D/FW' (which means Dallas/Fort Worth, for the uninitiated), on which Jimmie and Stevie Ray blend and switch lines almost imperceptibly, and 'Hillbillies From Outer Space', where Jimmie on steel guitar delineates the melody and Stevie Ray adds a deft, lyrical solo over the top – are probably more in keeping with what most fans had been expecting.

Although Stevie Ray had developed as a vocalist, with a far more confident approach, Jimmie had never sung much. *Family Style* redressed that. "I always wanted to sing, but was always afraid to. I never sang, really. But everybody wants to be a singer, I guess. Here's the deal: everybody can sing – some people can sing a lot better than others. I just never did it. I always had a singer in the band, and I was always the guitar player. … It was kind of scary, but it was fun. I can sing songs as long as I pick them out or I write them. [When] Billy Swan gave me 'White Boots' when we [The Fabulous Thunderbirds] were making the *Powerful Stuff* album, we didn't use it, but I always liked it. Every time I'd play it for my wife and any girls, they always liked the song." Accompanied by Berry's thunderous bassline, 'White Boots' was potentially very commercial, despite the almost unbelievably cheesy sentiments of the lyrics.

As Jimmie commented to Dan Forte: "I want to have fun, and I want to get to the people out on the street. I want the people who don't even like music to like my music and buy my records.

They don't have to know anything about music. I just always remember how music sounded when I was a kid, before I could play. And if I'm gonna make a record, I want to be on the radio; I want people to hear it. I like selling records. What's wrong with it? I want to give those people on the top of the charts trouble. I want to be up there, too. Me and Stevie have just as much right to be up there as some of this other stuff that I don't necessarily care for. We just tried to have an open mind, and as long as we play on the record and we play songs we like and the way we want to play, no producer or no song can make it not sound like us."

In the months to come they would indeed sell records, and lots of them – but certainly not for the reasons anyone could have foreseen.

During a break in the recording schedule, Stevie Ray returned to Austin to collect an armful of awards at the *Eighth Austin Music Awards* ceremony; these included Album Of The Year for *In Step*, Album Of The Decade for *Texas Flood*, Single Of The Year for 'Crossfire', and not only Musician Of The Year, but Musician Of The Decade. It was quite a haul, and the future looked no less rosy when The Fabulous Thunderbirds and Double Trouble co-headlined the *New Orleans Jazz & Heritage Festival*. Jimmie seized the day by announcing his permanent departure from the band.

In the months to come they would sell lots of records – but certainly not for the reasons anyone could have foreseen

Just before *Family Style* was released in September 1990, Stevie Ray and Double Trouble took to the road once again, this time with Joe Cocker. The 28-day tour – named *The Power & The Passion* – was scheduled to commence at the Shoreline Amphitheatre in Mountain View, California, passing through the Starplex outdoor theatre in Dallas, before climaxing in Vancouver. Cocker was no stranger to the routine madness of life on the road, and had famously been a focus for Leon Russell's *Mad Dogs And Englishmen* revue at the turn of the 1960s (later turned into a successful movie and soundtrack album). Originally from Sheffield in the north of England, ever since setting up home in Santa Barbara, just north of Los Angeles, Cocker's powerful gravel-throated vocals had become a regular feature of the summer season touring circuit across the US. Although later Cocker albums, such as *Sheffield Steel* (1982), *Civilized Man* (1984), *Unchain My Heart* (1987) and *One Night Of Sin* (1989), had suffered from too much padding, Cocker could still cut it live on stage as well as anyone.

By the time the tour ended in July, Stevie Ray was exhausted and needed a break, which he duly took by travelling to New Zealand with Janna. On his return he was ready, willing and able to get back on the road, and then into the studio again with Double Trouble.

"We were really looking forward to the next record," Chris recalled to *Guitar Player*. "Stevie and I were hot-rodding around LA in this [Mazda] 300ZX Turbo, and he said, 'Check this song out'. It was a John Hiatt tune – real cool, but different. Working through *In Step* and what he'd done up to that point with Jimmie on Family Style, he had this real comfort about working. All these fears had been put to rest – like can we do a record sober? We were going to make that all-important second record that's usually equated with somebody's second career record."

Stevie Ray and Jimmie were intending to go out on the road to promote *Family Style*, which meant Double Trouble were going to have their first extended break in a decade

Before starting work on another Double Trouble album, though, there were other things to be attended to first. Stevie Ray and Jimmie were intending to go out on the road to promote *Family Style*, which meant Double Trouble were going to have their first extended break in almost a decade. In the meantime there were a couple of gigs scheduled at the Alpine Valley Ski-Resort, near East Troy, Wisconsin, around 80 miles from Chicago's loop. Topping the bill over the two nights was Eric Clapton, then there was Buddy Guy, the Robert Cray Band, with the Memphis Horns, and Stevie Ray & Double Trouble, with Jimmie Vaughan guesting. The event provided a great opportunity for Fender guitars to gather together four of their most revered customers – Clapton, Cray and the Vaughan brothers – for an advertising photo-call.

At the end of the first night, Clapton was joined on stage by the Vaughan brothers, Robert Cray, and Buddy Guy, plus special guests Bonnie Raitt and Jeff Healey, both long-time Clapton fans. The following day, as night drew in and showtime came around, fog rolled in off Lake Michigan and settled in the mountains. By the end of the show, the fog was lowering, but for the 30,000 people or so in the audience, the encore with Clapton, Guy, Cray and the Vaughan brothers was worth enduring any climatic conditions. Appropriately Clapton chose 'Sweet Home Chicago' – after all, most of the audience would be braving the weather and the traffic jams to get back home in that direction.

Stevie Ray was not just a big occasion player: he could shine any time, any place. But by all accounts on that evening – bearing in mind of course that nothing colours the memory more than sentiment – Stevie Ray was on the top of his game, and played like a man possessed.

As the gig concluded and the fans made their way back home, helicopters were on hand to ferry the performers back to hotels in Chicago, or to meet connecting domestic flights to other destinations from Chicago airport. Stevie Ray was keen to pick up a connection from Chicago to New York to see Janna: after returning from their vacation in New Zealand the two of them had rented an apartment in New York, where Janna was working regularly as a model. Though places were in short supply on the helicopters, Stevie Ray managed to get a seat on a flight with members of Eric Clapton's entourage – these included Bobby Brooks, agent from International Creative Management, Colin Smythe, assistant tour manager, bodyguard Nigel Browne, and the pilot, Jeffrey Browne.

The helicopter left Alpine Valley at 12.40 am. The fog was dense by this time. Banking sharply, the helicopter (a Bell 206B Jet Ranger) failed to clear the brow of a hill, and crashed, killing everyone on board. It was the early hours of August 27th 1990 – four years to the day since Jimmie and Stevie Ray's father, Jimmie Lee Vaughan, had died. News of the accident spread like wildfire as Associated Press and local news networks picked up the story. Jimmie Vaughan and Eric Clapton were obliged to return to Wisconsin to the scene of the accident to help identify the victims.

Two days later, on August 29th, Stephen Ray Vaughan was buried alongside his father in the Veteran's Section 15 of the Laurel Land Memorial Park in Oak Cliff, Dallas. Tommy Shannon, Chris Layton, Reese Wynans, manager Alex Hodges, guitar tech Rene Martinez, tour manger Skip Rickert, production manager Mark Routledge, and stage manger Bill Moundsey were pall-bearers. Stevie Wonder recited *The Lord's Prayer*, and eulogies were given by Nile Rodgers and Bruce Miller, Stevie Ray's sponsor at Alcoholics Anonymous. An a cappella rendition of 'Amazing Grace' was sung by Bonnie Raitt, Jackson Browne and Stevie Wonder.

Naturally there was speculation among the media that this was another spectacular 'rock-'n'roll death' involving drugs and alcohol. They were wrong. Stevie Ray had not fallen off the wagon. But as John Swenson succinctly summarised in his posthumous review of *Family Style* in *Rolling Stone*: "One of the most compelling myths surrounding rock'n'rollers who have died young is the notion that they were on the verge of a major stylistic breakthrough at the time of their death. *Family Style* shows Stevie Ray at exactly that point, emerging in a new context that suggests a number of directions open to him. We are left with this legacy – and left to wonder how much more this guitar genius might have accomplished."

CHAPTER 9

Stevie Ray & The Guitar

"In an age when musical tastes are shaped by technological innovations ... it's downright refreshing to hear a guitarist who plays straight from the gut."

FRANK JOSEPH, ON STEVIE RAY'S APPEAL AS A GUITARIST AND MUSICIAN, IN *GUITAR WORLD*, 1983

In January 2001, *Guitarist* magazine in the UK ran a readers' poll entitled 'The 50 Greatest Blues Guitarists'. In an astonishing demonstration of the way his legend has grown, Stevie Ray Vaughan came top in the vote, ahead of the blues masters who had influenced him. There's no question he was historically the most important blues guitarist of the 1980s, and almost single-handedly sparked a revival of interest in blues, reminiscent of the effect Clapton had on the British Blues Boom in the mid 1960s. Critic Bill Milkowski wrote, "His playing was imbued with the kind of spirit and honesty that could only signify the real deal."

Part of the initial appeal of Stevie Ray's rough-house, pummelling blues-rock lies in the fact that he emerged in the early 1980s, when the death of guitar music was trumpeted on the newsstands, and the charts were wired to synthesised pop. As rock critic Frank Joseph observed in 1983 in *Guitar World*, "In an age when musical tastes are shaped by technological innovations, and sensibilities are assaulted by arsenals of Linn drums and Fairlights, it's downright refreshing to hear a guitarist who plays straight from the gut."

STEVIE RAY WORKING MAGIC WITH A FENDER STRAT

Stevie Ray stood out as a player who was consciously low-tech. In the 1980s guitarists would witness many technological advances that opened up new musical territory – from synth-guitars and sampling right down to the humble partial-capo. Stevie Ray preferred just an electric guitar plugged into an amplifier, with maybe a distortion box and a wah-wah. In other words, the gear he used wasn't the latest technology, but it was fit for his purpose – it was all he needed to express his music with force and a ram-rod directness.

And this struck a chord with many listeners. By 1984, if the first rush of Eddie Van Halen's frenetic tapping technique had lost some of its arpeggiated sparkle, rock fans could listen to the equally forceful but more traditional licks of Stevie Ray Vaughan. If they admired another early 1980s guitar hero, Mark Knopfler, but wanted more fire, they could go to Stevie Ray. If they were young and just discovering Hendrix they could see Vaughan in concert and get the full megawatt thwack of a live 'Voodoo Chile'.

Stevie Ray also understood the importance of image. On the cover of *Couldn't Stand The Weather* he clutches his Strat in mid-chord, and we see a tornado coming towards him – an idea that builds on an old on-stage favourite, 'They Call Me Guitar Hurricane'. The cover of *Texas Flood* has him peering out from under his ubiquitous black hat like Clint Eastwood's Man With No Name. On *Live Alive* he's in gold lamé; and as we've seen, he wasn't averse to wearing an Indian head-dress... To reach millions, technique is not enough. His image helped people feel Stevie Ray must be better than most because he looked the part. He looked how a guitar hero is meant to – larger than life.

But the image was backed-up by a no-nonsense style that was like a fury unleashed. *Guitar Player*'s Dan Forte once described Stevie Ray's playing as "a textbook … of incandescent licks streaming forth like a thunder shower". There's no doubt his effect as a guitarist was grounded in the sheer force of his playing. While other guitarists of the time were either developing a very technical style, or pushing the guitar into new sonic territory with sound effects and tailoring their playing to fit, Stevie Ray ploughed on regardless. It was simply because neither approach would have suited the music he wanted to play. His choice was to stick with the blues-based musical menu that rock guitarists had feasted on since lead guitar went centre-stage in the mid-1960s, and yet somehow find his own recipe. He garnished the meat and potatoes of the blues with chords more usually found in jazz-rock. What he didn't achieve in the way of breaking new ground, he made up for in finding what most guitarists search for – an unmistakable flavour in his playing. The paradox is that even when he's playing traditional blues phrases common to generations of electric guitarists, you can always tell it's Stevie Ray Vaughan.

His unique guitar sound was less to do with the actual guitars he played than with the unusually heavy strings he chose. Most rock players use light-gauge strings to facilitate string-bending: Stevie Ray favoured a monstrous 13,15,19,28, 38,58 combination – some 70 per cent thicker than standard light-gauge electric guitar strings. This has a very considerable effect on the tone of a guitar. The pickups have more signal to work with, because each note has more metal vibrating, and that gets fed to the amp. Such strings lend more body and sustain to the guitar's output. Odd as it may sound, non-players must take it on trust that most of Stevie Ray's up-tempo songs just don't feel right played on light-gauge strings.

He also tuned all the strings down a semitone, so E major chord shapes actually sounded at the pitch of E*b*. He may have picked this up from working out Hendrix songs. Stevie Ray liked the detuning because it helped with singing melodies, it partly reduced the additional tension of the heavy strings, and he felt it added tonal colour. His guitars were set with higher than normal actions (the clearance between strings and guitar neck), which eliminated fret buzz, and the necks themselves had wide 'jumbo' Gibson frets, which he wore out and had to have replaced every year. Few guitarists would have been comfortable with his guitars. He attacked the strings with the wrong end of the pick – the blunt, thick part – and often grabbed and pulled them with his fingers. He once quipped, "Like my brother Jimmie says, I play like I'm breaking out of jail."

Even when he's playing traditional blues phrases common to generations of electric guitarists, you can always tell it's Stevie Ray

Much of what makes Stevie Ray Vaughan distinctive as a guitarist is down to the level of physical attack with which he played. This is unusual in an electric guitar player. Unlike their acoustic brethren, most of the volume of an electric guitar is generated by the amplifier, and rock guitarists tend to like big, powerful amps. A chord hardly has to be touched on a highly amplified, lightly strung electric guitar for it to crash its way round a 10,000-seater auditorium. This means the rock guitarist can create a huge sound by stroking the strings in a (suitably) elegantly wasted manner, and cause less wear-and-tear to the hands. Contrast that with the way a flamenco guitarist thrums and smashes at his nylon-strung small-bodied Spanish acoustic, to generate musical harmony and percussive whacks to accompany dancing – the physical engagement with the instrument is far greater. Stevie Ray's approach to the electric guitar had a comparable intensity. He didn't just strike notes with the pick, he scrubbed and battered them. The heavy-gauge strings and high tension/high action could just about cope, but it's a wonder his fingers did.

This physicality in his playing may partly explain Stevie Ray's longer-term immunity to the seductive appeal of the Gibson Les Paul, a guitar famous among rock guitarists for its smooth action and sustain. Early in his career Stevie Ray owned a black 1954 Les Paul TV model and a 1952 goldtop with 'soap-bar' pickups, but neither remained with him. He didn't care for the 'dirty' sound of the standard Les Paul's humbuckers. Pete Townshend notwithstanding, the Les Paul doesn't really invite an aggressive, rhythmic style of playing. Many players talk about the workmanlike nature of Fender's Telecaster and Stratocaster, about how they enjoy having to 'dig' the music out of the neck. Fenders, they say, make you work harder. You can't imagine Stevie Ray doing 'Pride And Joy' on a Les Paul any more than it feels right trying 'Rude Mood' on one.

For Stevie Ray, the guitar of choice was the Fender Stratocaster. Along with Irish blues-rock hero Rory Gallagher, Stevie Ray Vaughan played the most famous battered Strat in rock history. His so-called 1959 Strat had little of its original sunburst finish left. As mentioned in Chapter Three, it was actually a hybrid constructed from pieces dating to different years. (Its reverse tremolo, rosewood neck, and 'SRV' logo were faithfully reproduced on the Fender SRV signature model – the guitar company's tribute to one of its most admired customers.) Stevie Ray had large hands and was comfortable with the neck's 'D' profile, which suited his grip. Eerily, its neck was snapped in half on July 9th 1990 (when some scenery collapsed at a theatre), only a month before its owner's death.

I'm not really trying to sound like Hendrix – but I'm not going to avoid what I do understand about how he played

He had several other Strats too, including a yellow '64 with a hollowed-out body, which was later stolen; another with a reverse headstock; another fitted with Danelectro pickups; and a white Strat, custom-made for him by Charley Wirz. Although he didn't like Les Pauls, he did have a Gibson dot-neck 335 and a Gibson Johnny Smith archtop.

His amplification wasn't as obvious as might be expected. He once said, "My amps are backwards: I use the Fenders for distortion and the Marshall for clarity" – the opposite of those famous amps' traditional roles. On *Texas Flood* he borrowed a Howard Dumble amp that belonged to Jackson Browne, and eventually bought a 150-watt Dumble Steel String Singer. At various times he used a Marshall combo amp with two 12″ JBL speakers, and two Fender Vibroverbs with one 15″ JBL, Mesa-Boogies, a Fender Bassman, and a Groove Tubes pre-amp. He often recorded with the guitar running through two amps at once – if you listen to his albums on headphones it's possible to hear this because they are set to give different tones, usually one of them with more distortion.

His effects included an Ibanez Tube Screamer distortion box, a Leslie revolving speaker – normally employed with Hammond organs, creating a swirling sound across any chord or note – and a Vox wah-wah pedal that his hero Hendrix had used on 'Up From The Skies'. He sometimes hooked more than one of each together to get additional effects: for instance using two wah-wah pedals at the same time, rocking them back and forth in different directions to each other – which meant he'd have both hands and both feet engaged at once.

To understand Stevie Ray Vaughan's rise from obscurity to guitar herodom, it's essential to grasp the Hendrix connections. This was where Stevie Ray found the bridge between rock and blues and to a wider audience. Austin guitarist Van Wilks once said, "It just seemed like Hendrix was always in his thoughts … He was certainly in his heart and fingers." Some saw Stevie Ray as Hendrix's heir. In a July 1986 interview he said, "I'm not really trying to sound like Hendrix. But I'm not going to avoid what I do understand about how he played … [It was] one of the first times in a long time when rock music was played with soul."

It often happens that a new guitar player isn't always recognised for what is individual about their own musical voice: the audience always hears first what elements have come from the past, because those are the bits it can recognise. Take, for instance, Mountain's Leslie West, whose career never recovered from comparisons with Clapton. It was the same with Stevie Ray: when rock critics and audiences heard him doing Hendrix, some were put off by what they heard as carbon-copy playing, and the apparent pastiche in his own 'original' songs. This was premature and a little unwarranted.

This early response is captured in the less-than-enthused tone with which Hendrix devotee Charles Shaar Murray talks about Stevie Ray in his book *Crosstown Traffic* (1989), calling him Hendrix's "greatest living imitator". He particularly chastises him for his 1985 recreation of 'The Star Spangled Banner' – an incendiary statement when performed by Hendrix at *Woodstock*, but when reproduced in a different context by Stevie Ray, for the opening of a baseball game in Houston, it seemed reduced to mere guitar pyrotechnics. Murray's opinion mellowed somewhat in his 1993 book *Blues On CD: The Essential Guide*, when he rates *In Step* as important because in it Stevie Ray "discovered how to use his formidable vocabulary to say something that was genuinely important to him".

It's clearly unfair to judge anyone against Hendrix – who was, after all, the highest achiever in the realm of the electric guitar – though it's a comparison Stevie Ray himself obviously invited, and an assessment his legend now requires us to make. The significant difference between them is ironically less to do with guitar-playing and more to do with boundaries of musical vision. It's certainly possible that Stevie Ray's musical talents could have blossomed even more if he had been willing to look further beyond the formulae and constraints of the blues – as Hendrix had done.

The fact is, for a music that associates itself with honesty and passion, with rebellion and the outsider, beneath the surface the blues can seem pretty conservative. The inevitable repetition of chord sequences, and often of templated guitar solos, can make some blues numbers almost indistinguishable. As we've seen, Stevie Ray always tried to play something different, but it could be argued he was fundamentally restricted by the genre he was working within. On *In Step*, for example, on three songs with contrasting lyric themes and emotions, the guitar licks are almost identical. But then again it's the very simplicity, familiarity and 'honesty' of blues that's at the heart of its appeal. As Buddy Guy put it, "When you come see a blues player, you're not gonna get anything fake ... you're not gonna see any buttons get pushed or hear guitars playing one note while you see him playing another." Stevie Ray Vaughan gave you this same reassurance. No buttons or machines. The 'real deal'.

There's a noticeable tension in his guitar-playing nonetheless, which – over and above the man's personal tribulations – may to some extent stem from his own self-taught, instinctive musicianship. Proudly unschooled in music, Stevie Ray confessed that he often didn't know what key he was writing in. Like many self-taught players, he worried that if he studied music, he'd lose his spontaneity and spark. In an October 1989 interview with Timothy White (heard on the reissued *Texas Flood*) Stevie Ray said: "If I start trying to pay attention to where I am on the neck, [or] the proper way to do this or that, then I end up thinking that through ... instead of playing from my heart I play from my mind – and that's where I get in trouble. If I just go with what's in my heart and let it come out, then I'm OK." Ironically this blind trust in what's in the heart, and fear of what's in the mind, can sometimes be stifling to a musician – especially one as talented as Stevie Ray.

So we'll never know if he could have achieved even greater heights – but we can certainly still enjoy the recordings he did leave, and which in their turn have influenced a new crop of guitar players and blues fans. He did of course dabble in other styles – occasionally incorporating elements of rock, funk and a touch of rhythmic jazz-rock into his beloved blues – and he liked to play around with the accepted conventions of the blues genre.

Here's a guitar-playing analysis of a few of his tracks, spotlighting some of the key moments of the Stevie Ray Vaughan recorded legacy...

'Let's Dance' (from David Bowie's *Let's Dance* album, 1983)
"I don't know what kind of music you'd call it," said Stevie Ray of his Bowie collaboration, "but I tried to play like Albert King and it seemed to fit." This was the first time many non-blues fans had heard Stevie Ray Vaughan, and it's a highly disciplined contribution. In the artful setting of Bowie's sharp-edged minimalist pop, Stevie Ray's Albert King-type multiple string bends on a single note gained a fresh colour, and in turn added a reassuring warmth to what was otherwise a fairly clinical production.

'Love Struck Baby' (from *Texas Flood*, 1983)
From his own debut album, recorded 'as live', 'Love Struck Baby' has typical thick chording over shuffling drums, and the guitar break has plenty of Chuck Berry-style double-stops (playing two notes at a time on the higher strings, moving around several such pairs). Stevie Ray also uses some distinctive ninth chords in the style of Freddie King: in a lot of blues music, simple major or minor chords dominate, but players will sometimes add extra notes to these chords, most often the tough seventh or the mildly jazzy ninth, as here.

'Pride And Joy' (*Texas Flood*, 1983)
A classic Texas shuffle. The main riff combines a bassline with chord mutes (stopping the strings as they're struck, for a percussive effect) played in huge rhythmic scoops that sound like someone shovelling coal. Stevie Ray makes a difficult guitar figure seem easy. The three guitar breaks have his trademark scorching high thirds (a double-stop with a sweet, appealing quality) fingered on strings 2 and 3 so the open top E-string will thicken the sound, and also abrupt switches of position from the 12th fret to the open E pentatonic scale position at the bottom of the neck. Stevie Ray ingeniously extracts extra sound from the guitar by choosing finger shapes that allow the maximum number of strings to ring at a time (often the top E-string). And listen too for his signature bottom E 'snap' at the end, made by pulling the string away from the guitar and letting go so it thwacks against the frets (comparable to the 'slap-bass' of Mark King et al in the 1980s).

'Rude Mood' (*Texas Flood*, 1983)
All lead guitarists have their own sense of phrasing – a certain inner rhythm that determines where phrases start and end, how they fit with the beat, how long they are, and so on. Stevie Ray's guitar work is generally typified by an obsessional rhythmic charge verging on monomania. 'Rude Mood' is the perfect expression of this, and allows him full opportunity to let rip. It starts with a frenetic riff and a burst of lead that comes on like Freddie King's 'Hideaway' on speed. Fluency,

sheer stamina, and force help obscure the repetitions, and there are inspired moments – like after one minute and six seconds (1:06), where there's a terrific run of two-octave alternations, to achieve which, Stevie Ray has to span the whole guitar-neck and move this stretched hand position rapidly downwards. There's another great moment at 3:18 where he plays 'ping-pong' with the beat, timing his stuttering notes so they bounce off the rhythm section, giving an effect that's exciting and funny at the same time. Along the way his single-note leads are beefed up with plenty of double-stop ideas.

It's worth stating that Stevie Ray was genuinely fond of the guitar instrumental, and usually found room on each of his albums for at least one. Later albums featured tracks like 'Scuttle Buttin'', 'Travis Walk', and the jazzier 'Stang's Swang', all of which develop the possibilities opened up by 'Rude Mood', even if they are not as super-charged.

'Dirty Pool' (Texas Flood, 1983)

Playing in a power trio, where the guitar has to fill a lot of harmonic space as well as generate lead, may have encouraged Stevie Ray to develop two-note figures like the double-stops previously described. 'Dirty Pool' is a slow minor-key blues in which this idea is pushed to the extreme. Stevie Ray shows incredible stamina to keep the 16th-note triplets going bar after bar, and considerable imagination in building a whole solo from these thirds – unusually low-pitched – though after a while they can become oppressive. Given this song's lyric about love and betrayal, this oppression is relevant – but in any case there's often a feeling of emotion compressed and trapped in Stevie Ray's music, revealing the darker side of his nature.

'Couldn't Stand The Weather' (from the album *Couldn't Stand The Weather*, 1984)

Stevie Ray had already ventured a hyper-funk riff on 'Testify' from his debut album, but the title track of the group's second album goes one better. It's among his most inventive compositions, where the harmony and structure are up to the standard of the guitar-playing, and very much in the style of Hendrix's later funk-rock tracks like 'Dolly Dagger', without being derivative. The listener's ear is tickled by the rhythm and the variety of chords on offer. Listen for the mix of guitar tones Stevie Ray uses on the guitar parts to differentiate them.

'Voodoo Chile' (*Couldn't Stand The Weather*, 1984)

Stevie Ray's love and respect of Hendrix was genuine, and he had sufficient confidence in his own ability and musical ambition to regard Hendrix classics like 'Voodoo Chile' as not off-limits. But even when he's at his most accurate in re-tracing Hendrix's musical footsteps, he still sounds like himself. There's no mistaking the difference in guitar tone, musical dynamic, and the underlying spirit.

Above all, taken at a quicker tempo, Stevie Ray's 'Voodoo Chile' has a forward drive and busy feel which is his own signature. You can hear it straight off in the way he shifts the emphasis on the wah-wah intro: he plays the E7#9 chord more rhythmically and on top of the beat, and cuts out the space between the first and second lyric lines. The relentlessness is evident in the manner that he worries away at the Hendrixy bend at 4:41, and in the characteristic chordal idea at 6:02. Stevie Ray's playing has a more tactile quality than Hendrix's: listening to Hendrix you can sometimes forget he's holding a piece of wood and metal in his hands – Stevie Ray never lets you forget it, whether because of the sheer physical attack, the raking (dragging the pick harshly across the strings) and sudden sliding of a single note or chord, or pulling the strings with a right-hand finger.

'Say What?' (from *Soul To Soul*, 1985)

This was Stevie Ray's take on 'Still Raining, Still Dreaming', Hendrix's (almost) one-chord wah-wah workout. As might be expected, Stevie Ray's version is not at all laidback, but pretty pumping. He toys with some standard blues bends and figures, altering the timing and rhythm with which they're played, so even if you know them they come out differently to what you expect. Some of this time-stretching is done by making emphatic use of the tremolo arm to shake the pitch of chords, plus finger vibrato and the wah-wah pedal to string out the notes. There are plenty of rakes, and some feedback – this is Stevie Ray more in rock guitar territory.

'Superstition' (from *Live Alive*, 1987)

This was an inspired choice of cover version, not only because Stevie Ray was equipped to do a fine job of growling the vocal, but because he could 'Hendrixify' Stevie Wonder's keyboard funk – in the main riff he employs the minor 7 and 7#9 chords associated with Hendrix songs like 'Foxy Lady', 'Crosstown Traffic' and 'Purple Haze'. The track is driven by Stevie Ray's 16th-note strumming – though the guitar could be a little higher in the mix.

'The House Is Rockin'' (from *In Step*, 1989)

On Stevie Ray's clean-up, comeback album, the production was slicker, and the guitar not always as up-front as in the past. But 'Crossfire' and 'Tightrope' showed him expanding his range of chords, while on the energetic 'The House Is Rockin'' there's an exhilarating moment toward the end of the first guitar solo where he stays on the same chord for several bars longer than you imagine he will, creating an exciting crescendo.

'Wall Of Denial' **(*In Step*, 1989)**

Another of Stevie Ray's funkier numbers, this boasts a long funk riff in E, with chordal ninth fills, reminiscent of James Brown, inserted at unpredictable points in the sequence of single notes and heard throughout the verse. This is more sophisticated than most of his earlier work, with plenty of tricky timing – so the band would certainly have to concentrate when they played it – though the production is not as hard as it could be. It's not far from the sort of stuff Living Colour might have played, if it were heavier and there were a few more guitar pyrotechnics. Past the four-minute mark, after the last vocals, the closing solo is strong, sounding tonally like the raw Stevie Ray of the early albums, bouncing off the open bottom E-string and milking the characteristic warmer tone of the guitar's front pickup. There's hardly a breathing space between his phrases.

'Riviera Paradise' **(*In Step*, 1989)**

The longest and best-known track on the *In Step* album, recorded in a live first take. It's become a well-loved Stevie Ray classic, but to be picky, from a guitar-playing perspective, you could ask whether Stevie Ray takes enough advantage of the opportunities such jazzy harmonies and chords offer when he brings them into a song like this. The more chords a song has, the more freedom there is, theoretically, for the guitarist to play a greater variety of notes – but Stevie Ray often has a tendency to fall back on tried-and-trusted blues runs. Though less feted, another of his atmospheric instrumentals, 'Chitlins Con Carne' (from The Sky Is Crying), compares favourably with this one, in that it features more inventive guitar work.

'Life By The Drop' **(from *The Sky Is Crying*, 1991)**

This cover version, from Stevie Ray's posthumous album-full of miscellany, boasts a performance quite unlike anything else in his repertoire. It's a no-overdub, heartfelt rendition, with Stevie Ray accompanying himself on a standard-tuning 12-string acoustic (though he did apparently consider a National steel-body). He keeps things moving along, with the guitar-work busy enough to be interesting but not so complex as to distract from the fine vocal part – it makes quite a change to hear Stevie Ray singing over an acoustic backing.

No one taking up blues guitar after 1990 can avoid Stevie Ray Vaughan's impact, just as no one playing rock guitar in the 1970s and 1980s could avoid Hendrix. Chances are that many young blues guitarists coming through now and in years to come will have cut their teeth playing Stevie Ray's records, studying transcriptions of Texas Flood, and covering some of his songs in clubs – just as he himself did with Albert King and Hubert Sumlin.

To his great credit, Stevie Ray Vaughan turned a whole new generation of players and listeners on to the blues: he knew and respected the tradition in which he worked, and paid due reverence to the greats who came before him, encouraging others to seek out their music.

Stevie Ray was undoubtedly a magnetic performer: even his harshest critics, such as Charles Shaar Murray, conceded he was "a fine guitarist and a master showman". As well as having the electric guitarist's 'holy grail' of an unmistakable tone, he displayed an astonishing energy and dexterity – he was a guitarist whose lead style actually incorporated a huge amount of rhythm, which helped give his soloing a propulsive power.

Stevie Ray Vaughan was a bona fide guitar hero who appealed to blues and rock fans alike, and did much to remind people of the electric guitar's roots – demonstrating the directness and drama of the instrument's appeal afresh for a new audience. He also penned a handful of tracks that will remain on the set-list of club bands for as long as there are guitar players ornery enough to want to shred their fingers with his patterns. Stevie Ray's finest guitar moments will undoubtedly stand the weather.

CHAPTER 10

Legacy

"The music was a good place to get lost in. That's what music is for."

JIMMIE VAUGHAN, ON COPING AFTER STEVIE RAY'S DEATH

In the months and years following Stevie Ray Vaughan's demise, there has been a renewed focus on music coming out of Texas. It perhaps can't be claimed this is exclusively due to Stevie Ray's influence, but he made a huge difference, no question. Immediately after his death, and the subsequent release of the Vaughan brothers' *Family Style*, there was every indication that he was being accorded the type of status usually reserved for those that self-destruct in mysterious and unexplained circumstances. There was no mystery about the helicopter accident: the coroner returned a verdict of death by misadventure, caused by pilot error (and thick fog). But the tragically early curtailment of such an exciting talent had the effect of pushing his name and music out into a wider public consciousness.

Family Style became the most successful album either of the Vaughan brothers ever made, and although it wasn't a typical Stevie Ray record – which meant many of his biggest fans were not so keen on it – others now recognised that Stevie Ray was more than just another noisy blues guitarist. What's more, *Family Style* brought Jimmie Vaughan's playing to a bigger audience.

Fans of Stevie Ray were not necessarily fans of The Fabulous Thunderbirds, and vice versa, but the success and circumstances of *Family Style* encouraged a new degree of open-mindedness. It seemed to coincide with many groups and musicians becoming more adventurous in their choice of repertoire. 'Alternative country' bands began harking back to traditional acoustic instruments such as the fiddle, mandolin or banjo. Blues bands were more likely to feature acoustic material in their sets or on their albums. Tex-Mex (or tejano) groups also started to experiment with material and instrumentation. The return to traditional styles and presentation was certainly assisted by the growing awareness and interest in 'world music' – audiences suddenly seemed to be more open to different sounds and styles.

In Texas, because the indigenous music has such a strong identity and incorporates so many styles, it seemed that anything and everything was possible. And Texas also became the place where many musicians moved to if they were trying to revive their careers or try something different. For instance, in the 1990s, Steve Earle's first record after being discharged from prison was an acoustic country record. And Emmylou Harris, who had made several very traditional sounding country albums such as *The Cowgirl's Prayer* and *Live At The Ryman Auditorium*, hooked up with Daniel Lanois to make *Wrecking Ball* in New Orleans – many country fans hated it, but just as *Family Style* had done for the Vaughans, it brought Harris to a new audience. More recently, in 2000, the success of the movie *O Brother Where Art Thou?* has fuelled interest in traditional American music styles.

Nonetheless blues music, in particular, has seemed to lack a leader, a trailblazer, since the death of Stevie Ray in 1990. Bruce Iglauer, boss of Chicago's Alligator label, lamented the effects of this in *Downbeat* magazine in the summer of 2002, when he admitted: "There has been a downturn in the sales of blues records because there isn't a major figure like Stevie Ray Vaughan around to get record buyers into the shops."

The fact is, sales of blues records have never been massive by mainstream standards. Certainly *Family Style* hit the US Top Ten, climbing to Number Seven on its release, and all of Stevie Ray's records have sold over a million units each – but compared to Hendrix or The Eagles, the Stevie Ray Vaughan back catalogue is an unremarkable performer. It ticks over very nicely, but the volume of sales is hardly commensurate with that of a performer who, for many people, was a giant in terms of talent and influence.

Still, the Stevie Ray legend continues to develop. Having first become an icon of the Texas music scene, his posthumous profile wasn't harmed by the gradual elevation of his home state in the eyes of the wider music business. This came about largely thanks to Austin's *South By South West (SXSW)* becoming one of the industry's premier annual beanos, matched only by *MIDEM* at

Cannes in the south of France. Indeed many industry bigwigs in the US no longer bother going to Cannes because they know all the serious European players will travel to *SXSW*.

Since the foundation of *SXSW* in 1987, Austin has become a centre of influence that can almost rival the likes of Nashville, Los Angeles or New York. What actually happens in Austin now has far-reaching repercussions elsewhere. Yet the quality of music coming out of Austin and Texas has not been compromised or diluted. Sure, there may be many more Texan bands than there were before, but unlike Nashville, for example, the bands in Texas are doing what they do because it's what they want to do. Chasing a buck may be important, but it's not the-be-all-and-end-all, as it can be elsewhere.

Since the foundation of *SXSW* in 1987, Austin has become a centre of influence almost rivalling Nashville, LA or New York

People seem to view Texas music differently now – the awareness of what it means to be a Texas-based musician has undergone a sea-change since the release of *Family Style*. Acts such as George Strait, a long-time favourite of Nashville and country fans, or Willie Nelson, a genuine maverick who, ever since moving back to Texas in the early 1970s, has ploughed his own very idiosyncratic furrow, certainly retain a flavour that fans can relate to. But elsewhere the combination of blues, country, R&B, Tex-Mex, zydeco and rock has conspired to create a unique hybrid. And naturally enough the number of bands or individuals that fit this profile is extraordinarily large – take, for example, The Flatlanders and Joe Ely, The Texas Tornados, or even Delbert McClinton.

The Flatlanders are a great example of disparate enthusiasms finding a common link and combining to create something unique. In 1970 three songwriters – Joe Ely, Jimmie Dale Gilmore and Butch Hancock – found themselves back in Lubbock, kicking their heels and watching paint dry. So they did what any normal red-blooded males would do under the circumstances: they formed a band, calling themselves The Flatlanders. They played a few gigs around Lubbock, with Steve Wesson on autoharp and saw, Sylvester Rice on acoustic bass, Tommy Hancock on fiddle and Tony Pearson on mandolin all joining to flesh out the sound. They even appointed a manager, Lou Driver, and he sorted out sessions in Nashville, with Shelby Singleton, then owner of the Sun label, and they recorded arguably one of the classic, must-have albums (if you like that sort of thing) of the early 1970s. It took country-rock out into the backwoods, gave it a quick scrub down back to basics, and left the musicians to do the rest.

A quirky, lo-fi hybrid of traditional country and country-rock, the *Flatlanders* album was a clarion call for putative songwriters, especially in Texas. Gilmore, Ely and Hancock all had different strengths: Gilmore was the more cerebral type, able to meditate on the perfidy of contemporary culture; Hancock, with the eye of a photographer, took snapshots of his milieu; Ely took on the blues and country and wrapped it all up into his own distinctive style. The resulting album was issued in 1973 on Singleton's Plantation label – a seriously tacky bargain-basement affair – and they chose to release it on eight-track cartridge. For those that don't remember, the eight-track cartridge was going to be the 'next big thing', before it was superseded by the compact cassette as we know it today. Unfortunately most eight-track machines were installed in cars, so most of the cartridges ended up lying on the floor where they were duly smashed to smithereens as people got in or out of their cars.

A quirky, lo-fi hybrid of traditional country and country-rock, the *Flatlanders* album was a clarion call for putative songwriters, especially in Texas

Being signed to such an obscure, cheap label did not in itself alter the group's ambitions. But when the eight-track sold a pathetically small number of copies – discerning record buyers tend not to buy their listening material at gas stations – the Flatlanders just did a few more gigs and then went their separate ways. Hancock went back to cutting predominantly acoustic albums, as and when the mood took him, and Gilmore retired from live performance as he was studying under an Indian guru. Ely though – perhaps taking his cue from the 'outlaw movement' of Willie Nelson and Waylon Jennings – put together a band that fused border ballads with country weepers, rockabilly with cajun, and rockin' R&B with western swing, and was consequently snapped up by MCA.

He remained with MCA for six years, until he was dropped in 1983. But during that time he cranked out a string of top-notch albums that were as eclectic as they were brimming with ideas. Cutting material by former Flatlanders' Hancock ('She Never Spoke Spanish To Me' and 'If You Were A Bluebird') and Gilmore ('Treat Me Like A Saturday Night'), Joe Ely's self-titled debut was a magnificent contrast with the back-to-basics raw energy of British groups like Dr Feelgood or The Clash. The next album, *Honky Tonk Masquerade* (1978), was another stone classic. The band this time included Ponty Bone on violin, Jesse Taylor on guitar and Lloyd Maines on steel guitar – a line-up that would remain substantially unchanged for the next few years or so.

A European tour with The Clash followed in the late 1970s, and although this introduced him to a lot of new fans abroad, his band's heavy rockin' style made it difficult for MCA to sell him to country fans in the United States. After he was dropped he remained without a record deal until 1987, when he was signed by Hightone, who had a fairly clued-up approach to marketing Ely. *Lord Of The Highway* (1987) – which included one of Ely's finest songs, 'Me And Billy The Kid' – and *Dig All Night* (1988) were not quite up to the impossibly high standard of *Honky Tonk Masquerade*, but they were pretty good. MCA saw what had they had let slip, and signed him up again. Touring constantly, Ely – like the Texas Tornados and another idiosyncratic Texan, Lyle Lovett – proved impervious to the fickle finger of fashion.

Ely's first set in the new deal with MCA was *Live At Liberty Lunch*, recorded at the popular Austin music venue. The contrast between this and the earlier *Live Shots* album was marked, and with the arrival of new guitarist David Grissom (later of Storyville) to replace the long-standing and much under-rated Jesse Taylor, Ely's style seemed as flexible as Austin itself. The following year he recorded *Love And Danger*, which had Double Trouble's Reese Wynans on keyboards, and included Robert Earl Keen's bittersweet and close-to-the-bone anthem, 'The Road Goes On Forever' (and, as the refrain goes, "the party never ends").

Joe Ely - like The Texas Tornados and another idiosyncratic Texan, Lyle Lovett – proved impervious to the fickle finger of fashion

A few more albums for MCA followed, including *Letter To Laredo*, where the Hispanic influences, mostly courtesy of flamenco guitarist Teje, served to emphasise Ely's diversity within the broader context of Texan music. But he eventually tired of MCA and moved to the independent Rounder label for *Live At Antone's*. More Ely goodies were rattled out with customary aplomb and joie de vivre.

In the meantime The Flatlanders had reconvened. Rounder had acquired the tapes of the earlier album and reissued it as *More A Legend Than A Band* in 1990 (an album that had surfaced in the UK in 1980), and it had been hailed as a classic. Then the group was approached to record a song for the Robert Redford film *The Horse Whisperer*. By all accounts they had such fun doing this that they decided to record another album together. *Now Again* emerged in 2002, and was followed buy a European Tour, culminating with a triumphant concert at London's Barbican centre.

The Texas Tornados were formed in 1989 by Doug Sahm, and featured Augie Meyers, one of Sahm's longest and most eclectic collaborators from the Sir Douglas Quintet; Freddy Fender, who had scored a massive country and pop hit in 1975 with 'Before The Next Teardrop Falls'; and

Flaco Jimenez, the accordionist that had sparked Ry Cooder's imagination and prompted him to record the album *Chicken Skin Music*. Working at first locally, and then across the US, the Texas Tornados managed to appeal to the more liberal Hispanic and country audiences, as well as the rock'n'roll and college student audiences. Albums such as *The Texas Tornados* (1990) (of which there was a Spanish version as well), *Zone Of Our Own* (1991), and *Hangin' On By A Thread* (1992), confirmed their pre-eminence. They were not just accomplished instrumentalists, they also had that rare knack of being able to fashion disparate styles into an homogeneous identity, with the possibility that anything might happen at any minute. Indeed Sahm once remarked to *Rolling Stone* and *Mojo* writer Ed Ward that, "They got me so busy I ain't got no time to smoke pot no more."

After disbanding the Tornados to resume solo careers, Sahm revived his Last Real Texas Blues Band project for an eponymous album in 1994. Recorded at Antone's – with an impromptu line-up of Derek O'Brien and Denny Freeman on guitars, Jack Barber on bass and George Rains on drums, as well as a substantial horn section – *The Last Real Texas Blues Band* displayed a facet of the Sahm persona that was often forgotten, or at least less celebrated than some of his other more iconoclastic experiments.

He then joined up with the other Tornados for *Four Aces* (1996), before reforming Sir Douglas Quintet for *SDQ '98* (1998), and then gathering in the Tornados once more for *Live From The Limo* (1999). Throughout this time the multi-faceted Sahm was, not surprisingly, cranking out solo albums such as *Get A Life* and *The Return Of Wayne Douglas*. But his sudden death on November 18th 1999 put paid to all that. Sahm's inspirational career, especially since returning from California, had been central to Texan music. Like Stevie Ray, Sahm managed to fire the enthusiasm of the young, with his liberal, freewheeling attitude, while retaining the respect and affection of his contemporaries. His former colleague Augie Meyers, in the meantime, found himself another gig, this time with Bob Dylan.

Delbert McClinton, a former employer of Reese Wynans, initially made his mark in the early 1960s when he played harmonica for Bruce Channel. On the strength of Channel's massive hit 'Hey Baby', McClinton toured the UK, on the same package tour as a bunch of young hopefuls from Liverpool called The Beatles. It's one of those great, often thought apocryphal stories that it was McClinton who taught John Lennon how to play harmonica. "He wanted to play the harmonica, so we spent some time together," McClinton confirmed in an interview in 1994. "I don't know long we spent together, but I just showed him some different things."

But McClinton's career had started long before that, back in Fort Worth where he grew up – though he'd been born in Lubbock on November 4th 1940. In Fort Worth he was exposed to everything from Hank Williams to Bob Wills, Nat 'King' Cole to Big Mama Thornton, and The Coasters to Hank Ballard & The Midnighters. "Deep blues to R&B to a smattering of country to rootsy rock'n'roll – grew up with all of that," McClinton told Art Tipaldi in *Children Of The Blues*. "I never saw the reason to pick one and shut the others out."

After first learning the guitar, he then turned his attention to the harmonica, and as Fort Worth had such a hectic local club scene he was soon playing in The Straitjackets. This group's stock-in-trade was backing visiting bluesmen such as Jimmy Reed, Sonny Boy Williamson and Howlin' Wolf at a gig called Blue Monday that took place at the Skyline Ballroom on Jacksboro Highway. By 1960 McClinton had made his recording debut, cutting a cover of Sonny Boy Williamson's 'Wake Up Baby', which had the distinction of being the first blues record by a white artist to be programmed on the local blues station KNOK. After his stint with Channel, he played in an early version of a garage band, The Rondells, whose claim to fame was a minor hit with 'If You Want Me To I'll Go' in 1965. But McClinton spent much of the 1960s playing roadhouses and local clubs throughout Texas.

Doug Sahm's inspirational career had been central to Texan music. Like Stevie Ray, Sahm managed to fire the enthusiasm of the young, while retaining the respect and affection of his contemporaries

In 1972 he moved to Los Angeles where, with another Fort Worth native, Glen Clark, he cut a brace of albums as Delbert & Glen for the Atlantic subsidiary, Clean. A hard-edged AOR, much tougher than anything The Eagles could have dreamed of, *Delbert & Glen* (1972) and *Subject To Change* (1973) both slipped beneath the radar – although they did enough to secure a new deal for McClinton with ABC. Again, his next three albums, *Victim Of Life's Circumstances* (1975), *Genuine Cowhide* (1976) and *Love Rustler* (1977), were too tough for prevailing trends, but marked him out as a distinctive writer. Emmylou Harris covered his 'Two More Bottles Of Wine', which she took to the top of the country charts. But none of this was good enough for ABC, who dropped him, and he then moved to Capricorn, home of the Allman Brothers Band. He managed to record two albums for Capricorn, *Second Wind* (1978) and *Keeper Of The Flame* (1979) – the latter included his composition 'B Movie Boxcar Blues', which the Blues Brothers made their own – but the Capricorn label went to the wall.

Having recorded extensively at Muscle Shoals Sound Studios with the famed in-house band,

McClinton decided to chance his arm by releasing *The Jealous Kind* (1980) on their new MSS label; the label wouldn't last, but 'Givin' It Up For Love' became one of the year's most surprising hits, climbing to Number Eight on the national charts. The next album, *Plain From The Heart*, featured a couple of great McClinton songs, 'I Want To Thank You Baby' and 'Sandy Beaches', but they weren't enough to stop the MSS label shutting up shop.

For the next five years McClinton worked hard, touring and keeping his head down, until in 1986 he contributed a cameo to Roy Buchanan's highly rated *Dancing On The Edge* album. This in turn prompted Bruce Iglauer to offer him a deal with Alligator. The resulting *Live From Austin* album (recorded for the PBS show *Austin City Limits*) confirmed his credentials as a bluesman of the highest order; and this paid dividends when he was lined up alongside Bonnie Raitt for the duet 'Good Man, Good Woman' on Raitt's album *Luck Of The Draw* – a performance that picked up a joint Grammy for Best Rock Vocal.

Sahm and McClinton spent years forging their own styles, at heart informed by the landscape and traditions of Texas

This in turn helped spread McClinton's name as a songwriter, and while he was spending much of his time in Nashville or on the road, his songs were being covered by country artists like Martina McBride, Vince Gill, and Lee Roy Parnell. Albums such as *I'm With You* (1990), *Never Been Rocked Enough* (1992), and *Delbert McClinton* (1993) all sold well, demonstrating his finesse when it came to fusing his influences into a polished yet highly individual style.

In 1997, McClinton's *One Of The Fortunate Few* attracted a cast of thousands – with guests like B.B. King, Patty Loveless, Lyle Lovett, John Prine and Mavis Staples, among others – but McClinton was still in control, ensuring he was not overshadowed by his famous friends. He then successfully moved to the Austin-based New West label, and recorded *Nothing Personal* (2001) and *Room To Breathe* (2002) – the former winning a Grammy for Best Contemporary Blues Album. It's indicative of McClinton's far-reaching influence that his songs have been covered by artists from Clarence 'Gatemouth' Brown to Garth Brooks; Eric Burdon to Taj Mahal, Anson Funderburgh to Waylon Jennings, and Jimmy Witherspoon to Marcia Ball.

Both Sahm and McClinton had spent years forging their own styles, at heart informed by the landscape and traditions of Texas – they no doubt benefitted from the general enthusiasm for Texas music (in all its motley manifestations), which had been largely fostered by Jimmie and

Stevie Ray Vaughan with *Family Style*. So surely now it was time for the surviving Vaughan brother to reap some of the benefits he and Stevie Ray had helped sow.

In spite of the success of *Family Style*, Jimmie Vaughan suddenly had a lot of other business to take care of after Stevie Ray's death. His first job was to sort out his brother's estate. After some searching, a will was located, and it was necessary to inventory the assets, which included: $173,000 scattered through different bank accounts; a music publishing company, Ray Vaughan Music Inc; 34 guitars, 31 amplifiers and 12 speaker cabinets; a 1975 Chevrolet Caprice; and sundry other personal effects. Then of course there were 132 video and audio tapes of unreleased recorded material...

The executors and beneficiaries of Stevie Ray's estate were his mother Martha and Jimmie, who established three charities: The Stevie Ray Vaughan Music Scholarship Fund, which provides funding for music students at his old school, the W.E. Greiner Middle School in Oak Cliff, Texas; The Stevie Ray Vaughan Charitable Fund, which donates funds to the Dallas Area Parkinsonian Society and the Ethel Daniels Foundation, a Dallas halfway house for drug addicts and alcoholics; and The Stevie Ray Vaughan Memorial Fund, which would provide funds for the maintenance of the statue of Stevie Ray to be erected in Austin.

But the rigmarole of touring or doing press interviews was not something Jimmie could face. "I was really close to Stevie when he died. To be honest, that year is all sort of blurred," he told Art Tipaldi later. "Everybody wanted to tell me how sorry they were, and I just didn't want to talk to anybody. ... [But] I didn't stop playing then. Back then I played every day. I had these ar top [jazz style] acoustic guitars that I played at home constantly. The music was a good pl get lost in. That's what music is for." But he determined to put The Fabulous Thu behind him for good.

Jimmie remained out of sight for around six months, emerging only to Clapton's concerts at London's Royal Albert Hall alongside Buddy Guy and R prisingly, they chose to play 'Sweet Home Chicago' in memory of Stevie R with Clapton when his American tour reached Dallas and New Orlean Bob Dylan appeared in Austin, but by and large he kept a low pro

Eventually he had to turn his attention to sorting out some posthumous album, *The Sky Is Crying*. Although some of it h in the studio, *The Sky Is Crying* is a fine cross-section o sions spanning *Couldn't Stand The Weather* (1984) to into the emotional range of Stevie Ray's talent. Ji 'Chitlins Con Carne' show Stevie Ray at his m

'May I Have A Talk With You' and 'The Sky Is Crying' it's the deep-down bluesy facet of his personality that's to the fore; and on 'Wham!' he cranks out those plangent chords with an awesome power and ferocity. All of that is in stark contrast with the lilting ballad 'Life By The Drop', penned by Doyle Bramhall and his partner Barbara Logan, and featuring Stevie Ray on acoustic guitar. It's almost as if Jimmie deliberately assembled *The Sky Is Crying* to complement *Family Style*, such is the album's richness and diversity. It was certainly a far-cry from the one-dimensional *Live Alive*.

This was followed by a video of Stevie Ray and Double Trouble filmed in concert in 1983 at El Mocambo in Toronto, Canada. Both *The Sky Is Crying* and *Live At El Mocambo* were huge financial as well as artistic successes, with the former reaching Number Ten on the national charts. Epic were so thrilled that they cajoled Jimmie into putting out another Stevie Ray set. Entitled *In The Beginning*, it was a radio broadcast from a concert in 1980 at Austin's Steamboat 1874: with the rough and ready attack of the group, rudimentary compositions, and rather unsophisticated axe-wielding guitar style, it was hard to believe this was the ...e person who went on to record *In Step* or *Family Style*.

Epic were so thrilled with the successes that they cajoled Jimmie into

...fter contributing to the John Lee Hooker album *Boom* ...92), Jimmie started recording his own solo debut, ... A-W...*ures*. Using Nile Rodgers as producer once ... the chance to develop some of the ideas ...lthough never a prolific writer, and not ...m people he had known for ages to ...uted bass, piano and vocals, as ...enny Freeman also came in ...en René Martinez, a fine fla... ...even opened the odd gig for ...asy familiarity of the set-up ... equal measure. But despite ... economy of Jimmie's guitar ... his potential.

...nationwide tour with the Tilt... ...organ, and George Rains on drums, Jimmie had at his disposal a synthesis of R&B, ancient and modern. Willis had played a gig at Antone's, caught Jimmie's eye and had never left town. Born on December 16th 1931, at one time he'd played with Billie Holiday, before wending his way to Cincinnati to become the in-house bassist at Sid Nathan's King label. After working with The Five Royales, Little Willie John, Hank Ballard & The Midniters, Bill Doggett and Freddie King (and yup, Willis is the man who plays bass on the original version of the King classic 'Hideaway'), Bill Doggett helped Willis develop a B3 that had additional bass built into the keyboard; Willis was so delighted with this eccentric piece of customising that he moved to Los Angeles to become something of a novelty act, and then worked in Las Vegas for over 25 years. After that he toured with the veteran R&B vocalist LaVern Baker, whose claim to fame was a lengthy stint with Atlantic, recording such priceless pieces as 'Tweedle Dee', 'I Cried A Tear', 'Saved' and 'Jim Dandy'.

George Rains' resumé, apart from working with Doug Sahm, was a musical compendium, having worked in Los Angeles with Screamin' Jay Hawkins, Roy Brown, J.J. Cale, Van Morrison and Jimmy Witherspoon. Since moving to Austin, Rains had worked with the best that Texas had to offer, which included Snooks Eaglin, Hubert Sumlin, Hank Crawford, Mose Allison, Albert Collins, Buddy Guy, Otis Rush, Dr John, David 'Fathead' Newman and Robert Ward – the list is endless. In 1996 Billy Pitman, from The Useless Playboys, joined Jimmie's touring band as an additional guitarist – he still puts in appearances with the Reverend Horton Heat and Tusco Del Rey. Since that time Jimmie seems to have struck a balance between playing live and developing his solo career, maximising the potential of his brother's catalogue, and working on his collection of Fifties and Sixties cars.

One of the things Jimmie got involved in was a special tribute to his brother. Taking the form of a concert at the studios of the TV show *Austin City Limits*, it was indicative of the esteem in which Stevie Ray was held that not only were Eric Clapton, Buddy Guy, Robert Cray and Jimmie present, but so were Bonnie Raitt, B.B. King, Dr John and Art Neville of The Neville Brothers. Carefully arranged and programmed, with accompaniment from Double Trouble, joined by Denny Freeman, Bill Willis and George Rains, the resulting album allowed each contributor to apply their own very specific styles to a range of compositions associated with Stevie Ray.

It starts with 'Pride and Joy', on which Bonnie Raitt's soulful vocals are underscored by her atmospheric guitar work, which sometimes seems eerily foreboding. Jimmie then picks up the pace with a taut, economical version of 'Texas Flood', before B.B. King enters the fray with a characteristically understated reading of 'The Telephone Song'. Buddy Guy's reworking of 'Long Way From Home' somehow seems restrained compared to what we've come to expect from Guy, but that should not be regarded as a criticism. 'Ain't Gone 'N' Give Up On Love' provides a platform for Eric Clapton, who proceeds to turn it into a mini-epic of brevity and succinctness. 'Love Struck Baby' becomes a vehicle for Cray, enabling him to show off the extent to which his style had been shaped by Albert Collins. 'Cold Shot' is a cunning subversion, this archetypal Austin anthem given a resounding makeover from one of New Orleans's most distinctive characters, Dr John. But the coup-de-grace is a three-pronged collaboration between Raitt, Clapton and Jimmie on the final three tracks: although Jimmie had already composed 'Tick Tock' for *Family Style*, his two new songs, 'Six Strings Down' and 'SRV Shuffle', are emphatic reminders that his compositional powers were developing rapidly. Indeed the following year, 'SRV Shuffle' received a Grammy for Best Instrumental. The bottom line is that this set has a power and passion that Stevie Ray Vaughan would have understood. In short, it's a fitting tribute – a celebration.

After the release of the tribute album, Jimmie continued trawling through his brother's collection of tapes, and decided to issue the Double Trouble concert at the Carnegie Hall from 1984. Again this was a timely release, because as well as complementing the tribute album, there was continuity in the presence of Dr John and Jimmie himself. The Roomful Of Blues' horn section added another, under-exposed dimension to Stevie Ray's sound. Featuring a cross-section of his most popular material, the power, urgency and vitality of this recording jumps out and grabs you by the throat, almost wrestling you into submission. By the end of *Live At The Carnegie Hall* the listener is left limp and lifeless, virtually gasping for breath.

One of the highlights is the old Guitar Slim stand-by, 'Things That I Used To Do', which, despite being played regularly by Stevie Ray over the years, had only been recorded for the studio set *Couldn't Stand The Weather*. 'Iced Over' was a discreet tribute to the influence of Albert Collins, who had died in 1993, while 'Honey Bee', one of Stevie Ray's lesser compositions, sounds like some hoary old classic only just unearthed from the Mississippi mud. No bad achievement.

After this Jimmie was ready to return to the studio again on his own account, to record the follow-up to *Strange Pleasures*. Unfortunately, *Out There* is not Jimmie's finest hour. It shows a newly-found confidence in penning his own material, but suggests he had not quite reached the point of knowing what to keep, what needed more work, or what to bin. That may sound harsh, but Jimmie had set himself very high standards up to this point, so when some of his material was run-of-the-mill it was glaringly apparent. Having said all that, it's not a bad record – many lesser talents might be persuaded it was the highpoint of their career. Accompanied by his regular crew of George Rains and Bill Willis, with Dr John, Denny Freeman and Junior Brantley adding a variety of keyboards, Nile Rodgers took on his now familiar role as producer, while adding little bits of rhythm guitar here and there. Despite the quality of some of the songs,

Jimmie's guitar work was as crisp and economical as ever – it just would have been better to include a couple of cover versions.

By this time Jimmie was thoroughly established as a key player, contributing to high-profile sets such as John Lee Hooker's *Best Of Friends* (1998), Willie Nelson's *Milk Cow Blues* (2000), Don Henley's *Inside Job* (2000), and the Eric Clapton and B.B. King collaboration *Riding With The King* (2000).

Then there was the collation of the four-CD boxed set *SRV*, which included a DVD of live footage and principally live material that had yet to see the light of day. While the quality of playing was wildly erratic, the fact that the set started with Stevie Ray's performance of 'Thunderbird' with Paul Ray & The Cobras from 1977, and climaxes with 'Leave My Girl Alone' from 1990 gives a good impression of the progress of his musical development. It was also good to see some of the top notch collaborations included, such as 'Don't Stop By The Creek, Son' with Johnny Copeland, 'Don't Ask Me No Questions' with Albert King, 'If You Have To Know' with Lonnie Mack, 'These Blues Is Killing Me' with A.C. Reed (who used to play with both Buddy Guy and Albert Collins), and 'Goin' Down' with Jeff Beck. Tony Russell in *Mojo* summed up the *SRV* box-set when he said: "A band that does its job year-in year-out without posturing is easy to take for granted, but this collection also celebrates Vaughan finding Tommy Shannon and Chris Layton … who stoked his band Double Trouble."

The *SRV* collection also celebrated Vaughan finding Tommy Shannon and Chris Layton, who stoked his band Double Trouble

Live At Montreux 1982 & 1985 was released in 2001. Mainly due to the distant geographical location of the venue, many dedicated Stevie Ray followers had not been able to attend these gigs, so this was their first official chance to hear them. The 1982 gig has become the stuff of legend, not just because Stevie Ray played amazingly well, but also because this was the gig that catapulted him onto the international stage. Although much of the material is well-known enough to his fans, Stevie Ray cranks it out with an awesome plangent ferocity. By contrast the second concert is routine, lacking the hunger of its predecessor. Even so, you're left in no doubt that in 1985 Stevie Ray was technically streets ahead of his closest competitors, and that his playing style was as highly developed as it was ever likely to become. As he grew older he simply added more strings to his bow (as it were), becoming more varied in the process.

On Jimmie Vaughan's third solo album, *Do You Get The Blues?*, his self-assurance was far more evident. "After I learned how to get the sounds right, and how to work all the stuff … it's a real pleasure working in the studio," he told Art Tipaldi in *Children Of The Blues*. "It's like you got this big blank canvas and you got all this paint. When you get into the studio, you've got to be creative. … Usually I try to bring the song and try to get a certain thing going and get the band to help me bring it out. As long as I know the melody and what the song is about it usually works. … It's real expressive to write the song, pick the band, write the arrangement, sing it, play the solo, and end it when you're damn good and ready."

The studio craft of *Do You Get The Blues?* is apparent from the opening track. Lots more work has gone into fashioning an overall sound that reflects Jimmie's strengths. Again you'd be hard-pressed to isolate individual songs that are sure-fire killers, but like his brother, he's sorted out the vital dynamic of how tracks are going to sound, and what will work together. In other words, even without consistently great material, he knows now how to make an album sound better than it actually is – the sum is greater than the individual parts.

Like his brother, Jimmie knows how to make an album sound better than it actually is – even without consistently great material

Jimmie Vaughan's forte has always been his economy, allied with an instinctive awareness of when a bit of experimentation may be effective, or when – in tennis parlance – you just knock it back down the tramlines. There's just enough variety to preclude the predictable: for instance Lou Ann Barton's vocals on 'Out Of The Shadows', 'Power Of Love' and Johnny 'Guitar' Watson's 'In The Middle Of The Night' – which also featured the Double Trouble rhythm section of Tommy Shannon and Chris Layton; plus the contributions of Greg Piccolo on tenor sax and James Cotton on harmonica.

"I wanted to make a romantic blues album," Jimmie explained. "I was listening to a lot of Sarah Vaughan and a lot of jazz. So I wanted to put my dirty blues guitar and the romantic feelings and the ins-and-outs of love together on one album. It's got a lot of gospel stylings, it's got blues, it's got R&B. I don't consciously think, 'OK, we need to put some of this in here; I like that beat, that's cool'. I don't plan it out or try to decipher what it is. I just try to create what I feel." Jimmie's gut feelings about *Do You Get The Blues?* were vindicated when it picked up the Grammy for Best Traditional Blues album in 2002.

CHAPTER 11

Walk That Walk

"My job is showing people who don't know anything about the blues that it has substance to it."

KIM WILSON OF THE FABULOUS THUNDERBIRDS

If Jimmie Vaughan had a tough time reconciling the death of his brother, it was also a difficult period, personally and professionally, for the former members of Stevie Ray's band. Double Trouble were a unit, and recognised as such – everyone knew they were one of the best rhythm sections in the country. The choice now was either simply to split up, or to form their own band and start again.

Organist Reese Wynans was in the easiest position: he had always played a lot of sessions, and with more and more people now streaming into Austin to record, he could not have been better placed. At first he joined Joe Ely's Band, but soon he was making regular trips across the country to Nashville to record with country performers such as John Michael Montgomery and Suzy Bogguss. Most of the time Reese was kept busy by kindred spirits such as Delbert McClinton, guitarists Mike Henderson, Lee Roy Parnell and Stephen Bruton, Omar & The Howlers, Buddy Guy, Doug Sahm, and Tracy Nelson, who used to be in the band Mother Earth in San Francisco during the late 1960s.

KIM WILSON, LEADER OF THE FABULOUS THUNDERBIRDS, AND VOCAL ADVOCATE OF 'REAL BLUES'

Chris Layton and Tommy Shannon opted to form a new group – which could have been a traumatic process, but in the event happened quite naturally. One afternoon Layton was practising at the Austin Rehearsal Complex with Shannon, guitarist and songwriter Charlie Sexton, and Doyle Bramhall's son, Doyle Bramhall II. Things went so well that, on the spot, they decided to start a band, calling themselves The Arc Angels.

Doyle Bramhall II was born on December 24th 1968, and had made his performing debut when he was about nine. An enthusiastic and disciplined guitarist, young Bramhall had the potential to go far, but he had grown up very rapidly and now he had a drug problem. Charlie Sexton was also born in Austin, on August 10th 1968. He too had had to grow up very fast, spending most of his childhood in clubs like Antone's and the Soap Creek Saloon. His talent as a guitarist meant he cut his first album in 1985: entitled *Pictures For Pleasure*, it was over-produced and tried too hard to push Sexton in the direction of the Bryan Adams' audience. Surprisingly, one of the tracks, 'Beats So Lonely', was picked up by MTV – but Sexton's subsequent intention to break into the movies as some sort of teen idol failed to materialise. After returning from Los Angeles to Austin he went back to doing what he knew best, playing a sort of rootsy blues rock on the album *Charlie Sexton* (1989).

For Shannon and Layton, the idea of being in a band with Bramhall and Sexton seemed almost too close to the bone – and Bramhall's spiralling use of drugs meant that history seemed to be repeating itself with unerring accuracy. Yet The Arc Angels debut, augmented by the keyboards of former Small Faces/Faces man Ian McLagan (who had followed his former colleague Ronnie Lane to Austin) was a finely balanced set, allowing both Bramhall and Sexton the chance to hallmark each title with their respective stamp. But it was Shannon and Layton that provided the unifying muscle, while Mac's tasteful fills on piano and B3 gave variety. Even so, the spectre of Stevie Ray Vaughan seemed to hover, especially on 'Sent By Angels', which was dedicated to him, and 'Livin' In A Dream'. Although it was a good album, the clash of egos between two guitarists of similar backgrounds and persuasions proved insurmountable, and The Arc Angels duly split up.

Bramhall went into detox in 1993. When he came out, he helped his father on the latter's long-awaited solo album, *Bird's Nest On The Ground* (1994), before cutting his own first solo set, *Doyle Bramhall II*, for the Geffen label. Featuring Wendy & Lisa and Sheila E, who had all worked with Prince during the 1980s, as well as drummer Brady Blade, who would go on to work with Daniel Lanois and Emmylou Harris, the album's weak point was nonetheless its one-dimensional song writing. But it was a start. His next two albums, recorded for RCA, were more convincing: despite a lack of consistency in the songwriting department, they show there's plenty of potential waiting to be tapped – although perhaps the involvement of Wendy & Lisa, and this time Mitchell Froom on keyboards, made the overall sound too busy. *Welcome* (2001) was beset by similar problems as its predecessors.

In the meantime Bramhall founded The Mighty Zor with Shannon and Layton in 1998 – though they don't seem to have recorded under that name to date – and when Sexton has sat in with the band it's suggested that another Arc Angels album may come first. Although his solo albums are patchy, Bramhall II's reputation continues to improve, helped by some high-profile sessions, including on the Eric Clapton and B.B. King vehicle, *Riding With The King* (2000), Clapton's *Reptile* (2001), and Sheryl Crow's *C'mon, C'mon* (2002).

As for Charlie Sexton, he returned with another solo album, *Under The Wishing Tree* (1995), on which he reflected the diversity of Austin, drawing on bluegrass as well as the blues, while some critics have detected a Celtic influence. Whatever the style, *Under The Wishing Tree* goes some way towards realising a potential that has been threatening for some years now. Sexton also settled into the steady groove of playing sessions around Austin with the likes of the Austin Lounge Lizards, singer-songwriter and conceptual artist Terry Allen, guitarist and singer-songwriter Alejandro Escovedo, and Lucinda Williams. He was also summoned to session for Bob Dylan's *Love And Theft* album, and then take part in the ensuing tour.

After the demise of The Arc Angels, Shannon and Layton's next, more productive project was when they formed Storyville

After the demise of The Arc Angels, Shannon and Layton's next, and more productive project was when they hooked up in 1994 with guitarists David Holt and David Grissom and vocalist Malford Milligan to form Storyville. Not unusually, the band came together after an informal jam session at Antone's. Holt had made his recording debut on the Mavericks' album, *From Hell To Paradise* (1992), while Grissom had been a fixture in Austin for a number of years, playing with Joe Ely, Lou Ann Barton, singer-songwriter James McMurtry and The Texas Tornados. He'd even played on sessions for Ringo Starr's album *Time Takes Time* (1992), as well as for John Mellencamp and John Mayall. Singer Milligan was the only novice.

It didn't take long for Storyville to cut their debut album for the independent November label. *The Bluest Eyes* predicated the vitality of Austin's local music scene, and so when it won a slew of prizes at the *Austin Music Awards* in 1995, including Best Album, it seemed certain Storyville were on a roll. They were, and they were duly signed to Atlantic subsidiary Code Blue.

Their next album, *A Piece Of Your Soul*, was one of the best outings of the genre in recent years – largely due to the fact that they didn't try to dilute the rawness and aggression with sophisticated studio gimcracks. They succeeded in distilling the essence and integrity of what a bar band is supposed to sound like. Milligan's vocals were especially noteworthy, while the twin guitars of Holt and Grissom were measured and resourceful, and the addition of Reese Wynans on Hammond added texture to an already rich palette.

The group's third album, *Dog Years* (1998), was issued on the parent label Atlantic. Although a thoroughly laudable offering, it seemed to lack the punch of *A Piece Of Your Soul*. Stephen Bruton had been brought in as producer, and his erstwhile employer Bonnie Raitt added backing vocals, alongside Sweet Pea Atkinson, with Don Was playing upright bass. The result was a classic case of too much money being lavished in the wrong areas. The material was of a type – not bad, but certainly not great. Overall a tried-and-tested formula that had worked well for countless years, sometimes yielding extraordinary results, but more often than not proving merely efficient.

Inevitably it was only going to be a matter of time before Double Trouble cut an album under their own name

Inevitably it was only going to be a matter of time before Double Trouble cut an album under their own name. When it came to pass in 2001, the Boston-based Tone-Cool label were the lucky recipients. Very sensibly, Shannon and Layton resisted the temptation to do everything themselves, attempting to turn themselves into vocalists or lead guitarists, or even producers. Instead, Stephen Bruton was invited to take the controls, and they had a quick look through their address books to come up with a bunch of chums who could handle vocals and guitar, leaving them to do what they knew best.

It could well have been a recipe for disaster, but *Been A Long Time* is a very effective calling card (if one were needed), confirming Double Trouble's position as one of the top-notch rhythm sections in the business. And apart from long-time friends and collaborators like Jimmie Vaughan, Willie Nelson, Dr John, Lou Ann Barton, Reese Wynans and Denny Freeman, they confined themselves to bringing in younger musicians with talent and potential, such as Jonny Lang, Eric Johnson, Susan Tedeschi and Kenny Wayne Shepherd, and those whom they already knew well and admired, like Doyle Bramhall II, Malford Milligan and Charlie Sexton.

Jonny Lang, from North Dakota, had already established himself as one of the most vital of the new generation of guitarists. He'd started his career in 1995 (when he was only 14) with

Smokin' for the independent Oarfin label. This had prompted a ferocious bidding war, which A&M eventually won. *Lie To Me* (1996) was a solid effort, but the follow-up, *Wander This World* (1998), was far better. Although his guitar work was what everyone had been bidding to get a piece of, his vocals seemed to carry even more weight and gravitas. So it was in that capacity he was recruited by Shannon and Layton.

A native of Texas, Eric Johnson was born on August 17th 1954, and is one of the few guitarists to emerge who has fashioned a technique at the expense of popular acceptance. His technique drew sharp in-takes of breath of admiration from guitarists as varied as Johnny Winter, Jeff 'Skunk' Baxter, Joe Satriani, Chet Atkins and Steve Vai – indeed Vai later paid him the ultimate compliment of signing him to his own Favoured Nations record label. But a string of albums that have included *Tones* (1986), *Ah Via Musicom* (1990), *Venus Isle* (1996), *Seven Worlds* (1998), and *Alien Love Child: Live And Beyond* (2000) have shown Johnson does not plough a furrow just to sell a few albums.

Ah Via Musicom showed Johnson at his best, and one of the tracks, 'Cliffs Of Dover', managed to win him a Grammy for Best Rock Instrumental. Probably no one was more surprised than Johnson. And then his debut for Vai's label, *Alien Love Child: Live And Beyond*, saw him taking the provident step of recruiting Storyville's Malford Milligan to provide vocals on tracks such as 'Don't Cha Know' and 'Once A Part of Me'.

Tone-Cool labelmate Susan Tedeschi's *Just Won't Burn* was one of the highpoints of 1998, securing a Grammy nomination for Best New Artist. While her vocals sometimes suggest Janis Joplin, there's a lot more to her vocal range than that might imply. As for her guitar work, she seems comfortable with electric or acoustic, which gives her a head-start over many contemporaries who seem ill-disposed to mix it up much. Her contribution to the Double Trouble album included 'In The Garden, which she co-wrote with Shannon – and which she later re-recorded in a new version on her album *Wait For Me* (2002).

When it came to interesting contributions, however, young guitarist Kenny Wayne Shepherd, from Shreveport, took pride of place. Born on June 12th 1977, Shepherd had been influenced by Stevie Ray Vaughan, Robert Cray, Duane Allman and Albert King. His career started in earnest at the tender age of 13 when he was invited on-stage by the New Orleans-based blues man Bryan Lee. After that his reputation kept on building until his father worked out a deal with the Eagles' manager Irving Azoff, who signed him to his record label, Giant. The resulting *Ledbetter Heights* (1995) sold over half-a-million copies by word-of-mouth alone. More importantly, Shepherd tempers his influences with his own style, so that whether he's playing blues or rock, the fingerprints of New Orleans and the Texas Triangle are clearly discernible. Later albums, such as

Trouble Is (1997) and *Live On* (1998) show he is still growing, though his compositional powers remain somewhat stilted. But it's his clean, ringing tone that has always attracted guitar buffs.

Considering the range of performers (and the potential for clashing egos), Double Trouble's *Been A Long Time* was a remarkably successful endeavour. It was to Shannon and Layton's great credit that they managed to keep a firm handle on the way the album developed, despite the range of personalities contributing. The mix of material, such as Johnny 'Guitar' Watson's 'In The Middle Of The Night' and Muddy Waters' 'She's Alright', complemented Led Zeppelin's 'Rock And Roll', even though some of the group's original compositions were very routine. In the end it proved once again that a great rhythm section will never turn a bad album into a good album, but it will make all the difference to a reasonable one...

As mentioned earlier, after Stevie Ray's death Jimmie Vaughan confirmed to Kim Wilson that he would not be returning to The Fabulous Thunderbirds. But as Kim had been writing most of the material anyway, he saw no reason why this should spell the end for the T-Birds – in theory all that was required to keep the band going was to hire another guitarist. Yet finding someone to replace the elegant economy of Jimmie was no easy matter. In the end Kim resolved the matter by hiring not one but two guitarists, Duke Robillard and Kid Bangham, for what was to be the T-Birds' final album for Epic.

Bangham was the new kid on the block, and had been working with revival R&B outfit Sugar Ray & The Bluetones. Robillard was by now an elder statesman – and he was also perhaps a rather unusual choice as a part-replacement for Jimmie Vaughan, specialising as he did in post-jump, pre-rock'n'roll R&B, in which he had an almost scholarly, academic preoccupation. He was very much his own man, yet he was clearly in touch with the ethos of The Fabulous Thunderbirds. He was, after all, a founder member of Roomful Of Blues, and the two groups had always been on a par, playing on the same club circuits, and generally seen as kindred spirits. There were other links between the two groups too: not only had the former Roomful Of Blues rhythm section of Fran Christina and Preston Hubbard earlier joined the T-Birds, but the Roomful Of Blues horn section had been frequent contributors to both the Vaughan brothers' recordings, whenever the need arose.

Duke Robillard was born on October 4th 1948 at Woonsocket, near Providence, Rhode Island. This may seem a particularly inauspicious place to get a grounding in the blues, but in fact, through attending the *Newport Jazz & Blues Festivals*, and then through the clubs of Boston and Providence, Robillard witnessed some of the finest blues musicians of the post-war era, including Muddy Waters, Otis Spann, Howlin' Wolf, John Lee Hooker, Buddy Guy and Junior

Wells. It wasn't just bluesmen that happened along either – Count Basie, Duke Ellington, Illinois Jacquet and Teddy Wilson, and many others, turned up in the neighbourhood as well. By the time he was 19, in 1967, Robillard had soaked up enough to form the first line-up of the Roomful Of Blues, with himself on guitar, Al Copley on piano, Hubbard on bass, and Fran Christina behind the traps. This first attempt only lasted a short while, but the following year the group reconvened in earnest and began gigging regularly up and down the east coast.

"When I started the Roomful Of Blues," Robillard later recalled, "what had always got to me was the hard, swinging style of T-Bone Walker and Louis Jordan. That's what really interested me, and nobody else was playing that type of rhythm & blues at all. There were plenty of the new-breed of bluesmen like the Paul Butterfield Blues Band, Taj Mahal, Canned Heat and John Hammond [Jr], but nobody seemed interested in the hard-rockin' R&B of Big Joe Turner or Roy Milton. So I would go and check out all these record stores, buying as much as I could get hold of. There was one store I remember and this guy had a basement that was stacked with old 78s by people like Wynonie Harris, Roy Brown, Big Joe Turner – anyone you can think of – and I asked the guy if I could go into his basement and look through the records. He said, 'OK here's the deal, you give me 20 dollars, and if you don't find anything you want I'll still keep the 20 dollars. But if you do find things you want, then we'll work it out'. So I said 'OK', and when I went back to him I had my arms full of records."

Nobody else was playing that type of rhythm & blues at all – the hard, swinging style of T-Bone Walker and Louis Jordan

Around 1970, after hearing Buddy Johnson's Orchestra, Robillard expanded The Roomful Of Blues to include a horn section, which initially featured Greg Piccolo on tenor, Rich Lataille on alto, and Doug James on baritone (James is still a member of Robillard's band). While the addition of horns greatly enhanced the group's popularity, it also made them much jazzier, enabling Robillard to distance himself still further from the contemporaneous trend among blues-based guitarists for playing millions of notes at high volume in no particular order. To this day Robillard swings effortlessly, with a succinctness born out of knowing that economy is the key.

Throughout the 1970s the Roomful Of Blues developed their reputation in the States on the festival and club circuits, playing with, among others, 'Red' Prysock, Eddie 'Cleanhead' Vinson, B.B. King, Maria Muldaur and Count Basie. With such a busy schedule, it wasn't until 1977 that they made their debut album, *Roomful Of Blues*, for Island. Produced by Joel Dorn and songwriter Doc Pomus, and featuring another Rhode Island native, Scott Hamilton, on tenor sax, it was packed with classics like Larry Davis's 'Texas Flood' and T-Bone Walker's 'Stormy Monday', as well as Robillard's 'Duke's Blues'.

Still the gigs continued to pour in, including an appearance at the *New Orleans Jazz & Heritage Festival*, opening for Professor Longhair. Consequently they didn't get back into the studios until the following year to record their second album. Again produced by Joel Dorn, *Let's Have A Party* (1979) was not quite as flamboyant as the title suggested, but it did show the band was sticking by its guns, and allowing little compromise along the way. So it came as something of a surprise when Robillard announced he was leaving the band for a solo career.

"We had been touring solidly," Robillard explained, "and there was some friction in the band. When you're touring constantly it does place a strain on friendships, but very gradually I found that the band was moving in a direction that didn't interest me. It was time to go."

After leaving the Roomful Of Blues, Robillard hooked up with rockabilly revivalist Robert Gordon, before moving on to the Legendary Blues Band for a spell. He remained a hired hand until 1981 when he formed his own band again, which would become the Pleasure Kings. This was initially a trio, featuring bassist Thomas Enright and drummer Tom DeQuattro – at least for the first two albums, *Duke Robillard & The Pleasure Kings* (1983) and *Too Hot To Handle* (1985); but later albums, such as *You Got Me* (1988), were supplemented by special guests like Dr John and Jimmie Vaughan.

Robillard's tenure with Rounder also enabled him to develop another facet of his career – working behind the scenes in the studio. At first this involved session work, most notably with R&B vocalist Johnny Adams, but in the fullness of time Robillard would be producing, engineering, mastering, taking photographs, and writing liner notes, as well as playing guitar.

Despite this restless energy, he continued developing his guitar style, paying tribute to one of his early idols, Charlie Christian, on the album *Swing* (1987) with Scott Hamilton. Then in 1990, with his former bandmates from Roomful Of Blues, Robillard cut *After Hours Swing Session* (1990). In some respects this is Robillard's defining moment, not only neatly encapsulating his remarkable style, but also capturing his infectious enthusiasm. Listen out for Al Basile's use of the mute on Nat King Cole's 'The Trouble With Me', while Rich Lataille's alto suggests more than a passing affection for Johnny Hodges. Even 'Sweet Georgia Brown' gets revived – "kind of like Count Basie meets Les Paul", according to Robillard in the liner notes. This is Robillard as catalyst.

The same year, having disbanded The Pleasure Kings, he put together another line-up for *Turn It Around* (1990). This incarnation of the band featured Susan Forrest (vocals), Scott

Applerouth (bass), and Doug Hinman (drums), but it proved short-lived. Then came the call to join the T-Birds. Although he only stayed for the one album, *Walk That Walk, Talk That Talk* (1991), it cemented a friendship with Kim Wilson that would see the two of them working together regularly in the future.

By 1994, Robillard had signed with Virgin/Pointblank. Although Virgin was by this time a major label and not an independent, they had the commendable good sense to let him do what he wanted; he even got to produce and play guitar on John Hammond's excellent *Found A Love* album. Three albums followed – *Temptation* (1994), *Duke's Blues* (1996) and *Dangerous Place* (1997) – but only *Duke's Blues* seems to be currently available.

Although still signed to Virgin, Robillard started to record for Canada's Stony Plain label in 1996, after producing Jimmy Witherspoon's *Spoon's Blues* in 1995 (Duke's Blues was the first album to appear under the Stony Plain banner). Pretty soon Robillard was right back into the swing of working behind the scenes. "I worked with Jay McShann," he recalled. "We made two albums together, *Hootie's Jumpin' Blues* [1997] and *Still Jumpin' The Blues* [1999], which I was very pleased to do." With his customary understatement, Robillard failed to mention that not only did he play guitar and produce these two sets, he also mixed and mastered them, and wrote the liner notes. "Then I did *Memphis, Tennessee* [1998] with another veteran, Rosco Gordon. He hadn't recorded for a long time, and so he had a lot of songs he had never recorded before." Again Robillard took on the engineering duties, as well as playing guitar; as it turned out this was to be Gordon's swansong – he passed away in the summer of 2002.

Robillard would often be involved in producing, engineering, mastering, writing sleeve notes, and taking photographs, as well as playing guitar

As the collaborations with McShann and his longtime association with Scott Hamilton signified, Robillard's enthusiasm for jazz had always influenced his guitar style. In 1999 he teamed up with swing veteran Herb Ellis for *Conversations In Swing Guitar*. Accompanied by rhythm guitar, bass and drums, Ellis and Robillard discourse on standards like Benny Goodman's 'Flying Home', Ellington's 'Just Squeeze Me' and Coleman Hawkins' 'Stuffy'. Elegant and refined, Ellis's ineffable swing complements Robillard's economical warmth to a fault, but it's Robillard's empathetic production that makes the difference, making the session seem more like an informal jam.

Still ringing the changes, the following year he came back with *Explorer*. "Although playing the blues is something I like to do, there are other styles of music I like to listen to," he said. "*Explorer* gave me a chance to do different styles." Some listeners may have found the variety on offer here confusing – with jazz tunes such as 'You Mean Everything To Me' and 'Jumpin' With The Duke' lining up alongside the Memphis soul of 'Just Between Me And You' and a New Orleans rumba, 'Sayin' Don't Make It So' – it certainly emphasised Robillard's eclecticism. "[He] knows jazz theory beyond the blues," Jimmie Vaughan admitted in *Children Of The Blues*. "I'm more primitive. He can play along with a jazz group because he sat down and studied it."

More recently, *Livin' With The Blues* (2002) showed Robillard returning to familiar territory – the first time he'd cut a traditional blues album since 1996. Again the material was as eclectic and sometimes obscure as one would expect, but Robillard is such a relaxed, as well as incisive, practitioner that he transcends categorisation, and is quite unlike anyone else around at the moment.

Robillard is such a relaxed, as well as incisive practitioner that he transcends categorisation

The T-birds' *Walk That Walk, Talk That Talk* also featured the Memphis Horns and the veteran gospel group The Dixie Hummingbirds. It should have been a business-as-usual set, but neither Duke Robillard nor Kid Bangham, despite some fine contributions (Robillard even wrote 'Born To Love You' for the album), could rescue what must have been a very difficult album to make. Despite the T-Birds' return to straightforward R&B, abandoning the more commercial approach of the three preceding albums, *Walk That Walk, Talk That Talk* was a lacklustre affair.

Following its release, Epic dropped The Fabulous Thunderbirds, and Kim mothballed the group while he undertook solo projects. The first of these, *Tigerman* (1993), for the Antone's label, drew from the same core of musicians as The T-Birds, with Fran and Preston providing the backdrop, and Gene Taylor contributing support on keyboards. The biggest departure was Kim's use of four different guitarists: Robillard, Junior Watson, Derek O'Brien and Rusty Zinn. Despite these subtle differences *Tigerman* followed pretty much the same pattern as the T-Birds' albums, combining a mix of original compositions, blues classics (Willie Dixon's 'When The Lights Go Out' and Sonny Boy Williamson's 'Trust Me Baby') and R&B numbers like 'You Got Me' and Johnny Guitar Watson's 'Don't Touch Me'. Even so it was a zesty affair, confirming Kim's undimmed passion for the blues, and the selective use of the Antone's horn section, led by Ronnie Cuber added an extra spark and punch.

By the time he got around to cutting *That's Life* (1994), it had become apparent that, with Kim the undisputed focus in the T-Birds (since Jimmie's departure), Kim Wilson the solo performer and frontman of The Fabulous Thunderbirds were interchangeable roles.

That's Life was a textbook rendering of Texas roadhouse blues and gritty blues-rock. Although a few of Kim's own songs lacked a little something, re-workings of Sonny Boy Williamson's 'She's My Baby', Howlin' Wolf's 'Ooh Baby (When You Squeeze Me)' and Slim Harpo's 'Teach Me (How To Love You)' were on the button. As on *Tigerman*, there were a bunch of different guitarists, with Clarence Holliman joining Robillard, Watson, O'Brien and Zinn. The rhythm section of Preston and Fran was used for the most part, but there are tracks featuring other bassists, such as Canned Heat's Larry Taylor or drummer Richard Innes. The whole set was fleshed out by Taylor and the Antone's horn section.

After *That's Life*, in late 1994, Kim reconvened The Fabulous Thunderbirds and cut *Roll Of The Dice*. Released on Private Music, and supported by some intensive touring across the United States, the band seemed more on the ball and more interested in what they doing; their reworking of the Bert Berns classic 'Here Comes The Night' may not be quite as portentous as Them's version, but that's no real criticism. But it has to be said their version of 'Zip-A-Dee-Doo-Dah' – presumably done just for a laugh – should have been left in the vaults. The really interesting addition to the band's line-up at this point was the arrival of Danny 'Kootch' Kortchemar.

Kim Wilson the solo performer and frontman of The Fabulous Thunderbirds had become interchangeable roles

Kortchemar, a very old friend of singer-songwriter James Taylor, is one of the shadowy figures that have lurked around the periphery of the LA session circuit for years. Kootch is often viewed as a 'Mr Fix-it', being not just a fine economical guitarist but also a good songwriter, able to work in almost any style. Indeed on *Roll Of The Dice* Kootch co-wrote half of the dozen tracks.

There were other changes as well, with former Electric Flag bassist Harvey Brooks coming in for Preston, alongside guitarists David Grissom (from Storyville) and David 'Kid' Ramos. Hailing from California, Ramos had spent his early years touring with the James Harman band before leaving the music business to concentrate on raising a family. Wilson was persuasive, though, and tempted him back into the fray. By the time the tour with T-Birds was over, Ramos was hooked, and has gone on to cut several solo albums for the Evidence label, including *Kid Ramos* (1999) and *Greasy Kid's Stuff* (2001). The other major modification on the *Roll Of The Dice* album was the recruitment of Steve Jordan as producer.

Kim was sufficiently encouraged by the success of *Roll Of The Dice* that he applied essentially the same formula to its follow-up, *High Water*. This is essentially a Kim Wilson solo album, with Kootch and Jordan helping out, so why it's credited to The Fabulous Thunderbirds is something of a mystery. It's certainly the only album in the T-Birds canon to be comprised of exclusively original material, and its R&B influence is almost subliminal. As with so many albums, there is little here to get excited about, but little to be excessively critical of. It's innocuous and quite pleasant – yet with the focus on Kim's vocals and harmonica playing, the absence of some characteristically incisive guitar work makes it feel unfinished.

At this point Kim teamed up with bluesman Snuff Johnson for *Will The Circle Be Unbroken?* With Johnson handling the vocals and acoustic guitar, and Kim accompanying on harmonica, this is a neat, unassuming set. Johnson is no frantic axeman, and his understated style seems to complement Kim very effectively – and of course being essentially an acoustic set it creates an intriguing counterpoint to the rest of Kim's work.

Too many people are getting away from the real blues ... Modern-day blues, which is one guy playing a 20-minute solo, usually on a guitar, is ludicrous to me

It was, on the face of it, a somewhat drastic departure for Kim, given the Fabulous Thunderbirds' most recent album. "There'll always be people out there who want to hear the rock'n'roll, hit record side of the band," Wilson told Art Tipaldi. "Lately we're introducing more of the blues side. In the old days it was balls-to-the-walls all the time. The T-Birds are getting deeper into the blues. We're getting more into the dynamics of it, and the interplay between the bandmembers. It's a natural thing that too many people are getting away from the real blues, because they haven't been exposed to it. Modern day blues, which is one guy playing a 20-minute solo, usually on a guitar, is ludicrous to me."

Kim backed up these comments with *My Blues* (1997), which he cut for his own label, Blue Collar. This featured a range of material from a variety of performers, such as Sonny Boy Williamson ('Your Funeral And My Trial'), Little Walter ('Break It Up Baby', 'Everything's Gonna Be Alright' and 'Oh Baby'), Eddie Boyd ('Five Long Years'), Dave Bartholomew ('Gumbo Blues'), Roy Milton ('Everything I Do Is Wrong' and 'Hop

Skip And Jump) and Roosevelt Sykes ('Date Bait' and 'West Helena Woman') – and there were just two Wilson originals, 'My Blues' and 'Tell Me Why'.

The modest combo accompanying him featured bassist Larry 'The Mole' Taylor, formerly of Canned Heat, Fred Kaplan on piano, and Rusty Zinn and Junior Watson on guitars, as well as Scott Steen (trumpet) and Tom Fabre (tenor sax). "My job is showing people who don't know anything about the blues that it has substance to it," Wilson claimed. "Right now, I really want to cater to the hardcore people, because I think there are a lot of people out there who didn't believe that real blues records could be made anymore." No one can doubt Wilson's sincerity, and *My Blues* does tend to make you go back and dig out the originals – so from that point of view Wilson's role as educator and motivator is irrefutable.

Kim's next solo album, *Smokin' Joint*, was another familiar blend of ancient and modern, with several guitarists – Bill Flynn, Kirk Fletcher and Troy Gonyea – lined up alongside Rusty Zinn, while Larry Taylor was joined by Richard Innes on drums. This was followed by a live album with The Fabulous Thunderbirds, which effectively reprised the highlights of the band's career. Despite the patchiness of the T-birds' albums since Jimmie Vaughan left the group, Kim Wilson's zeal about the position of the blues sometimes takes on an almost evangelical fervour. And with two separate avenues for expression – solo albums on the one hand and touring and recording with the T-Birds on the other – he has, as they say, the best of both worlds.

CHAPTER 12

Here To Stay

"All this business stuff ain't worth nothing. Let's just get out there and play the blues."

JOHNNY COPELAND

At the beginning of 2003, many of the changes on the musical map that Stevie Ray Vaughan helped to bring about had become an established part of the scenery. The Vaughan brothers' album *Family Style* had played its part in encouraging a more open-minded atmosphere, but more crucially the positive effect that Stevie Ray had on other guitarists and the blues scene in general was awesome.

Superficially it might appear that the main beneficiaries of the blues revival Stevie Ray helped kick-start in the 1980s were young white kids intent on becoming respected (or otherwise) rock stars. But the most important by-product was the general wealth of new opportunities presented to musicians and songwriters who were languishing in obscurity, unable to break beyond the confines of their immediate environment.

Of course this wasn't just down to the influence of Stevie Ray or the growth of interest in the blues per se – what ultimately made the difference was the advance of technology: first of all the availability and falling price of digital recording equipment, aimed at the home studio market,

STEVIE RAY – A TALENT, AND A PROFILE, THAT WILL ALWAYS BE REMEMBERED

and then the growth of the internet as a means of distributing music. Despite the protestations of established record labels, cutting a CD or downloading an MP3 file is cheap and easy, so traditional distribution methods are less crucial in breaking new artists. Even the smaller, independent record labels who always had a tough time getting international or indeed national distribution of their wares, can these days use websites to develop the mail order side of their business. In turn this has had a knock-on effect on large distributors and wholesalers, who have seen some of their power eroded – which is perhaps no bad thing. Maybe now we'll see records selling on merit, instead of relying on whether or not a wholesaler/distributor is inclined to handle them.

The expansion of the internet has meant that niche market artists who don't necessarily have mainstream commercial appeal can still get a decent hearing. Whereas previously they were dependent on the benevolence (or otherwise) of record labels to get their careers moving, they can now sell their self-made albums and promote their tours and shows to fans via websites – making a living while building their profile, and even putting themselves in a stronger position should they still decide to seek a major record deal at some stage.

New artists seem to be coming out of the woodwork all the time – some young, some not quite so young. Whatever the particular route taken in each case, the fact is that since the end of the 1990s we've witnessed a number of guitarists and bands, some of whom never had a chance to record before, now getting long overdue opportunities. And while Austin has mainly been the focus of activity, the Dallas-Fort Worth circuit has still been providing much of the raw material.

The unlikely partnership between Anson Funderburgh and Sam Myers – a contemporary of Stevie Ray linking up with a bluesman from an earlier generation – turned out to be an auspicious and mutually beneficial arrangement. Funderburgh was born on November 15th 1954 in Plano, Texas, and received his first guitar when he was seven or eight. "The lady my mother bought the guitar from gave me a box of singles," Funderburgh states in *Children Of The Blues*. "In that box were Freddy King's 'Hideaway', Bill Doggett's 'Honky Tonk', Albert Collins' 'Sno Cone; Parts 1 & 2', and Jimmy Reed stuff." Like the Vaughan brothers he picked up most of his knowledge by listening to records by bluesmen such as Blind Lemon Jefferson and Lightnin' Hopkins – he actually played with the latter in the late 1970s – and seeing guys like Albert Collins, Freddie King and Jimmy Reed.

In 1978 Funderburgh formed The Rockets, with Darren Nulisch on harmonica and vocals, and they immediately tapped into the same network as The Fabulous Thunderbirds. Playing a hard-driving brand of electric blues, The Rockets blended Mississippi delta blues with jump blues, underpinned by the characteristic churning funk of New Orleans. The analogy with the

T-Birds stretched further when Funderburgh made his recording debut with them on their second album, *Butt Rockin'*. "Jimmie's two years older than I am," said Funderburgh, "and I played with Stevie several times. ... He and Jimmie did so much to help me. I played on that *Butt Rockin'* record with the T-Birds; Jimmie didn't have to do that." Funderburgh was later signed in his own right to the Black Top label, out of New Orleans, and made his solo debut with the curiously titled *Talk To You By The Hand* (which still sounds like a typographical error) in 1981.

Funderburgh first met Sam Myers in 1982, at a small venue in Jackson, Mississippi, and they got together again regularly whenever schedules coincided. "I knew Sammy from his work with Elmore James in the 1950s," Funderburgh expanded, "and I had a copy of his 1950s single 'My Love Is Here To Stay'. After that meeting I thought a recording session with a stand-up bass and swing-style drums would be great."

Myers was born in Laurel, Mississippi, in 1936. Although he went to school locally (learning to play the trumpet there) his vacations were spent in Chicago, where he came in to contact with legends such as Muddy Waters, Willie Dixon and Little Walter. After joining Elmore James as a drummer in 1949, Myers started playing harmonica as well: he said later, "[I] transformed what I knew from the trumpet to the harmonica." Myers remained with James up until the latter's death in 1964. Then during the early 1960s he recorded for Bobby Robinson's New Orleans labels, Fire and Fury, and even toured with Robert Lockwood Jr and played on the chitlin' circuit for years before linking up properly with Funderburgh in 1985.

Their first album together came to fruition in 1986, after the release of *She Knocks Me Out* and the departure of Darren Nulisch from The Rockets. Calling the album, naturally enough, *My Love Is Here To Stay*, Funderburgh and Myers showed themselves to be an ideal partnership: Funderburgh's snazzy fluid licks complemented the gruff, down-home style of Myers, whose harmonica work seemed to echo that of Sonny Boy Williamson II (aka Rice Miller).

Since then the two of them have gone from strength to strength, and Funderburgh's songwriting gains in gravitas and authority with each album: some of the high points include *Sins* (1987), and especially *Tell Me What I Want To Hear* (1991) – on the latter, the title track and 'Rent Man Blues' affirm their own take on the traditional form.

In 1999 Funderburgh moved over to the Rounder subsidiary Bullseye Blues for *Change In My Pocket*, but the previous year's collaboration with guitarists Otis Grand and Debbie Davies, *Grand Union* (1998), recalled other great team-works such as *Showdown!*, the seminal Grammy-award-winning set with Albert Collins, Johnny Copeland and Robert Cray...

Just as Jimmie and Stevie Ray Vaughan had been influenced by a range of traditional bluesmen and bands, they too in their turn have cast their influence on both contemporaries and younger players. For instance, guitarist Mike Morgan, another Dallas native (born November 30th 1959), started his own band, The Crawl, after working in studios for a while. His 1990 debut on the Black Top label, *Raw And Ready*, was strong on atmosphere, but the second release, *Mighty Fine Dancin'*, with its robust horn section and a rhythm section of Frankie Meyer on bass and Marc Wilson on drums, set up a fine duel of wills and temperament between Morgan and Lee McBee on harmonica and vocals.

Some critics have argued that *Mighty Fine Dancin'* is too polished and sophisticated for its own good. This is a fallacy – it's not sophistication that jeopardises integrity, only a lack of focus or direction. Perhaps the biggest threat to the group's future is the lack of variety in the choice of material: some of it feels just too familiar. After McBee left the band in 1995, Morgan chose to replace him with (neatly-named) saxophonist Chris Whynaught, whose energetic vocals fired up *Looky Here*. Whynaught did not last long, though, and was replaced by the returning McBee, who picked up where he had left off, making the next release, *The Road*, a potent blend of rock and R&B.

Although Mike Morgan and The Crawl have yet to crack open the European festival circuit, Omar & The Howlers are long-time favourites. Based in Austin since 1976, Omar Kent Dykes was born in 1950 in McComb, Mississippi, the hometown of Bo Diddley. He learned to play the guitar and started doing odd local gigs while still at high-school. After moving to Austin he formed The Howlers – a generally loose-knit aggregation, although Bruce Jones on bass and Gene Brandon on drums have the longest term association with Omar. But it's Omar's band, and his robust earthy vocals complement the incisive economy of his guitar work.

Instead of trying to compete with contemporaries like the T-Birds or Double Trouble, Omar & The Howlers fashioned their own style

Like The Fabulous Thunderbirds, Omar & The Howlers toured the south west solidly, cultivating a thorough reputation with a punchy blend of original compositions and covers. They recorded their debut with Big Leg Beat in 1980, but their second set, *I Told You So* (1984), confirmed the group's position as one of the most compelling purveyors of Texan R&B – mainly because they were prepared to draw inspiration from other centres such as Chicago. Also, rather than trying to compete head-to-head with contemporaries like the T-Birds or Double Trouble, Omar & The Howlers concentrated on fashioning their own style and their own musical identity. This was rewarded when they were signed by Columbia

– although, like many other bands, their services were dispensed with when, after two very likeable albums, *Hard Times In The Land Of Plenty* (1987) and *Wall Of Pride* (1988), Columbia was bought by Sony. In the long run, being dropped by Sony was a blessing in disguise, as the band were able to pursue their own objectives without interference.

Through the 1990s, Omar & The Howlers' strike rate was impressive, knocking out an album every year or so for Rounder's Bullseye Blues subsidiary and the Austin-based Watermelon label. They also developed their reputation across Europe by appearing at festivals or on the club circuits there. The group's subsequent recording deals seem to have been negotiated on a per-album basis – and thus freed of contractual obligations they can devote their time and energies to playing live. One of their albums, *Big Delta* (2002), which featured bassist Roscoe Beck and drummer Terry Bozzio (a member of Jeff Beck's band on *The Fire And The Fury* tour with Stevie Ray Vaughan), was a perfect opportunity for Omar to reprise some of his best-known compositions with a cracking rhythm section that rivalled Double Trouble.

Smokin' Joe Kubek, from Dallas, and B'nois King, from Monroe, Louisiana, have developed a strikingly symbiotic partnership built on a fundamental difference in approach. Kubek, with his powder-blue Fender Stratocaster, slashes and burns his way through each song, while King, with his hollow-bodied Gibson, drops in long melodic lines that echo Wes Montgomery or Kenny Burrell. Like the Vaughan brothers, Kubek started out early – he was a member of Freddie King's band in the last few months of King's life – and was on the treadmill of low-paying bar gigs in and around Dallas from the age of 14. B'nois King's route was no less arduous, though his first gigs were in jazz groups whose haunts were hotel bars or night clubs. "Most of the time I played for people who didn't really care whether you were there," he recalled in *Children Of The Blues*. In 1988, Kubek and King met up and started playing together. "We just clicked right from the start," said King.

For the next three years or so the band toured and gigged constantly throughout the south west before making their debut on Bullseye Blues. A confident and well-balanced set, *Steppin' Out Texas Style* (1991) was the template for later albums such as *Texas Cadillac* (1993), *Got My Mind Back* (1996), *Take Your Best Shot* (1998) and *Bite Me* (2000). Although the repertoire – a combination of original compositions and covers from the usual sources (Willie Dixon, T-Bone Walker, Jimmy Reed, Littler Walter etc) – is on the surface unlikely to set many pulses racing, the performances are uniformly superb. King's vocals and rhythm guitar have enough grit and warmth to complement Kubek's abrasive attack. After nine albums for Bullseye, they moved to the Blind Pig label in 2002. *Roadhouse Research* was another finely judged set that augured well for the future. Perhaps the only downside is that now the group's fan-base in the US is of such a size that they really don't have much time to tour Europe. Shame.

Chris Duarte – born in San Antonio on February 16th 1963 – was once hailed as a wunderkind, and is still lumbered with comparisons to Stevie Ray, although his highly rhythmic take on blues-based rock has invited comparisons with Johnny Winter too. Duarte moved to Austin when he was 16, after several years knocking around on the San Antonio club circuit. At first he played in a jazz group, before moving on to Bobby Mack & Night Train. Then in 1994 he was picked up by the Silvertone label, who issued his debut solo album, *Texas Sugar/Strat Magik* – a passionate and intense affair, even if the self-composed material was rather prosaic. The follow-up, *Tailspin Headwhack*, showed a distinct improvement in the standard of the content: the single 'Cleopatra' was ear-catching to say the least; the cover of B.B. King's ' The Thrill Is Gone' was quite exceptional; and The Meters' 'People Say' was an added twist to the potent mix. Then he was dropped by Silvertone, and didn't have a deal until 2000, when *Love Is Greater Than Me* was released by the Zoe label. Full of original material, it lacked consistency – but it seemed at least he was shrugging off the dual spectres of Hendrix and Stevie Ray.

Sherman Robertson, a singer, songwriter and guitarist of some repute, must have thought all his Christmases had come at once when he was signed to Atlantic's affiliate Code Blue in 1994, when he was already in his late forties. But he managed to cut just two albums before Code Blue shut up shop in 1996. Both albums, *I'm The Man* (1994) and *Here & Now* (1995), were warmly, indeed glowingly received by some members of the press, but perhaps he just had the 'wrong sort of haircut' for mainstream success at the time. Whatever the reason, despite years plying his trade throughout the south west, Robertson was almost back to square one.

Born in Breaux Bridge, Louisiana, in 1948, Sherman Robertson was raised over the border in Houston, in the Fifth Ward, just down the block from the Duke & Peacock recording studios. This meant that from an early age he had such august personages as Junior Parker, Bobby 'Blue' Bland, 'Gatemouth' Brown, Albert Collins, Freddie King and Johnny Copeland making music just minutes from his home. Over the years he got to know and play with some of them himself: indeed Copeland was appropriately encouraging many years later when he said to him, "Sherman, all this business stuff ain't worth nothing. Let's just get out there and play the blues."

Notwithstanding such influential blues giants lurking in the background, Robertson's own music incorporated elements of zydeco, swamp blues, R&B and electric blues, and was largely fashioned by spells with Clifton Chenier in the 1980s. "I learned a great deal from him," Robertson explained to Art Tipaldi in *Children Of The Blues*. "He's the one who taught me how to do a crowd, how to get it happening every night, no matter who you are." Then there were stints with Rockin' Dopsie and Terrance Simien & The Mallet Playboys – through Rockin' Dopsie, Robertson was introduced to Paul Simon, which led to session work on Simon's *Graceland*. This was all enough to convince Robertson that a solo career was beckoning, and the two albums for Atlantic and Code Blue followed. Both sets were full of heart, topped with fluid playing and astute song selection, no doubt learned from years on the road. The 1998 offering for the Audioquest label, *Going Back Home*, was far less sophisticated than its predecessors, lacking the high-gloss production values that recording for a major label affords. But the rough and ready rawness of *Going Back Home* imparts an urgency that only comes when cutting a studio set 'live' – almost as it might be done on stage. Robertson even managed to gather into the fold Little Feat's Bill Payne and Richie Hayward on keyboards and drums, with Bob Glaub on bass and Joe Sublett on tenor sax.

Clifton Chenier taught Sherman Robertson how to work a crowd – how to get it happening every night

Long John Hunter had to wait even longer than Robertson, but when his opportunity came, there were few better equipped to make the most of what was on offer. Hunter was born in 1931, over the border in Louisiana, but moved to Beaumont in the early 1950s, where he worked in a box factory. One evening B.B. King came to town and Hunter was smitten – so smitten he went and bought himself a guitar. Practising in the evenings, he soon picked up a recording contract with Don Robey's Duke label; his first single, 'She Used To Be My Woman', came out in 1954, just as he was about to move down to the border town of El Paso. Although he played nightly, entertaining soldiers (from Fort Bliss) and anyone else that drifted by, there was little recording activity, apart from odd singles such as 'El Paso Rock' and 'Border Town Blues'. In fact Hunter remained something of a closely guarded secret for much of the next three decades – he did not record again properly until 1993, when he cut *Ride With Me* for the now defunct Spindletop label. Even this didn't cause many ripples.

Alligator boss Bruce Iglauer picked up on the record, though, and Hunter made his debut for his label in 1996 with the appositely titled *Border Town Legend*. Although it featured a horn section, this didn't distract from the distinctive flavour and potency of the brew. Hunter's vocals and guitar work perfectly conjured up the hot and steamy atmosphere of the downtown 'road-house' bar, while retaining a worldly sophistication. Perhaps the biggest difference was the mostly self-composed repertoire, with songs such as 'Nasty Ways' and 'T-Bone Intentions' –

Hunter's songs benefited from being reworked on-stage every night for years: the numbers had evolved and were knocked into shape, so when he started recording the playing came easily.

Swingin' From The Rafters (1997) was an even more assertive offering, if anything, with the horn section playing an auxiliary role and long-time Austin denizen Derek O'Brien chipping in with some elegant rhythm guitar work. Despite the guest credits, this is Hunter's work, and it places him – albeit belatedly – up there with the best.

Roy Gaines did not have to wait quite as long as Hunter, but not far off. Born in 1934 in Houston, his brother Grady joined Little Richard's road band, The Upsetters, but Roy's idol was T-Bone Walker. As a teenager he even graced the same stage as his role model when the legendary guitar battles between Walker and 'Gatemouth' Brown took place; the youthful Gaines was so well known he was even known as 'T-Bone Junior' for a spell.

With such a mighty reputation, Gaines was employed by Roy Milton when a vacancy for a guitarist arose. Based first in Los Angeles and then in New York City, Gaines moved into Chuck Willis' band, and even accompanied T-Bone Walker in the years up to T-Bone's death in 1975. Gaines also played sessions for Coleman Hawkins, Big Mama Thornton, Bobby 'Blue' Bland, The Jazz Crusaders, Jimmy Rushing, Junior Parker and Ray Charles, among others – but surprisingly his solo career has been patchy. At first he recorded the odd 78 or 45 here and there – the most notable being 'Gainesville', an extraordinarily robust piece of work that can almost cause genuine enthusiasts to give up playing the guitar altogether and take up stamp collecting instead. But his solo career did not really start until 1982, when he cut the album *Gaineling* (put together by an English label), after which another hiatus ensued until 1996. Since then, though, Gaines has recorded at fairly regular intervals, cutting albums such as *Bluesman For Life* and I *Got The T-Bone Walker Blues*.

For Andrew 'Junior Boy' Jones, the route was somewhat serpentine. Initially a protégé of Freddie King, Jones played with the maestro for around ten years, usually at weekends. That was followed by stints with the under-rated soul and R&B vocalist Bobby Patterson, and then a spell with Johnnie Taylor (one of the Stax label's finest vocalists, Taylor's biggest hit, 'Disco Lady' was also one of his least impressive performances). In 1987 Jones moved out to Los Angeles where he recorded and toured with the Texan R&B vocalist Katie Webster, before taking on the role of bandleader for harmonica player Charlie Musselwhite, a job he held down for around eight years. In the mid-1990s he returned to Dallas, where he has become something of a stalwart on the local club circuit. Effectively Jones is a journeyman, but his solo debut, *I Need Time*, is a powerful testament to the durability of a breed of musician that is often neglected.

Although a generation younger than 'Junior Boy' Jones, John 'Tutu' Jones (born in Dallas on

September 9th 1967) shares analogous influences. At first Tutu was a backing vocalist, before moving over to drums, in which role he accompanied the great R&B singer Z.Z. Hill; then when Hill died in 1984, Jones took on similar duties for R.L. Burnside, the North Mississippi blues guitarist. When he was not behind the traps Tutu could be found practising his guitar work and composing songs: such diligence was rewarded in 1994 when he cut *I'm For Real*.

Though Jones' guitar work carried the influence of Freddie King and his vocals suggested a combination of Bobby 'Blue' Bland and Z.Z. Hill, there's nothing wrong in role models of that quality. Later albums such as *Blue Texas Soul* and *Staying Power* were perfectly acceptable offerings, the latter featuring the Memphis Horns of Andrew Love and Wayne Jackson. Although there are so many guys touring out there now, playing soul and R&B, Tutu's individuality and enthusiasm is infectious and whole-hearted. The fact that he's also chosen to include Europe in his touring schedule seems to set him apart from his contemporaries.

Both T.D. Bell on guitar and Erbie Bowser on piano and vocals are musicians of the old school. For years they performed regularly at Austin's Victory Grill, and at last in 1992 they recorded the appositely titled *It's About Time*. With assistance from W.C. Clark on bass and George Rains on drums, Bell and Bowser rattled through choice selections such as 'T-Bone Shuffle' with all the alacrity of spring chickens. They were also on hand to contribute to Long John Hunter's album *Ride With Me* – a more telling gesture of solidarity would be difficult to imagine. Excellent though *It's About Time* was, it really was recorded just in time, because before they could go back into the studio to cut a follow-up, Bowser was taken ill, and he died on August 15th 1995.

Gradually the new generation replaces the old. The list of names goes on... Nowadays it's pleasing to say that not only race and age but even record company patronage is pretty much irrelevant to the spread and continued success of the blues. More than a decade since his death, it's clear that the legacy of Stevie Ray Vaughan will endure, but what we're also seeing is evidence of the world's long-running love affair with the electric guitar. And while there are Texan-born standard-bearers of the calibre of Charlie Christian, T-Bone Walker, Freddie King, Albert Collins, Billy Gibbons and the Vaughan brothers, there's no reason to suppose this love affair will ever end. Because for every kid like Stevie Ray, who managed to take blues to a whole new level, there are thousands more waiting in the wings – especially in Texas... stepping onto a makeshift stage in a little roadhouse somewhere, pumping out the latest slant on that age-old mix of blues and R&B for which their region of the US is famed around the globe.

Discography

Stevie Ray Vaughan & Double Trouble

TEXAS FLOOD

RELEASED: 1983
LABEL: Epic/Legacy
US CATALOGUE NUMBER: 65870
UK CATALOGUE NUMBER: EPC 494129

Tracklist: Love Struck Baby (S.R. Vaughan); Pride And Joy (S.R. Vaughan); Texas Flood (L.C. Davis/J.W. Scott); Tell Me (C. Burnett); Testify (G. Clinton/Taylor); Rude Mood (S.R. Vaughan); Mary Had A Little Lamb (B. Guy); Dirty Pool (D. Bramhall/S.R. Vaughan); I'm Cryin' (S.R. Vaughan); Lenny (S.R. Vaughan).
Bonus Tracks: SRV Speaks; Tin Pan Alley (AKA The Roughest Place In Town) – Live (Geddins); Testify – Live (G. Clinton/Taylor); Mary Had A Little Lamb – Live (B. Guy); Wham! – Live (L. Mack).

Performers: Stevie Ray Vaughan (guitars and vocals); Tommy Shannon (bass); Chris Layton (drums).

Recording: Downtown Studios, Los Angeles; Media Sound, New York City.
Executive Producer: John Hammond Sr.
Producers: Stevie Ray Vaughan, Chris Layton, Tommy Shannon, John Hammond, Richard Mullen, Jim Capfer.
Engineers: Richard Mullen, Lincoln Clapp, James Geddes.

Now re-mastered, and still the best album from Stevie Ray Vaughan and Double Trouble, mainly because it was recorded over just two or three days, which imparted a fresh vitality that's still as potent 20 years later.

COULDN'T STAND THE WEATHER

RELEASED: 1984
LABEL: Epic/Legacy
US CATALOGUE NUMBER: 65871
UK CATALOGUE NUMBER: EPC 494130

Tracklist: Scuttle Buttin' (S.R. Vaughan); Couldn't Stand The Weather (S.R. Vaughan); The Things That I Used To Do (Jones); Voodoo Chile (Slight Return) (J. Hendrix); Cold Shot (W.C. Clark/M. Kindred); Tin Pan Alley (AKA The Roughest Place In Town) (Geddins); Honey Bee (S.R. Vaughan); Stang's Swang (S.R. Vaughan).
Bonus Tracks: SRV Speaks; Hideaway ((King/Thompson); Look At Little Sister (H. Ballard); Give Me Back My Wig (S.R. Vaughan); Come On, Part 3 (King).

Performers: Stevie Ray Vaughan (guitars and vocals); Jimmie Vaughan (guitar); Tommy Shannon (bass); Chris Layton, Fran Christina (drums); Stan Harrison (tenor saxophone).

Recording: Power Station, New York City.
Executive Producer: John Hammond Sr.
Producers: Stevie Ray Vaughan, Chris Layton, Tommy Shannon, Richard Mullen, Jim Capfer.
Engineer: Richard Mullen.

Couldn't Stand The Weather *is the slightest of the SRV canon due to over-recording. While much of the material was familiar, the quest for perfection ultimately compromised the group's immediacy.*

SOUL TO SOUL

RELEASED: 1985
LABEL: Epic/Legacy
US CATALOGUE NUMBER: 65872
UK CATALOGUE NUMBER: EPC 494131

Tracklist: Say What (S.R. Vaughan); Lookin' Out The Window (D. Bramhall); Look At Little Sister (H. Ballard); Ain't Gone 'N' Give Up On Love (S.R. Vaughan); Gone Home (Harris); Change It (D. Bramhall); You'll Be Mine (Dixon); Empty Arms (S.R. Vaughan); Come On, Part 3 (King); Life Without You (S.R. Vaughan).
Bonus Tracks: SRV Speaks (live); Little Wing/Third Stone From The Sun (J. Hendrix); Slip Slidin' Slim.

Performers: Stevie Ray Vaughan (guitars and vocals); Jimmie Vaughan (guitar); Reese Wynans (keyboards); Tommy Shannon (bass); Chris Layton (drums); Joe Sublett (saxophones).

Recording: Dallas Sound Labs; Riverside Sound, Austin.
Executive Producer: John Hammond Sr.
Producers: Stevie Ray Vaughan, Chris Layton, Tommy Shannon, Richard Mullen, John Hammond Jr.
Engineer: Richard Mullen.

Now re-mastered, like each of the first four studio albums, with added bonus tracks, Soul To Soul *demonstrates the progress of Stevie Ray as a studio musician. No longer reliant on a basic trio, as Reese Wynans had joined to provide a counter-balance, but Stevie Ray's writing is still formulaic. Doyle Bramhall's contribution of two songs is a welcome fillip to the album's dynamic.*

LIVE ALIVE

RELEASED: 1986
LABEL: Epic
US CATALOGUE NUMBER: 40511
UK CATALOGUE NUMBER: EPC 40511

Tracklist: Say What (S.R. Vaughan); Ain't Gone 'N' Give Up On Love (S.R. Vaughan); Pride And Joy (S.R. Vaughan); Mary Had A Little Lamb (B. Guy); Superstition (S. Wonder); I'm Leaving You (Commit A Crime) (C. Burnett); Cold Shot (W.C. Clark/M. Kindred); Willie The Wimp (R. Ellsworth/B. Carter); Look At Little Sister (H. Ballard); Texas Flood (L.C. Davis/J.W. Scott); Voodoo Chile (Slight Return) (J. Hendrix); Love Struck Baby (S.R. Vaughan); Change It (D. Bramhall).

Performers: Stevie Ray Vaughan (guitars and vocals); Jimmie Vaughan (guitar); Reese Wynans (keyboards); Tommy Shannon (bass); Chris Layton (drums).

Recording: Live from Montreux; and Dallas, Austin.
Producers: Stevie Ray Vaughan, Chris Layton, Tommy Shannon, Richard Mullen.
Engineers: Kalifornia Kurt Kinzel, Gary Olazabal, Dave Richards.

Since Stevie Ray's demise there have been a slew of live albums that are always going to be more representative of the Stevie Ray 'concert experience'. Although Live Alive *is still available, tellingly it is yet to be re-mastered. If you want 'live' stuff, this is not the one to go for, because most of it was stitched together in the studio.*

IN STEP

RELEASED: 1989
LABEL: Epic/Legacy
US CATALOGUE NUMBER: 65874
UK CATALOGUE NUMBER: EPC 494132

Tracklist: The House Is Rockin' (D. Bramhall/S.R. Vaughan); Crossfire (T. Shannon/C. Layton/R. Wynans/R. Ellsworth/B. Carter); Tightrope (D. Bramhall/S.R. Vaughan); Let Me Love You Baby (W. Dixon); Leave My Girl Alone (B. Guy); Travis Walk (S.R. Vaughan); Wall Of Denial (S.R. Vaughan/D. Bramhall); Scratch N' Sniff (S.R. Vaughan/D. Bramhall); Riviera Paradise (S.R. Vaughan)
Bonus Tracks: SRV Speaks; The House Is Rockin' – Live (D. Bramhall/S.R. Vaughan); Let Me Love You Baby – Live (W. Dixon); Texas Flood – Live (L.C. Davis/J.W. Scott); Life Without You – Live (S.R. Vaughan).

Performers: Stevie Ray Vaughan (guitars and vocals); Reese Wynans (keyboards); Tommy Shannon (bass); Chris Layton (drums); Joe Sublett (saxophones).

Recording: Sound Castle Studios, Los Angeles; Summa Studios, Los Angeles; Kiva Studios, Memphis.
Producers: Stevie Ray Vaughan, Chris Layton, Tommy Shannon, Jim Gaines.
Engineers: Richard Mullen, Jim Gaines, Ryan Dorn.

Again re-mastered, the Vaughan and Bramhall writing team is shifting up a gear, and a 'clean' SRV has the chops to address anything he chooses. While this set lacks 'the up-and-at-em' quality of Texas Flood, its sophistication and completeness makes it an essential item for all SRV fanciers.

Stevie Ray Vaughan & Jimmie Vaughan

FAMILY STYLE

RELEASED: 1990
LABEL: Epic
US CATALOGUE NUMBER: ZK 46225
UK CATALOGUE NUMBER: EPC 46225

Tracklist: Hard To Be (D. Bramhall/S.R. Vaughan); White Boots (Leslie/Swan); D/FW (J. Vaughan); Good Texan (Rodgers/Vaughan); Hillbillies From Outerspace (S.R. Vaughan/J. Vaughan); Long Way From Home (D. Bramhall/S.R. Vaughan); Tick Tock (Rodgers/Vaughan/Williams); Telephone Song (D. Bramhall/S.R. Vaughan); Baboom (D. Freeman/S.R. Vaughan/J. Vaughan); Brothers (S.R. Vaughan/J. Vaughan).

Performers: Stevie Ray Vaughan (guitars and vocals); Jimmie Vaughan (guitar, steel guitar, organ and vocals); Nile Rodgers (guitar); Richard Hilton (keyboards, programming); Al Berry, Preston Hubbard (bass); Larry Aberman, Doyle Bramhall (drums); Steven Elson (baritone & tenor sax); Tawatha Agee, Curtis King, Curtis Rance King Jr, George Sims, David Spinner, Brenda White-King (backing vocals, vocals).
Horn Arrangements: Nile Rodgers.

Recording: Dallas Sound Labs.; Ardent Studios (Memphis).
Producer: Nile Rodgers.
Engineers: Patrick Dillett, John Goldberger, John Hampton, Richard Hilton.

To these ears, Family Style *is one of the most important albums of the 1990s. If some of the writing or material selection is slightly 'ho-hum',* the performances and the *spirit elevate it above the rough and tumble.*

THE SKY IS CRYING

RELEASED: 1991
LABEL: Epic
US CATALOGUE NUMBER: EK 47390
UK CATALOGUE NUMBER: EPC 47390

Tracklist: Boot Hill (Witherspoon); The Sky Is Crying (James/Levy/Lewis); Empty Arms (S.R. Vaughan); Little Wing (J. Hendrix); Wham! (L. Mack); May I Have A Talk With You (C. Burnett); Close To You (W. Dixon); Chitlins Con Carne (K. Burrell); So Excited (S.R. Vaughan); Life By The Drop (D. Bramhall/B. Logan).

Performers: Stevie Ray Vaughan (guitars and vocals); Reese Wynans (keyboards); Tommy Shannon (bass); Chris Layton (drums).

Recording: Various studios.
Producers: Stevie Ray Vaughan, Chris Layton, Tommy Shannon, Richard Mullen, Jim Gaines, Jimmie Vaughan, Jim Capfer.
Engineers: Richard Mullen, Jim Gaines.

A live album – albeit live tracks compiled from across the years by Jimmie Vaughan – this is a fine set that catches the many moods of Stevie Ray.

IN THE BEGINNING

RELEASED: 1992
LABEL: Epic
US CATALOGUE NUMBER: EK 53168
UK CATALOGUE NUMBER: EPC 472624

Tracklist: In The Open (King/Thompson); Slide Thing (S.R. Vaughan); They Call Me Guitar Hurricane (Jones); All Your Love I Miss Your Loving (Rush); Tin Pan Alley (AKA The Roughest Place In Town) (Geddins); Love Struck Baby (S.R. Vaughan); Tell Me (C. Burnett); Shake For Me (Dixon); Live Another Day (S.R. Vaughan).

Performers: Stevie Ray Vaughan (guitars, vocals); Jack Newhouse (bass); Chris Layton (drums).

Recording: Radio broadcast from Austin, Texas, April 1st 1980.
Producer: Wayne Bell.
Engineers: Malcolm Harper, Wayne Bell.

This radio broadcast has a rough and ready feel about it that's rather appealing. Hearing this it's difficult to understand why SRV had to wait three further years before cutting Texas Flood.

GREATEST HITS

RELEASED: 1995
LABEL: Epic
US CATALOGUE NUMBER: 66217
UK CATALOGUE NUMBER: EPC 481025

Tracklist: Taxman (G. Harrison); Texas Flood (L.C. Davis/J.W. Scott); The House Is Rockin' (D. Bramhall/S.R. Vaughan); Pride And Joy (S.R. Vaughan); Tightrope (D. Bramhall/S.R. Vaughan); Little Wing (J Hendrix); Crossfire (T. Shannon/C. Layton/R. Wynans/ R. Ellsworth/B. Carter); Change It (D. Bramhall); Cold Shot (W.C. Clark/M. Kindred); Couldn't Stand The Weather (S.R. Vaughan); Life Without You (S.R. Vaughan).

Performers: Stevie Ray Vaughan (guitars, vocals); Reese Wynans (keyboards); Tommy Shannon (bass); Chris Layton (drums).

Recording: Various studios.
Executive Producer: John Hammond Sr.
Producers: Stevie Ray Vaughan, Chris Layton, Tommy Shannon, Richard Mullen, Nile Rodgers, Jim Gaines, Jimmie Vaughan, Jim Capfer.
Engineers: Richard Mullen, Jim Gaines.

The performances here are fine and make a sensible introduction to SRV's career. But I can't help thinking that anyone who was really interested would have the salient records already. Texas Flood *or* The Sky Is Crying *would in fact provide the novice with a much more cogent view of what Vaughan was about.*

LIVE AT CARNEGIE HALL

RELEASED: 1997
LABEL: Epic
US CATALOGUE NUMBER: 68163
UK CATALOGUE NUMBER: EPC 68163

Tracklist: Intro; Scuttle Buttin'(S.R. Vaughan); Testify (G. Clinton/Taylor); Love Struck Baby (S.R. Vaughan); Honey Bee (S.R. Vaughan); Cold Shot (W.C. Clark/M. Kindred); Letter To My Girlfriend (Jones); Dirty Pool (D. Bramhall/ S.R. Vaughan); Pride And Joy (S.R. Vaughan); The Things That I Used To Do (Jones); COD (Gooden); Iced Over (S.R. Vaughan); Lenny (S.R. Vaughan).

Performers: Stevie Ray Vaughan (guitars and vocals); Jimmie Vaughan, John Hammond Jr (guitar); Dr John (keyboards); Tommy Shannon (bass); Chris Layton, George Rains (drums); Bob Enos (trumpet); Porky Cohen (trombone); Rich Lataille (alto sax); Greg Piccolo (tenor sax); Doug James (baritone sax); Angela Strehli (vocals).

Recording: Live at Carnegie Hall.
Executive Producer: John Hammond Sr.
Producers: Stevie Ray Vaughan, Chris Layton, Tommy Shannon, Richard Mullen.
Engineer: Richard Mullen.

Recorded around SRV's 30th birthday, the addition of the Roomful Of Blues horn section adds a different dimension, making it atypical – but that shouldn't detract from its intrinsic merit.

THE REAL DEAL: GREATEST HITS VOLUME 2

RELEASED: 1999
LABEL: Epic/Legacy
US CATALOGUE NUMBER: 65873
UK CATALOGUE NUMBER: EPC 494133

Tracklist: Love Struck Baby (S.R. Vaughan); Ain't Gone 'N' Give Up On Love (S.R. Vaughan); Scuttle Buttin' (S.R. Vaughan); Wall Of Denial (D. Bramhall/S.R. Vaughan); Lenny (S.R. Vaughan); Superstition – Live (S. Wonder); Empty Arms (S.R. Vaughan); Riviera Paradise (S.R. Vaughan); Look At Little Sister (H. Ballard); Willie The Wimp – Live (R. Ellsworth/B. Carter); Pipeline (B. Spikard/ B. Carman); Shake For Me – Live (W. Dixon); Leave My Girl Alone – Live (B. Guy); Telephone Song (D. Bramhall/ S.R. Vaughan); Voodoo Chile (Slight Return) (J. Hendrix); Life By The Drop (D. Bramhall/B. Logan).

Performers: Stevie Ray Vaughan (guitars and vocals), Jimmie Vaughan (guitar); Reese Wynans (keyboards); Tommy Shannon (bass); Chris Layton (drums).

Recording: Various studios.
Executive Producer: John Hammond Sr.
Producers: Stevie Ray Vaughan, Chris Layton, Tommy Shannon, Richard Mullen, Nile Rodgers, Jim Gaines, Jimmie Vaughan, Jim Capfer.
Engineers: Richard Mullen, Jim Gaines.

It's rare for a second volume of 'Greatest Hits' to be anything other than a chance for the record label to gull the luckless record buyer, but The Real Deal *is a good set, cut through with curios such as 'Pipeline' or 'Superstition'. The variety is sufficient to make it a worthy companion piece to its predecessor.*

BLUES AT SUNRISE

RELEASED: 2000
LABEL: Epic/Legacy
US CATALOGUE NUMBER: 63842
UK CATALOGUE NUMBER: EPC 497858

Tracklist: Ain't Gone 'N' Give Up On Love (S.R. Vaughan); Leave My Girl Alone (B. Guy); Tin Pan Alley (AKA The Roughest Place In Town) – Live (Geddins); Chitlins Con Carne (K.Burrell); The Things That I Used To Do (Jones); The Sky Is Crying (James/Levy/Lewis); Texas Flood (L.C. Davis/J.W. Scott); May I Have A Talk With You (C. Burnett); Dirty Pool (D. Bramhall/S.R. Vaughan); Blues At Sunrise – Live (King)

Performers: Stevie Ray Vaughan (guitars and vocals); Jimmie Vaughan, Johnny Copeland, Albert King (guitar); Reese Wynans, Tony Llorens (keyboards); Tommy Shannon, Gus Thornton (bass); Chris Layton, Michael Llorens (drums).

Recording: Various studios.
Executive Producer: John Hammond Sr.
Producers: Stevie Ray Vaughan. Chris Layton. Tommy Shannon. Richard Mullen. Jim Gaines. Ian Anderson and Bill Belmont.
Engineers: Richard Mullen, Jim Gaines.

A slightly curious collection really, rounding up some of the overtly bluesy items from Stevie Ray's career. Much of it has surfaced elsewhere, so this set's raison d'etre is presumably to appeal to blues fans of a more purist bent. It's a valid exercise, perhaps, and hangs together well, even if it does smack of overkill.

SRV

RELEASED: 2000
LABEL: Epic/Legacy
US CATALOGUE NUMBER: 65714
UK CATALOGUE NUMBER: EPC 497858

Tracklist: Thunderbird (Nightcaps); I'm Cryin' (S.R. Vaughan); You're Gonna Miss Me Baby – Live (Stone/Young); They Call Me Guitar Hurricane – Live (Jones); All Your Love (I Miss Your Loving) – Live (Rush); Come On, Pt 1 (King); Letter To My Girlfriend (Jones); Lenny (S.R. Vaughan); Don't Lose Your Cool – Live (A. Collins); Crosscut Saw – Live (Ford); Manic Depression – Live (J. Hendrix); Texas Flood – Live (L.C. Davis/J.W. Scott); Collins Shuffle – Live (S.R. Vaughan); Pride And Joy (S.R. Vaughan); Love Struck Baby – Live (S.R. Vaughan); Hug You, Squeeze You – Live (Hooker); Don't Stop By The Creek, Son (J. Copeland); Don't Ask Me No Questions (King); Scuttle Buttin' (S.R. Vaughan); Couldn't Stand The Weather (S.R. Vaughan); Empty Arms (S.R. Vaughan); Little Wing/Third Stone From The Sun – Live (J. Hendrix); If You Have To Know (J. & M. Drummond); These Blues Is Killing Me (A.C. Reed); Boilermaker (Vaughan/Vaughan); Change It (Bramhall); Shake N' Bake (Bramhall/S.R. Vaughan); Mary Had A Little Lamb – Live (B. Guy); I'm Leaving You (Commit A Crime) – Live (C.Burnett); Rude Mood/Pipeline – Live (Spickard/S.R. Vaughan); The Sky Is Crying – Live (James/Levy/Lewis); Voodoo Chile (Slight Return) – Live (J. Hendrix); Lookin' Out The Window – Live (Bramhall); Look At Little Sister – Live (H. Ballard); Willie The Wimp – Live (R. Ellsworth/B. Carter); The House Is Rockin' (D. Bramhall/S.R. Vaughan); Crossfire – Live (T. Shannon/ C. Layton/R. Wynans/R. Ellsworth/B. Carter); Wall Of Denial (D. Bramhall/S.R. Vaughan); Dirty Pool (D. Bramhall/ S.R. Vaughan); Going Down (King); Rude Mood – Live (S.R. Vaughan); Pride And Joy – Live (S.R. Vaughan); Testify (Clinton/Taylor); Long Way From Home (D. Bramhall/ S.R. Vaughan); Tightrope – Live (D. Bramhall/S.R. Vaughan); The Things That I Used To Do – Live (Jones); Let Me Love You Baby – Live (Dixon); Leave My Girl Alone – Live (Guy).

Performers: Stevie Ray Vaughan (guitars and vocals); Jimmie Vaughan, Johnny Copeland, Albert King, Jeff Beck, Denny Freeman, Marvin Jackson, Joel Perry (guitars); Reese Wynans, Tony Hymas, Tony Llorens, Stan Szelest (keyboards); Richard Hilton, Ken Thornton, Ken Vangel (piano); Tommy Shannon, Jackie Newhouse, Al Berry, Gus Thornton, Freddie Dixon, Tim Drummond, Brian Miller (bass); Chris Layton, Larry Aberman, Terry Bozzio, Michael Llorens, Dennis O'Neal, Jimmy Wormworth (drums); Casey

Jones, Rodney Craig (drums and vocals); Angela Strehli, Paul Ray, Vicki Hardy, Miranda Louise (vocals); A.C. Reed (saxophone and vocals); Joe Sublett (saxophone).

Recording: Various studios.
Executive Producer: John Hammond Sr.
Producers: Stevie Ray Vaughan, Chris Layton, Tommy Shannon, Richard Mullen, Jim Gaines, Lonnie Mack, A.C. Reed, Wayne Bell, John Martin, Terry Lickona, Ian Anderson and Bill Belmont.
Engineers: Richard Mullen, Jim Gaines, David Hough.

This 49-track four-CD set of alternate takes and unreleased live material is aimed at completists and aficionados. While it is a bit of a ragbag in terms of the consistency of the performances, it is a good overview of SRV's career, with lots of exceptional moments.

LIVE AT MONTREUX 1982 & 1985

RELEASED: 2001
LABEL: Epic/Legacy
US CATALOGUE NUMBER: 86151
UK CATALOGUE NUMBER: EPC 5051-61200

Tracklist: Hideaway (King/Thompson); Rude Mood (S.R. Vaughan); Pride And Joy (S.R. Vaughan); Texas Flood (L.C. Davis/J.W. Scott); Love Struck Baby (S.R. Vaughan); Dirty Pool (D. Bramhall/S.R. Vaughan); Give Me Back My Wig (T.R. Taylor); Collins' Shuffle (S.R. Vaughan); Scuttle Buttin' (S.R. Vaughan); Say What! (S.R. Vaughan); Ain't Gone 'N' Give Up On Love (S.R. Vaughan); Pride And Joy (S.R. Vaughan); Mary Had A Little Lamb (B. Guy); Tin Pan Alley (AKA The Roughest Place In Town) (Geddins); Voodoo Chile (Slight Return) (J. Hendrix); Texas Flood (L.C. Davis/J.W. Scott); Life Without You (S.R. Vaughan); Gone Home (E. Harris); Couldn't Stand The Weather (S.R. Vaughan).

Performers: Stevie Ray Vaughan (guitars and vocals); Johnny Copeland (guitar); Reese Wynans (keyboards); Tommy Shannon (bass); Chris Layton (drums).

Recording: Montreux, and mixed at Sony Music Studios, New York City.
Producers: Stevie Ray Vaughan, Bob Irwin.

An imposing juxtaposition: the gig where SRV and Double Trouble caught the attention of the rest of the world; followed by the gig where there was nothing left to prove.

THE ESSENTIAL STEVIE RAY VAUGHAN

RELEASED: 2002
LABEL: Sony
US CATALOGUE NUMBER: 86423
UK CATALOGUE NUMBER: 510019

Tracklist: Shake For Me – Live (Dixon); Rude Mood/Hideaway (S.R. Vaughan/ King/Thompson); Love Struck Baby (S.R. Vaughan); Pride and Joy (S.R. Vaughan); Texas Flood (L.C. Davis/J.W. Scott); Mary Had A Little Lamb (B.Guy); Lenny (S.R. Vaughan); Scuttle Buttin' (S.R. Vaughan); Couldn't Stand The Weather (S.R. Vaughan); The Things That I Used To Do (Jones); Cold Shot (W.C. Clark/ M. Kindred); Tin Pan Alley (AKA The Roughest Place In Town) (Geddins); Give Me Back My Wig (T.R. Taylor); Empty Arms (S.R. Vaughan); The Sky Is Crying – Live (James/ Levy/ Lewis); Voodoo Chile (Slight Return) – Live (J. Hendrix); Say What! (Vaughan); Look At Little Sister (Ballard); Change It (Bramhall); Come On Pt 3 (King); Life Without You (S.R. Vaughan); Little Wing (J. Hendrix); Willie The Wimp – Live (R. Ellsworth/B. Carter); Superstition – Live (Wonder); Leave My Girl Alone – Live (B. Guy); The House Is Rockin' (Bramhall/S.R. Vaughan); Crossfire (T. Shannon/C. Layton/ R. Wynans/R. Ellsworth/B. Carter); Tightrope (Bramhall/ S.R. Vaughan); Wall Of Denial (Bramhall/S.R. Vaughan); Riviera Paradise (S.R. Vaughan); Telephone Song (Bramhall/S.R. Vaughan); The Long Way From Home (Bramhall/S.R. Vaughan); Life By The Drop (Bramhall/Logan).

Performers: Stevie Ray Vaughan (guitars and vocals); Jimmie Vaughan, Nile Rodgers (guitars); Reese Wynans, (keyboards); Tommy Shannon, Jackie Newhouse, Al Berry, (bass); Chris Layton, Larry Aberman, (drums); Joe Sublett (saxophone)

Recording: Various studios.
Producers: Stevie Ray Vaughan, Chris Layton, Tommy Shannon, Richard Mullen, Jim Gaines, Nile Rodgers, Wayne Bell, Jim Capfer, Bob Irwin.
Engineers: Richard Mullen, Jim Gaines.

Reasonable balance of material, but only essential if you've never got around to buying an SRV album before.

Stevie Ray Vaughan's contributions to other releases

The Unplugged Collection, Vol 1, Various, Warner Bros (1994)
Bird Nest On The Ground, Doyle Bramhall, Antone's (1994)
Under The Red Sky, Bob Dylan, Columbia (1990)
Distant Drums, Brian Slawson, CBS (1988)
Loaded Dice, Bill Carter, CBS (1988)
Characters, Stevie Wonder, Motown (1987)
I'm In The Wrong Business, A.C. Reed, Alligator (1987)
Back To The Beach, Various, Columbia (1987)
Emerald City, Teena Marie, Epic (1986)
Famous Blue Raincoat, Jennifer Warnes, Cypress (1986)
Gravity, James Brown, Scotti Bros (1986)
Heartbeat, Don Johnson, Epic (1986)
Living For A Song, Roy Head, Texas Crude (1985)
Strike Like Lightning, Lonnie Mack, Alligator (1985)
Twilight Time, Bennie Wallace, Blue Note (1985)
Blues Explosion, Various, Atlantic (1984)
Let's Dance, David Bowie, EMI-America (1983)
Soulful Dress, Marcia Ball, Rounder (1983)
Texas Twister, Johnny Copeland, Rounder (1983)
A New Hi, Cast of Thousands, Tempo (1971)

Other discographies

ARC ANGELS

Arc Angels, Geffen (1992)
Probably a collector's item by now, which means there's even greater cause to hunt it down.

MARCIA BALL

Soulful Dress, Rounder (1984)
Hot Tamale Baby, Rounder (1985)
Gatorhythms, Rounder (1989)
Dreams Come True, Antone's (1990)
Ball with Lou Ann Barton and Angela Strehli.
Blue House, Rounder (1994)
Let Me Play With Your Poodle, Rounder (1997)
When left to her own devices, Ball makes very solid albums, mainly because she knows when to be understated. If push comes to shove, *Gatorhythms* is probably the best of the Rounder albums.
Sing It, Rounder (1998)
Lined up alongside Irma Thomas and Tracy Nelson, Ball comes out reasonably well, but the material and the arrangements are pedestrian.
Presumed Innocent, Alligator (2001)
Slide guitarist Sonny Landreth gives Ball's first set for a new label an extra boost.

T.D. BELL/ERBIE BOWSER

It's About Time, Antone's (1992)
A real little gem that should be bought while it's still available.

LOU ANN BARTON

Old Enough, Discovery (1982)
Read My Lips, Discovery (1989)
Barton's solo sets are well worth looking for, not least for contributions from the Vaughan brothers.
Dreams Come True, Antone's (1990)
With Marcia Ball & Angela Strehli. Pleasant but predictable.

ZU ZU BOLLIN

Texas Bluesman, Antone's (1989)
The solitary set from an important influence on Texas R&B.

DOYLE BRAMHALL

Bird's Nest On The Ground, Discovery (1994)
Fitcherburg Street, Yep Roc (2003)
Drummer and songwriter Bramhall only records when he has something to say; both these sets are well-crafted and real little gems.

DOYLE BRAMHALL II

Jellycream, RCA (1997)
Welcome, RCA (1999)
While Bramhall Junior is a fine guitarist, the material is sometimes insubstantial. Still worthing checking out.

CLARENCE 'GATEMOUTH' BROWN

The Original Peacock Recordings, Rounder (1990)
This set covers the cream of the crop from 1948-1959 – it could do with being longer, but there is no filler at all.
Just Got Lucky, Evidence (1985)
Material from the 1970s, including the French Black & Blue label. Jus' fine.
Pressure Cooker, Alligator (1985)
Recorded in 1973 with an all-star cast, Brown makes no bones about his ability to cut it with the great and the good.
Alright Again!, Rounder (1981)
Cut in 1981, Brown's versatility and apparent indefatigability is intoxicating.
Real Life (Live), Rounder (1985)
Captured live in Fort Worth and pretty representative of a Brown concert.
Standing My Ground, Alligator (1989)
Diverse but effective.
Okie Dokie Stomp, Bullseye Blues (1999)
This collection, taken from the three Rounder albums of the 1980s, is a good starting point for those just discovering Brown.
American Music, Texas Style, Verve (1999)
The title says it all..
Back To Bogalusa, Blue Thumb (2001)
Still going strong after all these years, Brown shows little aptitude for settling back.

CLIFTON CHENIER

Out West, Arhoolie (1971)
Bon Ton Roulet, Arhoolie (1981)
The Chenier catalogue is vast. These two fine sets give an impression of what he was about
Zydeco Dynamite: The Clifton Chenier Anthology, Rhino (1993)
Spanning from 1954 until his death, this 40-track overview is excellent.

CHARLIE CHRISTIAN

Solo Flight (1939-41), Vintage Jazz (1993)
Radio broadcasts with the Benny Goodman Sextet, live and untampered with; the sound is fine too.
The Immortal Charlie Christian, Columbia/Legacy (2001)
Featuring Monk and Gillespie, among others, this complements Christian's work with Goodman.
The Genius Of The Electric Guitar (Box Set), Columbia Jazz (2002)
A defining set that is not just about context it is also sublime music. See, history does not have to be dull.

W.C. CLARK

Hearts Of Gold, Black Top (1994)
Texas Soul, Black Top (1995)
From Austin With Soul, Alligator (2002)
A defining influence in Austin who deserves far wider exposure; *Hearts Of Gold* is the classic.

ALBERT COLLINS

Truckin' With Albert Collins, MCA (1969)
This set originally emerged as *The Cool Sound Of Albert Collins* in 1965, and then it was re-issued by Blue Thumb in 1969. The signature sound of the 'master of the Telecaster' is fully developed.
Ice Pickin', Alligator (1978)
This could be one of the Iceman's defining hours. There are few more compelling chunks of contemporary electric blues around.
Frostbite, Alligator (1980)
Frozen Alive, Alligator (1981)
Don't Lose Your Cool, Alligator (1983)
These later Alligator sets show Collins extending his vocal

and compositional ability, but not at the expense of his guitar work, which remains focused and attacking.
Showdown, Alligator (1985)
Collins, Copeland and Robert Cray on this Grammy-award-winning collaboration that must be heard.
The Complete Imperial Recordings, EMI (1991)
These sessions were recorded at the end of the 1960s, before he acquired the following of later years.
Collins Mix: The Best, Pointblank (1995)
Fine performances, with cameos from admirers, make this collection a fitting tribute.
Live 92/93, Pointblank (1995)
Good companion piece to *Collins Mix.*
Deluxe Edition, Alligator (1997)
Lots of albums from which to extract material; bought alongside *Truckin' With Albert Collins,* you are on the way to having a complete picture.

JOHNNY COPELAND

Make My Home Where I Hang My Hat, Rounder (1982)
Texas Twister, Rounder (1983)
Featuring a cameo from Stevie Ray Vaughan, Texas Twister is a top-of-the-range Copeland set.
Bringing It All Back Home, Rounder (1986)
Copeland digs back and draws in African elements.
Ain't Nothing But A Party, Rounder (1988)
A live set that picked up a Grammy nomination.
When The Rain Starts A Fallin', Rounder (1988)
Another worthwhile set.
The Collection Volume 1, Collectables (1988)
The Collection Volume 2, Collectables (1990)
These two sets cover the early years of Copeland's career, but Volume 2 carries on up to the Rounder years. So there are some very quirky stylistic shifts, but these only emphasise his eclecticism.
The Crazy Cajun Recordings, Edsel (1999)
More early recordings, this time with producer Huey Meaux.
Honky Tonkin', Bullseye Blues (1999)
Good round-up of the Rounder material, which is some compensation for the absence of the later Polygram output.

PEE WEE CRAYTON

The Things I Used To Do, Vanguard, (1971)
The first and best of Pee Wee's comeback albums.
Everyday I Have The Blues, Pablo (1982)
Another late session with such august types as Barney Kessel and Plas Johnson.
The Modern Legacy, Volume 1, Ace (1996)
The Modern Legacy, Volume 2: Blues Guitar, Ace (2000)
A comprehensive look at Pee Wee's tenure with the Modern label.
The Essential Pee Wee Crayton: Blues After Hours, Indigo (2002)
Less comprehensive, naturally, but succinct.

DOUBLE TROUBLE

Been A Long Time, Tone-Cool (2001)
Well-balanced post-SRV debut from SRV's backing band, with a cast of thousands guesting on guitar and vocals.

CHRIS DUARTE

Texas Sugar/Strat Magik, Silvertone (1994)
Tailspin Headwhack, Silvertone (1997)
Love Is Greater Than Me, Zoe (2000)
Texas Sugar/Strat Magick is the raw debut, though *Love Is Greater Than Me* has the better material.

EDDIE DURHAM

Blue Bone, JSP (1982)
Despite Durham's early incursions with the electric guitar, there is not much of the man himself available on record, so this set has a certain relevance.

JOE ELY

Joe Ely, MCA (1977)
Honky Tonk Masquerade, MCA, (1978)
First two albums from defining writer who transcends category.
Live Shots, MCA (1980)
Live At Liberty Lunch, MCA (1990)
Live At Antone's, Rounder (2000)
Ely is in his element live on-stage.
Lord Of The Highway, Hightone (1987)
Letter To Laredo, MCA (1995)
Twistin' In The Wind, MCA (1998)
Later studio albums from Ely, which illustrate his growth as a

writer and performer.
The Best Of Joe Ely, MCA (2000)
From Lubbock To Laredo: Best of (Live), MCA (2002)
Two anthologies, one from the studio, one live – both are equally good.

THE FABULOUS THUNDERBIRDS

The Fabulous Thunderbirds, Chrysalis (1979)
What's The Word, Benchmark (1980)
Butt Rockin', Benchmark (1981)
T-Bird Rhythm, Benchmark (1982)
The T-Birds first four albums are representative. The debut is very punchy and direct – a classic.The more albums they recorded the more polished they became.
Tuff Enuff, Epic (1986)
The first and most successful album for Epic.
The Essential, Chrysalis (1991)
Another round-up of the Chrysalis years.
Hot Stuff: The Greatest Hits (1992)
Collection of the more 'rock-oriented' material from the Epic years.
Wrap It Up, Sony (1993)
Another collection of the best material from the Epic years.
Girls Go Wild, Benchmark (2002)
This is the first album, *Fabulous Thunderbirds,* repackaged and retitled with three extra tracks.
Live, CMC (2002)
Self-explanatory and reasonably entertaining.

FLATLANDERS

More A Legend Than A Band, Rounder (1990)
Now Again, New West (2002)
Occasional aggregation that could only come from Texas

ANSON FUNDERBURGH

Sins, Black Top (1987)
Tell Me What I Want To Hear, Black Top (1991)
That's What They Want, Black Top (1997)
In partnership with Sam Myers, Funderburgh is one of the toughest and most authoritative blues guitarists to come around for years.
Thru' The Years: A Retrospective, Black Top (1999)
A pretty good cross section of Funderburgh's career

ROY GAINES

Bluesman For Life, JSP (1998)
T-Bone Walker is the role model for this survivor

JOE 'GUITAR' HUGHES

If You Want to See These Blues, Black Top (1989)
Texas Guitar Slinger, Bullseye Blues (1996)
Stuff Like That, Blues Express (2001)
Despite his journeyman status Hughes delivers high quality albums every time. Although long periods elapse between each release, every track is made to count.

LONG JOHN HUNTER

Ride With Me, Spindletop (1992)
Border Town Legend, Alligator (1996)
Swingin' From The Rafters, Alligator (1997)
Ooh Wee Pretty Baby!, Norton (1999)
Hunter's output is a model of consistency. *Ride With Me* lacks some of the polish of later sets – which might not be a bad thing.

ERIC JOHNSON

Tones, Reprise (1986)
Ah Via Musicom, Capitol (1990)
The first two official albums from Johnson, which vouch-safed an incredible guitar technique.
Seven Worlds, Ark 21 (1998)
Early demos that preceded *Tones.*
Alien Love Child: Live And Beyond, Favoured Nations (2000)
With a title like that, what more do you want?

ANDREW 'JUNIOR BOY' JONES

I Need Time, JSP (1997)
This is all the evidence you need that Jones deserves to be far better known.

TUTU JONES

I'm For Real, JSP (1994)
Staying Power, Bullseye Blues (1998)
Jones' material may be a little light on occasions and the productions too pristine, but his demeanour is as muscular as they come.

FREDDIE KING

Let's Hide Away And Dance Away, King (1961)
The early sides that influenced countless guitarists.
Freddie King Is A Blues Master, Atlantic (1969)
Accompanied by King Curtis , David 'Fathead' Newman and James Booker, King shows an early affinity with the 'rock legends' that will follow.
Gettin' Ready, Shelter (1971)
Texas Cannonball, Shelter (1972)
The 'rock' influences are in the ascendant, yet the charismatic King easily holds his own.
Hideaway: The Best of Freddie King, Rhino (1993)
King's take on the blues and R&B was eclectic to say the least but, because his style was heavily accented towards rock audiences, he was able to create a signature that was contemporary and potent. This collection chronicles that evolution.
Blues Guitar Hero, Ace (1994)
Early sides – plangent and pithy. Good stuff.
King Of The Blues, EMI/Shelter (1995)
All the Shelter stuff and a few unissued goodies on two CDs. A bit patchy.
Live At The Electric Ballroom 1976, Black Top (1996)
This uneven set is powerful and immediate, and gives a much better feel of how King performed in front of local crowds, instead of the big rock audiences he played for in later years.

SMOKIN' JOE KUBEK

Steppin' Out Texas Style, Bullseye Blues (1991)
Texas Cadillac, Bullseye Blues (1993)
Got My Mind Back, Bullseye Blues (1996)
Kubek and sidekick B'nois King at their most convincing.
Roadhouse Research, Blind Pig (2003)
Not a great front cover, but the music is up to par.

JONNY LANG

Lie To Me, A&M (1997)
Wander This World, A&M (1998)
Fine vocalist and songwriter, with taut economical guitar work, Lang is one of the best prospects for years

LONNIE MACK

Strike Like Lightning, Alligator (1985)
Produced by Stevie Ray Vaughan – not that you'd notice, particularly. Still, worth catching.
Memphis Wham!, Ace (1999)
Strictly speaking, Mack – the archetypal blue collar rocker – falls beyond the remit of this book, but there is the legitimate link to SRV. And there is some excellent stuff here.

DELBERT McCLINTON

Live From Austin, Alligator (1989)
Pure R&B that kicks like a mule.
Never Been Rocked Enough, Curb (1992)
Includes the Grammy-award-winning duet with Bonnie Raitt, 'Good Man, Good Woman'.
Delbert McClinton, Curb (1993)
Victim Of Life's Circumstances/Genuine Cowhide, Raven (1996)
Combining two of the ABC albums, back to back, presents a strong case for McClinton's durability
One Of The Fortunate Few, Rising Tide (1997)
Fine songwriting that draws from country, R&B and blues. Few do it better.
The Crazy Cajun Recordings, Edsel (1999)
Archive bits and bobs from the early 1960s.
The Ultimate Collection, Hip O (1999)
The title says it all, with material from the 1970s–late 1990s.
The Jealous Kind/Plain From The Heart, Raven (2001)
The two Capitol albums in one package.
Nothing Personal, New West (2001)
Room To Breathe, New West (2001)
Although McClinton always calls upon famous friends, his albums retain his own identity.
Second Wind/Keeper Of The Flame, Raven (2002)
The two Mercury albums, back to back.

MIKE MORGAN & THE CRAWL

Mighty Fine Dancin', Black Top (1991)
Full Moon Over Dallas, Black Top (1992)
Looky Here, Black Top (1996)
The Road, Black Top (1998)
Dallas-ite Morgan's finer moments – each as good as the other.

OMAR & THE HOWLERS

I Told You So, Austin (1984)
Hard Times In The Land Of Plenty, Sony Special (1987)
Two sets from early in his career which show his writing, vocals and guitar work evolving fast.
Live At Paradiso, Bullseye Blues (1991)
Omar and the boys on a stage, just where they like to be.
The Screamin' Cat, Provogue (2000)
Big Delta, Blind Pig (2002)
Thoroughly established now, Omar's records are reliable and always worthwhile. Try to see him play live first, though

KID RAMOS

Two Hands One Heart, Black Top (1995)
Kid Ramos, Evidence (1999)
West Coast House Party, Evidence (2000)
Greasy Kid's Stuff, Evidence (2001)
A recent collaborator of Kim Wilson's, Ramos' solo stuff is worth tracking down.

SHERMAN ROBERTSON

I'm The Man, Atlantic/Code Blue (1994)
Here And Now, Atlantic/Code Blue (1996)
Going Back Home, AudioQuest (1998)
Underexposed but supremely accomplished, Robertson's second album might just have the edge on the other two – it's a close thing.

DUKE ROBILLARD

Rockin' Blues, Rounder (1988)
You Got Me, Rounder (1988)
Robillard's forte is rockin' blues; *You Got Me* features an array of guest including Jimmie Vaughan.
Swing, Rounder (1989)
After Hours Swing Session, Rounder (1990)
The jazzy side of Robillard.
Turn It Around, Rounder (1990)
The robust Robillard with a rollicking rocker of a record.
Duke's Blues, Pointblank (1996)
A fine stylistic resumé of music that influenced Robillard.
Stretchin' Out Live, Stony Plain (1998)
Substantially the same set that he performed live during a tour of Canada with Jimmy Witherspoon.
Plays Blues: The Rounder Years, Bullseye Blues (1997)
Plays Jazz: The Rounder Years, Bullseye Blues (1997)
Two anthologies.
New Blues For Modern Man, Shanachie (1999)
Another solid set bursting with health and vitality.
Conversations In Swing Guitar, Stony Plain (1999)
With jazz guitarist Herb Ellis.
Explorer, Shanachie (2000)
Robillard casts his net a little further afield to embrace Afro-cuban rhythms and the sounds of New Orleans.
Living With The Blues, Stony Plain (2002)

ROOMFUL OF BLUES

Dance All Night, Bullseye Blues (1994)
Watch You When You Go, Rounder (2001)
Somehow the band's up-front live stage sound seldom translates onto album. Having said that, Roomful Of Blues have never tried to commercialise their sound. Which is to their credit.
The Blues I'll Make You Happy Too, Rounder (2000)
A thorough round-up of the group's recorded achievements to tie in with the 30th anniversary of the Rounder label.

DOUG SAHM (SEE ALSO SIR DOUGLAS QUINTET, TEXAS TORNADOS)

Texas Rock for Country Rollers, Edsel (1976)
Back To The 'Dillo, Edsel (1988)
Two samplings from the extensive Sahm catalogue dating from the 1970s.
Juke Box Music, Antone's (1989)
Sahm in R&B mode, with the house band at Antone's. Excellent
Doug Sahm & Friends: The Best Of Doug Sahm's Atlantic Sessions, Rhino (1995)
This overview provides an interesting glimpse into the weird and wacky world of Sahm. But his 1973 set with Bob Dylan, *Doug Sahm & His Band*, is a watershed performance, drawing together those elements that makes Texas R&B a hybrid.
She's About A Mover: The Best Of Crazy Cajun, Edsel (1999)
Early selections from Sahm and the Sir Douglas Quintet – but don't be misled, his early stuff is as important as the

later, it's just more rough around the edges.
San Antonio Rock: The Harlem Recordings (1957-61) Norton (2000)
Before Sir Douglas Quintet, Little Doug had his day, and then other bands with different line-ups. Interesting and quirky, providing a link between the R&B of Texas and the garage bands that would emerge in the mid 1960s.
The Return Of Wayne Douglas, Evangeline (2000)
Get A Life, Munich (2001)
Two of Sahm's final recordings – the quality is variable, but such is Sahm's cachet that it really doesn't matter too much.

CHARLIE SEXTON

Pictures For Pleasure, MCA (1985)
Charlie Sexton, MCA (1989)
Under The Wishing Tree, MCA (1995)
The most diverse of all Sexton's albums, but years of being a sideman have shown him the virtue of economy.

KENNY WAYNE SHEPHERD

Ledbetter Heights, Giant (1995)
Live On, Giant (1999)
A teenage axeman, hot and ready to strike...

SIR DOUGLAS QUINTET (SEE ALSO DOUG SAHM, TEXAS TORNADOS)

Mendocino, Acadia (2002)
Together After Five, Acadia (2002)
Sir Douglas Quintet + 2 = (Honky Blues), Acadia (2002)
The original Sir Douglas Quintet albums recorded for Smash, with tracks from the Mercury set *Rough Edges* liberally distributed as bonus tracks.

STORYVILLE

Piece Of Your Soul, Code Blue (1996)
A defining set of the genre.
Dog Years, Atlantic (1998)
A few too many guest stars and routine material means *Dog Years* lacks the focus of its predecessor.

SUSAN TEDESCHI

Just Won't Burn, Tone-Cool (1998)
Wait For Me, Tone-Cool (2002)
Versatile guitarist with a great voice and superior compositional skills.

TEXAS TORNADOS (SEE ALSO SIR DOUGLAS QUINTET, DOUG SAHM)

Texas Tornados, Reprise (1990)
Sahm almost in acoustic mode, with celebrated chums like Flaco Jimenez and Freddy Fender. There's a Spanish version of this set if you search hard enough.
Zone Of Our Own, Reprise (1991)
Hangin' On By A Thread, Reprise (1992)
Two last two albums before The Tornados took a break to do other things. Instrumentally and vocally they catch a rare spare spirit that still works.
The Best Of The Texas Tornados, Reprise (1994)
Good overview of the first three albums.
Four Aces, Reprise (1996)
The reformed Tornados – not their best album, but still knocks corners off most rivals.
Live From The Limo, Volume 1, Virgin (1999)
Another late set from the band, caught at Antone's. Sahm died later that year.

JIMMIE VAUGHAN

Strange Pleasures, Epic (1995)
It was a long time coming, but *Strange Pleasures* is an apt postscript to *Family Style.*
Out There, Sony (1998)
Not as convincing as the predecessor.
Do You Get The Blues? Artemis (2001)
A fine, fine set that gets better the more you listen to it.

T-BONE WALKER

T-Bone Blues, Atlantic (1959)
The Complete Recordings Of T-Bone Walker, 1940-1954, Mosaic (1990)
The Complete Imperial Recordings, Capitol (1991)
The Complete Capitol/Black & White Recordings, Capitol (1995)
Blues Masters: The Very Best Of T-Bone Walker, Rhino (2000)
The Original Source, Proper (2002)
Walker's catalogue is a minefield pitted with compilations

that cover essentially the same territory. The best course of action is to splash out on the Mosaic set, with six CDs, and consider your job almost done. Of the individual albums, *T-Bone Blues*, is worth hunting to ground.

JOHNNY 'GUITAR' WATSON

Lone Ranger, Fantasy (1996)
Essentially two albums from the 1970s combined – *Listen* (1973) and *I Don't Want To Be Alone Stranger* (1975).
The Very Best Of Johnny 'Guitar' Watson: In Loving Memory, Collectables (1996)
Extracted from the DJM catalogue, not typical of Watson as such but still a good example of the idiosyncratic guitarist.
The Very Best Of Johnny 'Guitar' Watson, Rhino (1999)
Top notch. Compiled by Jimmie Vaughan – can't think of a higher recommendation than that.
The Essential Johnny 'Guitar' Watson, Fuel 2000 (2002)
Early stuff, rather lacking a context – but then Watson recorded so much for so many different labels.

HOP WILSON

Steel Guitar Flash! Ace (1988)
Houston Ghetto Blues, Bullseye Blues (1993)
There's some overlap here, as Wilson was not the most prolific of recording artists – but either one of these would be fine.

U.P. WILSON

Attack Of The Atomic Guitar (Live), Red Lightnin' (1992)
Boogie Boy: Texas Guitar Returns, JSP (1995)
The Best Of Texas Blues Guitar Tornado, JSP (1998)
Alongside vocalist Robert Ealey, Wilson is a survivor of the Dallas-Fort Worth connection.

KIM WILSON

Tigerman, Antone's (1993)
That's Life, Discovery (1994)
My Blues, Blue Collar (1997)
Smokin' Joint, MC Records (2001)
The Wilson solo output has more of a traditional flavour than that of The Fabulous Thunderbirds – there's also a consistency here that is sometimes lacking in the T-Birds' catalogue.

JOHNNY WINTER

Johnny Winter, Columbia (1969)
Second Winter, Columbia (1970)
Despite what Winter may have achieved subsequently, these first two sets are the dog's dangly bits: Winter had plenty of time to work out where he was going, and what he wanted to do. These albums convey all the feral energy and aggression of a man at the top of his game. Blues and rock were genuine bedfellows hereafter.
Johnny Winter And … , DCC (1970)
Johnny Winter And … Live! , Columbia (1971)
Although there are some limitations to Winter's style, and the progress to a rock base rather than blues seems inexorable, these two albums (from the studio and stage respectively) are pretty good.
Still Alive And Well, Columbia (1973).
Saints And Sinners Columbia (1974)
A spell in rehab failed to quell the ardour. When *Saints And Sinners* was reissued it included the previously unreleased track, 'Dirty'.
Together – Live!, Blue Sky (1978)
With brother Edgar, and plenty of zip.
Nothing But The Blues, Blue Sky (1978)
Winter cut half-a-dozen albums for Blue Sky, all decent enough, but this set shows him moving back to playing the blues.
Guitar Slinger, Alligator (1984)
The best of the Alligator albums. No question.
Let Me In, Pointblank (1991)
Loads of famous friends join in for this amiable canter. Winter doesn't really push the envelope with much conviction, but he is still passionate about what he does.
Scorchin' Blues, Epic/Legacy (1992)
Early Columbia material up to and including selected items from the Blue Sky catalogue. Checking in at 45 minutes or so this is not the best value you're ever going to find, but OK nevertheless.
Johnny Winter: A Rock And Roll Collection, Columbia/Legacy (1994)
The title says it all: if you're approaching the blues from the 'rock' end of the spectrum, this is a good perspective of the Columbia years from 1969 until 1979.
Deluxe Edition, Alligator (2001)

The best from the three Alligator albums.
The Best Of Johnny Winter, Columbia/Legacy (2002)
16 tracks taken from the early years between 1969 and 1971, with a few exceptions. But if you only want one Johnny Winter record, either this or *Second Winter* are the ones to look for.

ZZ TOP

ZZ Top's First Album, Warner Bros (1970)
Rio Grande Mud, Warner Bros (1972)
The Top's first forays into the recording firmament have a gritty directness that indicate the band's bluesy beginnings.
Trés Hombres, Warner Bros (1973)
Not as sophisticated perhaps as some of the later efforts, but the tongue-in-cheek humour is very appealing. And Billy Gibbons shows he is probably one of the most underrated guitarist on the planet.
Fandango, Warner Bros (1975)
Half in the studio and half live, and features 'Tush'.
Deguello, Warner Bros (1979)
Top's best album by a stretch.
Eliminator, Warner Bros (1983)
Afterburner, Warner Bros (1985)
Swanky and sophisticated, despite their popularity these two sets are a little too contrived for their own good – but that's with the doubtful benefit of hindsight.
Greatest Hits, Warner Bros (1992)
It's all true. For those with a penchant for non-political correctness, *Greatest Hits* is also available on video.
Antenna, RCA (1994)
Impervious to the fickle finger of fashion, Top just keep right on doing what they have always done. Fair enough.
One Foot In The Blues, Warner Bros (1994)
Some have suggested this compilation of the Top's bluesy side is a cynical exercise in exploitation. They're wrong – the blues and Top are inseparable, and this proves it.
Rhythmeen, RCA (1994)
Minus the synths and drum machine and all that stuff, the only thing they need on this set is some decent songs. But the energy distracts from such quibbles.

Bibliography

Alexander, Charles (ed), *Masters Of Jazz Guitar*, Balafon, London, 1999

Bacon, Tony & Day, Paul, *The Fender Book*, Balafon, London, 1992

Betrock, Alan, *Girl Groups: The Story Of A Sound*, Delilah, New York, 1982

Booth, Stanley, *Rhythm Oil*, Pantheon, London, 1991

Brunning, Bob, *Blues In Britain*, Blandford, London, 1995

Carson, Annette, *Jeff Beck: Crazy Fingers,* Backbeat Books, San Francisco, 2001

Charles, Ray, with Ritz, David, *Brother Ray,* Dial Press, New York, 1978

Davis, Francis, *The History Of The Blues,* Secker & Warburg. London, 1995

Dixon, Willie, with Don Snowden, *I Am The Blues: The Willie Dixon Story*, Da Capo, New York, 1989

Feather, Leonard, *The Encyclopedia Of Jazz,* Da Capo, New York, 1960

Freeman, Scott, *Midnight Riders: The Story Of The Allman Brothers Band*, Little, Brown & Co, London, 1995

Gaar, Gillian, *She's A Rebel,* Blandford, London, 1993

George, Nelson, *The Death Of Rhythm & Blues,* Omnibus, London, 1988

Gillett, Charlie, *The Sound Of The City,* Souvenir, London, 1970; *Making Tracks: Atlantic Records & The Growth Of A Multi-Billion Dollar Industry Souvenir*, London, 1974

Greig, Charlotte, *Will You Still Love Me Tomorrow?* Virago, London, 1989

Gregory, Hugh, *Soul Music A-Z,* Da Capo, New York, 1995; *1000 Great Guitarists,* Balafon, London, 1994: *The Real Rhythm & Blues,* Blandford, London, 1998

Guralnick, Peter, *Sweet Soul Music,* Virgin, London,1986; *Feel Like Going Home,* Omnibus, London, 1981

Hammond, John, with Irving Townsend, *John Hammond On Record: An Autobiography*, Summit, New York, 1977

Hardy, Phil, and Laing, Dave, *The Faber Companion To 20th Century Popular Music*, Faber, London, 1990

Hirshey, Gerri, *Nowhere To Run,* Macmillan, London, 1984

Hoskyns, Barney, *Say It One Time For The Broken Hearted: The Country Side Of Southern Soul.* Fontana, London, 1987

Jackson, John, *Big Beat Heat,* Schirmer, Munich, 1991

Jones, Leroi, *Black Music,* William Morrow & Co, New York, 1968

Larkin, Colin (ed), *The Guinness Encyclopedia Of Popular Music,* Guinness Publishing, London, 1997

Marcus, Greil, *Mystery Train,* Omnibus, London, 1979

Marsh, Dave, *The Heart Of Rock & Soul,* Penguin, London, 1989

Murray, Charles Shaar, *Crosstown Traffic,* Faber, London, 1989

Obrecht, Jas (ed), *Rollin' And Tumblin': The Postwar Blues Guitarists,* Miller Freeman, San Francisco, 2000

Patoski, Joe Nick, and Crawford, Bill, *Stevie Ray Vaughan: Caught In The Crossfire,* Little, Brown & Co, New York, 1993

Sawyer, Charles, *B.B. King: The Authorised Biography,* Blandford, London, 1981

Shaw, Arnold, *Honkers And Shouters,* Collier, New York, 1978

Tipaldi, Art, *Children Of The Blues,* Backbeat Books, San Francisco, 2002

Tosches, Nick, *The Unsung Heroes Of Rock'N'Roll,* Secker & Warburg, London, 1991

Wade, Dorothy, and Picardie, Justine, *Music Man,* W.W. Norton, New York, 1990

Warner, Alan, *Who Sang What In Rock'N'Roll,* Blandford, London, 1990

Wexler, Jerry, with Ritz, David, *Rhythm And The Blues,* Random, New York, 1993

White, Forrest, *Fender: The Inside Story,* Miller Freeman, San Francisco, 1994

Williams, Richard, *The Sound Of Phil Spector: Out Of His Head,* Abacus, London, 1974

Index

A

A New Hi 48
A Piece of Your Soul 151
Aberman, Larry 116
Adams, Johnny 156
After Hours Swing Session 156
'Ain't Gone 'N' Give Up On Love' 90, 99, 143
Alcoholics Anonymous 104, 119
Alexander, John Henry 52
Allen, Terry 151
Allison, Luther 108
Allman Brothers Band, The 96
Alomar, Carlos 75
American Caravan 99
amplification 124
Anderle, David 50
Antone, Clifford 54
Antone's (club) 54, 58, 150
Arc Angels, The 150
Asleep At The Wheel 80
Atkinson, Sweet Pea 151
Austin City Limits 113
Austin Lounge Lizards 151
Australia and New Zealand tour 87

B

Back To The Beach 105
Bailey, Lenny 66, 105
Ball, Marcia 88
Ballard, Hank 91, 99
Bangham, Kid 154
Bartholomew, Dave 15
Barton, Lou Ann 58, 60-61, 64-66, 113, 142, 146, 151-2
Basie, Count 10
Beard, Frank 36
Beck, Jeff 111, 145
Beck, Roscoe 167
Been A Long Time 151
Bell, T.D. 170
Benno, Mark 49-50
Benson, Ray 81
Berry, Al 116
Berry, Chuck 111, 113, 127
Best Of Friends 145
Betts, Dickey 96
Big Delta 167
Bite Me 167
Blackbird 47, 49
Bland, Bobby 52, 58
Blue Texas Soul 170
Bluesman For Life 170
Bob Wills & His Texas Cowboys 113
Bogguss, Suzy 148
Bollin, Zuzu 33
Booker T & The MGs 113
Boom Boom 142
'Boot Hill' 111, 141
Border Town Legend 169
Bowie, David 74, 113, 127
Bowser, Ernie 170
Bramhall, Doyle 45, 50, 80, 91, 109, 116, 142, 150
Bramhall, Doyle (II) 150, 152
Brandenberg, Robert 'Cutter' 49, 68, 81, 87
Brandon, Gene 166
Brantley, Junior 145
Brooks, Bobby 119
Brooks, Harvey 159
Brooks, Lonnie 108
Broonzy, Big Bill 12
Brown, Clarence 'Gatemouth' 21-23
Brown, James 96, 130
Browne, Colin 119
Browne, Jackson 74, 119
Browne, Nigel 119
Bruton, Stephen 62, 148, 152
Bryant, Jimmy 113
Buck, Mike 58
Burrell, Kenny 110, 141
Bush, President George 111
Butt Rockin' 72, 165
Butterfield, Paul 105

C

Calloway, Cab 12
Canned Heat 159
Carnegie Hall 87
Carter, Bill 109
Change In My Pocket 165
'Change It' 90-1
Chantays, The 105
Charter programme 104
Chenier, Clifton 168
Chessmen, The 45
'China Girl' 75
'Chitlins Con Carne' 130, 141
Christian, Charlie 8, 10-12, 113
Christina, Fran 72, 154
Clapton, Eric 27, 40, 87, 105, 118, 141, 143, 145, 151
Clark, Glen 139
Clark, W.C. 60, 86, 113, 171
Clash, The 73
Clement, Jack 65
Clinton, George 79
Clouds of Joy 8
Cobras, The 44, 90, 145
Cocker, Joe 117
'Coffee Cup' 50
'Cold Shot' 86, 144
Coleman, Deborah 108
Collins, Albert 24, 27-30, 58, 108, 144
Colonna, Roddy 49
Columbia Records (CBS) 12, 106, 167
'Come On' 91
Commander Cody & his Lost Planet Airmen 54
Conversations In Swing Guitar 157
Cooder, Ry 138
Copeland, Johnny 24, 30-31, 75, 145
Copeland, Shemekia 31
Cotton, James 146
Couldn't Stand The Weather 86, 128
'Couldn't Stand The Weather' 128
Cox, Ida 12
Craig, Robert 52
Crawl, The 166
Cray, Robert 105, 118, 141, 143
Crayton, Pee Wee 16-20
Cream 46
'Crossfire' 109, 117, 129
Cuber, Ronnie 158

D

'D/FW' 116
Dale, Dick 105
Dangerous Place 157
Davies, Debbie 165
Davis, Kim 47
de Plicque, Christian 47
Deis, Noel 47
Delbert & Glen 139
Delta Blues Festival, Mississippi 87
DeQuattro, Thomas 156
Diddley, Bo 113
'Dirty Pool' 50, 80, 128
Dixie Flyers 50
Dixie Hummingbirds, The 158
Dixon, Willie 58, 91, 110
Do You Get The Blues? 145
Dog Years 151
Domino, Antoine 'Fats' 15
Don Johnson 96
'Don't Ask Me No Questions' 145
Double Trouble 62, 72, 99, 117, 118, 143, 145, 148, 152
Dr John 87, 142, 143, 144, 152
Duarte, Chris 168
Duckworth, Tim 96
Duke Robillard & The Pleasure Kings 156
Duke's Blues 157
Durham, Eddie 8
Dyer, John 65, 79
Dyke & The Blazers 111
Dykes, Omar Kent 166
Dylan, Bob 113, 151

E

Edmunds, Dave 92-93, 103
Ellis, Herb 157
Ellsworth, Ruth 109
Ely, Joe 135, 151
Emerald City 96
Enright, Thomas 156
Epic (label) 68, 78, 98, 105, 158
Escovedo, Alejandro 151
Etheridge, Billy 50
Explorer 158

F

Fabre, Tom 161
Fabulous Thunderbirds, The 58, 70, 92, 112-113, 117, 134, 141, 154, 159-161
Family Style 113-117, 132, 142
Fender amplifiers 124
Fender Stratocaster 124
Fender, Freddy 137
Ferguson, Keith 51
Ferguson, Keith 58
Flatlanders, The 135
Fletcher, Kirk 161
Flynn, Bill 161
Ford, Robben 113
Frame, David 47
Freeman, Charlie 50
Freeman, Denny 52, 57, 113, 142, 144, 152
From Hell To Paradise 151
Froom, Mitchelll 151
Funderburgh, Anson 164

G

Gaineling 170
Gaines, Jim 108
Gaines, Roy 170
Gibbons, Billy 36
Gibson 335 124
Gibson ES150 8
Gibson Jimmy Smith 124
Gibson Les Paul 124
Glaub, Bob 169
'Goin' Down' 111, 145
Going Back Home 169
Gonyea, Troy 161
'Good Texan' 116
Goodman, Benny 11
Gordon, Robert 156
Gordon, Rosco 157
Got My Mind Back 167
Graceland 169
Gracey, Joe 63
Grammy award 111
Grand Union 165
Grand, Otis 165
Greasy Kid's Stuff 159
Green, Grant 110
Greezy Wheels 63
Grissom, David 151, 159
Groove Tubes pre-amp 124
Guitar Player awards 84
Guitar Slim 14, 86, 144
Guitar World 120
Guitarist 120
Guy, Buddy 54, 58, 79, 110-111, 118, 141,143, 148

H
Ham, Bill 51, 99
Hamilton, Scott 156-7
Hammond, John 11, 77, 84, 90, 108
Hard Times In The Land Of Plenty 167
'Hard To Be' 113, 116
Harman, James 159
Harris, Emmylou 150
Harrison, George 113
Hayward, Richie 169
Healey, Jeff 118
Heart of Texas Music 51
Heartbeat 96
Henderson, Mike 148
Hendrix, Jimi 46, 86, 110, 125, 128, 141
Here & Now 168
Hiatt, John 118
High Water 159
Hill, Joe 36
'Hillbillies From Outer Space' 116
'Hip Hip Baby' 65
Hodges, Alex 80, 94, 119
Holliman, Clarence 159
Holmes, Richard 'Groove' 113
Holt, David 151
'Honey Bee' 86, 144
Hooker, John Lee 54, 108, 142, 144
Hornsby, Bruce 113
Hot Number 103
Howard Dumble (amp) 124
Howlin' Wolf 15, 79, 99, 110
Hubbard, Preston 116, 154
Huey Lewis & The News 81
Huff, John 47
Hughes, Joe 31-32
Humble Pie 50
Hunter, Ivory Joe 17
Hunter, Long John 169, 171

I
I Got The T-Bone Walker Blues 170
I Need Time 170
I Told You So 166
'I Wrote The Book' 111
Ibanez Tube Screamer 125
'Iced Over' 144
'If You Have To Know' 145
'I'm Crying' 80
I'm For Real 170
'I'm Leaving You (Commit A Crime)' 99
I'm The Man 168
Imperial (label) 15
In Step 106, 117, 125, 129-130
In The Beginning 67, 142
'In The Open' 67
Innes, Richard 159
Inside Job 145
Internet, music and 164
It's About Time 170

J
J.Geils Band 50
Jagger, Mick 73
Jeff Beck Group 111
Jefferson, Blind Lemon 12
'Jeff's Boogie' 111
Jimenez, Flaco 138
Jimmie on Stevie 114
John, Elton 113
John, Little Willie 111
Johnson, Eric 152
Johnson, Snuff 160
Jones, Andrew 'Junior Boy' 170
Jones, Bruce 166
Jones, John 'Tutu' 170
Jordan, Steve 159

K
Kaplan, Fred 161
Khan, Chaka 105
Kid Ramos 159
Kindred, Mike 60, 86
King, Albert 87, 105, 113, 127, 130, 145
King, B.B. 12, 58, 105, 113, 143, 145, 169
King, B'nois 167
King, Earl 91
King, Freddie 24-27, 46, 58, 111, 127
Kirk, Andy 8
Knight, Gladys 105
Kooper, Al 113
Kortchemar, Danny 'Kooch' 159
Krackerjack 49
Kubek, Smokin' Joe 167
Lang, Jonny 152
Lapidus, Janna 93, 118
Last Real Texas Blues Band, The 138
Layton, Chris 60, 63, 67, 108, 119, 145, 150
'Leave My Girl Alone' 110, 145
Legendary Blues Band 156
'Lenny' 80
Leslie speaker 125
'Let A Woman Be A Woman, Let A Man Be A Man' 111
'Let Me Love You Baby' 110
Let's Dance 74, 113
'Let's Dance' 75, 127
Liberation 47
'Life By The Drop' 130
'Life Without You' 91, 98-9
Lindley, David 113
Little Feat 169
'Little Wing' 141
Live Alive 96
'Live Another Day' 67
Live At El Macombo 142
Live At Montreux 1982 & 1985 145
Live At The Carnegie Hall 144
Livin' With The Blues 158
'Living In America' 96
Logan, Barbara 142
'Long Way From Home' 116, 143
'Look At Little Sister' 90, 99
'Lookin' Out The Window' 91
Looky Here 166
Love And Theft 151
'Love is Turning Green' 50
'Love Me Darlin'' 110
'Love Struck Baby' 65, 79, 127, 144
Lowe, Nick 81-82
Lunceford, Jimmie 9

M
Mack, Lonnie 88, 99, 104, 145
Madison Square Garden 111
Marshall amplifiers 124
Martinez, René 119, 142
'Mary Had A Little Lamb' 79, 99
Mavericks, The 151
'May I Have A Talk With You' 142
McBee, Lee 166
McClinton, Delbert 138-140, 148
McClure, Tommy 50
McLagan, Ian 150
McMurtry, James 151
McShann, Jay 157
Mellencamp, John 151
Memphis Horns 103, 118, 158
Mercury Records 13
Mesa Boogie 124
Meyer, Frankie 166
Mighty Fine Dancin' 166
Mighty Zor, The 151
Milk Cow Blues 145
Miller, Bruce 119
Miller, Mitch 99
Miller, Steve 20
Milligan, Malford 151-2
Millikin, Chesley 68, 73, 76, 88, 92, 94, 105
'Modern Love' 75
Montgomery, John Michael 148
Montreux International Jazz Festival 73-74
Moore, Jack 63
Morgan, Mike 166
Moss, Jerry 50
Mother Earth 148
Moundsey, Bill 119
Mountain 125
MTV 87
Mullen, Richard 84, 87, 90
Musicians, American Federation of 14
My Blues 160
My Love Is Here To Stay 165
Myers, Sam 164
Mystics, The 60

N
Napier, Alex 48-9, 52
Nelson, Tracy 148
Nelson, Willie 54, 144, 151
Neville, Art 143
New Blue Bird Nite Club 60
New Zealand 87
Newhouse, Jackie 67-69
Nightcrawlers, The 50, 91
Nix, Don 111
Nobs, Claude 73
Nulisch, Darren 164

O
O'Brien, Derek 113, 158, 170
Old Enough 66
Omar & The Howlers 148, 166
One Knite Dive & Tavern 51
Otis, Johnny 19
Out There 144

P
Parker, Junior 52
Parnell, Lee Roy 148
Paul Ray & The Cobras 51
Payne, Bill 169
Pennington, Drew 50
Pharoah, Freddie 60
Piccolo, Greg 146
Pickett, Wilson 52
'Pipeline' 105
Pitman, Billy 143
Pleasure Kings, The 156
Police, The 81
Pomus, Doc 65, 156
Power Station (studio) 86
Powerful Stuff 111
'Pride And Joy' 65, 79, 127, 143
Priestnitz, Joe 65
Prince 150
Ptacek, Rainer 38

R
Rainey, Ma 12
Rains, George 113, 142, 144, 171
Raitt, Bonnie 96, 99, 118-9, 140, 143, 152
Ramos, David 'Kid' 159
Raw And Ready 166
Ray, Paul 44, 108, 145
Recording techniques 90
Reed, A.C. 145
Reed, Jimmy 15, 58
Reed, Jimmy 54
Reno, Johnny 62
Reptile 151
Rickert, Skip 119
Ride With Me 169-170
Riding With The King 145, 151
'Riviera Paradise' 109, 130
Roadhouse Research 167
Robertson, Sherman 168
Robey, Don 21, 169

Robillard, Duke 154
Rockets, The 164
Rockin' Dopsie 169
Rodgers, Nile 113, 119, 142, 144
Roll Of The Dice 159
Rondells, The 139
Roomful of Blues 65, 144, 154-5
Routledge, Mark 119
'Rude Mood' 79, 127
Rush, Otis 58
Rush, Otis 58
Russell, Leon 49-50

S

Sahm, Doug 52-53, 56, 137, 148
'Say What?' 90, 129
'Scratch-N-Sniff' 109
'Scuttle Buttin" 86, 128
Serious Moonlight tour 75
Sexton, Charlie 150, 152
Shannon, Tommy 47, 49, 60, 69, 96, 108, 111, 119, 145, 150
She Knocks Me Out 165
Sheila E 150
Shepherd, Kenny Wayne 152
Showdown! 165
Simon, Paul 169
Sins 165
Sir Douglas Quintet 52, 138
'Six Strings Down' 143
Slash 113
Slim, Sunnyland 58
Smith, Floyd 8
Smokin' Joint 161
Smythe, Colin 119
Sony (label) 106, 167
Soul To Soul 90, 128
'Soul To Soul' 90
Soulful Dress 88
sound 122
SRV 145
'SRV Shuffle' 143
'Stang's Swang' 86, 128
Starr, Ringo 151
Staying Power 170
Steen, Scott 161
Steppin' Out Texas Style 167
Storm 50
Storyville 151
Strange Pleasures 142
Strelhi, Angela 57, 60, 87, 113
Strike Like Lightning 88
Sublett, Joe 52, 90, 142, 169
Sumlin, Hubert 58, 130
'Superstition' 99, 129
'Sweet Home Chicago' 118
Swing 156
Swingin' From The Rafters 170

T

Tailspin Headwhack 168
'Take Me Down Easy' 50
'Take My Love' 111
Take Your Best Shot 167
Takoma (label) 63
Talk To You By The Hand 165
Taylor, Hound Dog 58
Taylor, James 159
Taylor, Jesse 49
Taylor, Koko 58
Taylor, Larry 'The Mole' 159, 161
T-Bird Rhythm 82
technique 123
Tedeschi, Susan 152
Teena Marie 96
Tell Me What I Want To Hear 165
'Tell Me' 79
Temptation 157
Terrance Simien & The Mallet Playboys 169
'Testify' 79, 128
Texas Cadillac 167
Texas Flood 74, 77, 117, 127
'Texas Flood' 99, 143
Texas Storm 46
Texas Sugar/Strat Magic 168
Texas Tornados, The 137, 151
Texas Twister 75
Texas, musical culture of 8-24
That's Life 159
The Bluest Eyes 151
The Cellars (club) 48
The Fire Meets The Fury Tour 111
'The House Is Rockin" 109, 128
The Power & The Passion (tour) 117
The Road 166
The Sky Is Crying 130, 141
'The Sky Is Crying' 142
'The Star-Spangled Banner' 125
'The Telephone Song' 116, 143
'The Things That I Used To Do' 86, 144
'These Blues Is Killing Me' 145
'They Call Me Guitar Hurricane' 67
'Thunderbird' 145
'Tick Tock' 116, 144
Tigerman 158
'Tightrope' 109, 129
Tilt-A-Whirl Band, The 142
Time Takes Time 151
'Tin Pan Alley (AKA The Roughest Place In Town)' 67, 86
Too Hot To Handle 156
'Travis Walk' 109, 128
Travis, Merle 109
Trimmier, Jim 52
Triple Threat Revue 60
Trout, Walter 108
Tucker, Luther 58
Tuff Enuff 93
tuning 123
Turn It Around 156
Turner, John 47
Turner, 'Uncle' John 49

U

Under The Red Sky 113
Under the Wishing Tree 151
Useless Playboys, The 143

V

Varsity 13
Vaughan Brothers, The 113
Vaughan, Jimmie 40
- birth and childhood 43
- and death of Stevie Ray 141
- Fabulous Thunderbirds 58, 117
- guitar style 59
- on Stevie Ray 114

Vaughan, Stevie Ray
- as bass player 47
- birth 43
- collapse 100
- and David Bowie 75
- death 119
- debut album 77
- detox 101
- divorce 104
- drug arrest 66
- drugs 60, 90, 94, 99
- drying out 104
- eclecticism 110
- effects pedals 125
- fall from stage 102
- family background 40
- fine and probation 68
- first gigs 46
- first guitars 44
- first lead guitar gig 47
- forms Double Trouble 62
- funeral 119
- groupies 60
- *Guitar Player* awards 84
- guitar style 59, 122
- image 122
- influence 130, 162
- influences 44-45
- instruments 124
- on Jimmie 114
- live album 96
- marriage 67
- National Blues Awards 87
- radio listening 44
- recording in LA 50
- records in Nashville 65
- records own songs 65
- rejected by Stones 73
- second album 86
- stagecraft 108
- starts singing 65
- Stratocaster 'Number One' 51
- strings 123
- technique 123
- treatment for addiction 104
- tribute show 143
- tuning 90, 123
- videos 87
- vocals 86
- will & estate 141

Victor Bloom, Dr 101
'Voodoo Chile (Slight Return)' 86, 99, 128
Vox wah-wah 125

W

W.C.Handy National Blues Awards 88
Walk That Talk, Talk That Talk 157-8
Walker, Aaron 'T-Bone' 8, 12-16, 110, 113
'Wall of Denial' 109, 130
Wall Of Pride 167
Was, Don 151
Waters, Muddy 8, 16, 46, 54, 59
Watson, Johnny 'Guitar' 14, 19-21, 146
Watson, Junior 158, 161
Watts, Charlie 73
Wells, Junior 58
Wendy & Lisa 150
West, Leslie 125
West, Speedy 113
Wexler, Jerry 66, 72
'Wham!' 88, 142
What's The Word 70
'White Boots' 116
White House 111
Whynaught, Chris 166
Will The Circle Be Unbroken 160
Williams, Lucinda 151
Williamson, Sonny Boy 16
'Willie The Wimp' 99
Willis, Bill 142, 144
Wilson, Hop 32
Wilson, Kim 56-58, 154, 158
Wilson, Marc 166
Wilson, U.P. 32, 113
Winter, Johnny 34-36, 47
Wirz, Charlie 91
Witherspoon, Jimmy 157
Wonder, Stevie 98-99, 119, 129
Wood, Ronnie 96
Wynans, Reese 89, 91-92, 99, 108, 119, 148, 152

Y

'You Can Have My Husband (But Leave My Man Alone)' 65
You Got Me 156
'You'll Be Mine' 91

Z

Zinn, Rusty 158, 161
ZZ Top 36-38, 47, 51, 99

Photo credits

FRONT COVER: Ebet Roberts/ Redferns; **BACK COVER:** Rich Saputo / Retna Ltd; **p2/3:** David Redfern/ Redferns; **p6:** Robert Matheu / Retna Ltd; **p9:** Brian Smith/ Sylvia Pitcher Picture Library; **p25:** Andrea Laubach/ Retna Ltd; **p41:** background – Sylvia Pitcher Picture Library; foreground – Lucciano Viti / Retna Ltd; **p55:** Tony Mottram/ Retna Ltd; **p71:** Barry Morgenstein/ Retna Ltd; **p85:** David Redfern/ Redferns; **p97:** Sylvia Pitcher Picture Library; **p107:** Gary Gershoff/ Retna Ltd; **p121:** Gary Gershoff/ Retna Ltd; **p133:** Van Osdol/ Retna Ltd; **p149:** Sylvia Pitcher Picture Library; **p163:** background – Tony Mottram/ Sylvia Pitcher Picture Library; foreground – Patricia Steur Sunshine / Retna Ltd.

Acknowledgements

First and foremost thanks are due to Nigel Osborne, Tony Bacon and Phil Richardson and all at Backbeat Books for assistance and generosity over and above the call of duty. Paul Quinn deserves a big vote of thanks for his scrupulous editing skills. Rikky Rooksby also deserves a big hand for his technical deconstructions in Chapter 9. Paul Cooper's design is stylish and easy on the eye, so thanks for that.

John Stedman and Don Ottensman provided useful information and pointers. Paul Trynka gave me a pass to the Mojo Archive. Then other magazines such as Guitarist and Guitar Player provided a wealth of background detail. Casey Monaghan at the Texas Music Office was a regular source of useful information. My job would be almost impossible were it not for the many record labels that continue to ply me with CDs.

Finally a big round of applause to Sara-Jane, Caitlin, Luke and Oliver for their tolerance and forbearance in the face of adversity.

Hugh Gregory, **London 2003**